ONE NIGHT ONLY

KEN REID

CONVERSATIONS WITH
THE NHL'S ONE-GAME WONDERS

ONE
NIGHT
ONLY

Published by ECW Press
665 Gerrard Street East
Toronto, ON M4M 1Y2
416-694-3348 / info@ecwpress.com

Library and Archives Canada Cataloguing in Publication

Reid, Ken, 1974–, author
One night only : conversations with the NHL's one-game wonders / Ken Reid ; foreword by Jeff Marek.

Issued in print and electronic formats.
ISBN 978-1-77041-297-2 (paperback); ISBN 978-1-77090-912-0 (pdf); ISBN 978-1-77090-911-3 (epub)

1. Hockey players—Biography. 2. National Hockey League—History. I. Marek, Jeff, 1969–, writer of foreword II. Title.

GV848.5.A1R45 2016   796.962092'2   C2016-902385-0
C2016-902386-9

Editor for the press: Michael Holmes
Cover design: Michel Vrana
Cover images: © Aksonov / iStockPhoto
Unless otherwise stated, photos are from the author's personal collection or provided by the players themselves.
Printing: Marquis   5   4   3   2   1

The publication of *One Night Only* has been generously supported by the Government of Canada through the Canada Book Fund. *Ce livre est financé en partie par le gouvernement du Canada.* We also acknowledge the contribution of the Government of Ontario through the Ontario Book Publishing Tax Credit and the Ontario Media Development Corporation.

Printed and bound in Canada

To Jacoby and Langdon — DREAM BIG!

CONTENTS

JEFF MAREK *Foreword*

One.

This is a book about playing *one* game in the NHL. You know, the stuff any kid who's ever picked up a stick dreams about. (I know I did.)

What's it like to get the call?
How do you sleep the night before?
What was it like walking into the dressing room?
Who did you think of the moment your skates touched the ice in a real NHL game?

Hockey is, after all, a fast-paced meditation — there can be no distractions, only an intense, burning focus on a sequence of events — where the game plays you as much as you play it. This is probably why in-game hockey interviews are so horrible. You can't ask players what happened out there because they don't really know. Things just happened, and they reacted. Perspective and understanding come later.

It's a riddle: many of the men you're going to read about have probably spent their lives wondering what exactly happened. What did I do out there? What should I have done? If I could do it again, what would I change? After all, when you have but one game to dwell on and the rest of your life to do so, you tend to go deep.

The only thing I have a hard time with in Ken's book is the word "only."

In the following pages, you'll read stories of players who played *only* one NHL game — many wishing for more and feeling that the experience is incomplete because it happened just once. No second act, no encore. Thanks, son, that'll be all.

And when I hear some of these players use the word "only," I cringe a little. It's used to indicate regret rather than celebration. It makes me wonder, "What makes you feel that way?" This is an accomplishment that so few of us ever get to experience. Do you know how many of us wish we could have the word "only" on our hockey resume?

One is the beginning.

One is the initiation.

One is great.

It's not the loneliest number, as Three Dog Night would have you believe.

These players all brought to that one game their own language of sport, built on the years of sacrifice and repetition that got them there. But as all of them will tell you, it's still never enough to prepare you for the experience — the real thing. Nothing gets you ready for that jump; your training merely comforts you through any anxiety you have about it.

A second game is never like the first, can never be like the first — which is why we hold the first so sacred and are fascinated by it.

Nobody ever asks how your second game went.

If one man's ceiling is another man's floor, then to most of us hacks, who bang around glorified frozen cow patties in various adult leagues while our children and spouses have long gone to bed, playing a single NHL game is somewhat akin to scoring a Game 7 overtime Cup winner.

It's perfect.

Just don't call it *only* one game.

Introduction

This is a book for beer leaguers. For every kid who ever laced up their skates. It's for everyone who had to pick up a net and move it when somebody else yelled, "Car!"

This is a book for everyone who ever dreamed of making it — but didn't — and for everyone who ever dreamed of hitting the NHL ice for just one night or just one shift.

Like countless other Canadian kids, I dreamed of one day playing in the NHL. Those dreams quickly disappeared, when at the age of eight, I was assigned to a Novice 2 team instead of the uber-talented Novice 1 squad (at least I thought they were uber-talented). It was around that time that I decided to find a way to still be a part of the hockey world even though I wasn't good enough to play in it. Luckily for me, I found my way into *sports* broadcasting.

But that idea of strapping on the blades at the game's highest level has never really left my imagination. As a kid, you dream of scoring the winning goal in Game 7 of the Stanley Cup Final, but as you grow older reality begins to set in. Not everyone will get to do that. And then maybe you settle on just making it to the NHL for a few years. But not everyone can do that either.

I'm sure there were many others who, like me, settled on this thought: "I'd give anything to play just *one* game in the NHL."

In fact, about 350 men, give or take, managed to do just that — play in a single NHL game, not one game more. *One Night Only* comprises the stories of men who made it all the way to the best league in the world — if only for the briefest hockey moment.

So, was their one game a dream come true? Or did they feel more like Cinderella, their dreams cruelly snatched away? Were they bitter? Or were they simply satisfied to have defied the odds by making it to the sport's pinnacle?

Back in my minor-hockey days, a hockey school would visit my hometown in Nova Scotia at the start of each season. It was called Coach International. Every year, we were told an NHLer who had some Nova Scotian roots, Trevor Fahey, ran the school. I don't remember ever seeing Mr. Fahey, but I'm sure he was there — he just didn't stand out among the other instructors decked out in their maroon Coach International track suits. It wasn't like it is now; after a session with the guys from Coach International, we couldn't just head home and google the names of our instructors. I knew Bobby Heighton played for the Pictou Jr. C Mariners — but Trevor Fahey always remained a bit of a mystery. Many years later I learned that Trevor Fahey played in one contest for the New York Rangers in 1964–65. It was his only NHL game. He went on to play university hockey (imagine that, suiting up in university after making it all the way to the NHL) and was one of the first Canadians to head over to Russia to study how that country produced such great hockey players.

Fast forward to just a couple of years ago. I was up late one night, racking my brain for ideas. *Hockey Card Stories* was in stores and I was rummaging through my past, looking for something else to write about. I had been debating between writing another hockey-card book (I'm going to, for those who have been asking) or taking a different path. I was thinking of some of the guys from my neck of the woods who had made it to the NHL, when I thought of Trevor Fahey again. Suddenly I wanted to know more about him.

What was it like to make it all the way to the NHL for one game? A dream come true? Or was it heartbreaking? Could he even remember the actual game? Does it in any way define him all these years later? A quick online search showed me exactly how many men had played just a single game. I figured I was on to something.

A few days later in our wardrobe room at Sportsnet, Jeff Marek asked me about my next book idea and I told him. He said he'd had exactly the same idea. The original plan was for Marek and I to write this book together, but that didn't happen. Jeff's a busy guy. Luckily for me he did write the foreword. (Thanks, "Palm Isle.") It was good to find out that, like Jeff, I'm not the only freak out there who's not only obsessed with the superstars of the game but also the super stories of the game.

So I started making phone calls, tracking down the men who suited up in the world's greatest hockey league for just a single night. Playing detective and finding out where these guys are now was a lot of fun, but the true thrill of putting together a book like this is getting to know the men who, if for only the briefest moment, fulfilled all of our childhood dreams.

But does a dream really come true when it only lasts for a few hours, or, in some cases, a few seconds? Let's find out.

CHAPTER ONE
SCHOOL TIES

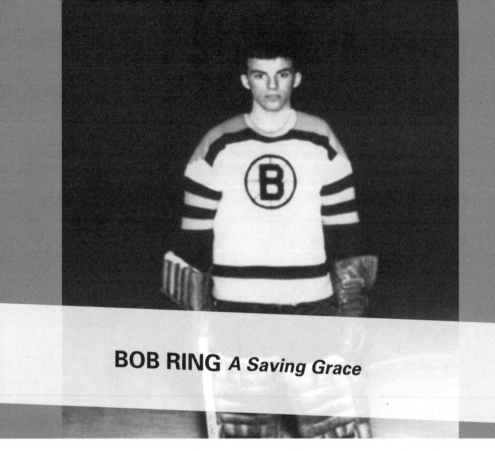

BOB RING *A Saving Grace*

The Boston Bruins, Acadia University and the Vietnam War. Those three things are part of Bob Ring's amazing hockey journey. His hockey story is unlike any I've ever heard. And it goes like this . . .

Bob Ring graduated from high school in Wakefield, Massachusetts, in 1964. Growing up, he used to watch the Bruins at the Boston Garden. Ring and his high school buddies would sit in some cheap seats right down by the ice, and on most nights, they'd watch the Bruins struggle. Then, in the summer of 1964, Bob Ring signed with the team as a goalie and became a part of the Bruins organization. His first assignment took him to the Ontario Hockey League to play junior with the Niagara Falls Flyers. They, along with the Oshawa Generals, were one of two Bruins-controlled teams.

Boston was retooling. Actually, that's putting things lightly. The team hadn't won a Stanley Cup since 1941 and had finished sixth in the six-team NHL four seasons in a row. When Ring joined the organization, their junior system was ripe with future NHL stars like Jean Pronovost, Derek Sanderson and Bernie Parent on the Niagara Falls Flyers and

Bobby Orr and Wayne Cashman on the Oshawa Generals. Ring spent the 1964–65 season playing mostly Junior A and Junior B in the Niagara Falls area. The next year, he was with the big club. But while the rest of Ring's teammates, all Canadians, were just going about their business, something else was hanging over Bob Ring's head: the Vietnam draft. "I had a slightly different situation going, because we had the draft in the U.S. at that time. Vietnam was going on so you really had to be in the top of your class in college to have a student deferment. So that sort of sets the stage."

In October 1965, Ring was in Niagara Falls when the team's general manager, Hap Emms, called the young American into his office. "He said that they were sending me to Boston." When Ring heard those words, he immediately thought the Flyers were sending him home and that his time with the team was over. No, when Emms said Boston, he meant the Bruins. A goalie was down with an injury, and Ring was on his way to the NHL. "So a year out of high school I was playing in the Garden, which was just a tremendous thrill."

Ring headed for home with a plan to surprise his parents with the big news. Unfortunately, the Boston papers got word of the local-boy-makes-good story first, and the Wakefield kid's arrival in his hometown was already making headlines by the time he returned. Apparently the news didn't make its way to the Garden's security though: when the youthful-looking Ring arrived for his first NHL practice, he had a little trouble getting into the building. "I went into the Garden through the main gate and I had my equipment with me. And the guard at the gate informed me that the high school practice was not until four o'clock and that the Bruins were practising. And of course, I'm trying to convince him that I'm going to practise with them." Security was having none of it but, luckily for Ring, along came a familiar face. It was Bruins centre Ron Schock, who Ring was more than familiar with from his time in the organization. "[Ronnie] sort of brushed me aside and said, 'Excuse me, kid, high school doesn't start until four.' He threw me under the bus," laughs Ring. "But I finally managed to talk my way in."

The Bruins' plan was to go with their veteran goalie Eddie Johnston in the crease with Ring on the bench until Cheevers came back to play, but plans don't always work out. On October 30, 1965, Johnston got the start against the New York Rangers. With the Bruins down, Ring got the word from Bruins head coach Milt Schmidt that he was going in. In those days, if you replaced a goaltender during the game the backup got a chance for a little warm-up. Ring loosened up. When the referee blew his whistle for the game to resume, Ring's old buddy Ron Schock showed up again. "Shocker had three pucks about 15 feet out in front of the net, so he skates over and he shoots one into the lower corner and one into the upper corner and another to the other side. Boom, boom, boom and they're in the net. He taps me on the pads and he says, 'Good luck, rookie.'" A really nice guy, that Ron Schock.

As play resumed, Bob Ring found himself in a surreal world. He was on the ice at the Gardens playing for the Bruins. He was now the guy that just a couple of years ago he had paid to watch. "I can remember it was like an out-of-body experience. You're looking out into the stands and you're seeing your old high school buddies that you used to sit with the year before. They're watching the game and you're sort of saying, 'This is weird.'"

It was Ring's first NHL game and it was the first NHL game for the Rangers goalie as well. Future Hall of Famer Eddie Giacomin was at the other end of the ice. Before Ring knew it, another future member of the Hall came barrelling in on him. "Leo Boivin was a defenceman who used to throw some big hip checks in those days. The first goal that was scored on me was from Jean Ratelle. He came up the right wing and Boivin threw a hip check at him at the blue line and Ratelle sort of jumped over him, danced over him, skipped over him, and then came in on a breakaway and went to the upper-right-hand corner."

Bob Ring ended up making nine saves on 13 Rangers shots that night in an 8–2 home loss for the Bruins. The next day Ring was back at the Garden and was getting ready to join the Bruins for his first NHL road trip. That's when Bob Ring got his first official NHL lecture. And it was from an unlikely source. "I had packed my bag to get ready for the trip, and the trainer went berserk. Because it was his responsibility to make sure that all of the equipment arrived at the city. It was his job to pack the bags. But you know, as a kid you always pack your own bag. You had no idea that somebody was supposed to pack it for you. You didn't realize just where you were." Bob Ring was in the NHL now — he didn't need to pack his own gear; someone else would do it for him. And someone packed Ring's bag for a while. He didn't see any more action, but he practised with team for another month. The Bruins eventually made a move with Ring, but they didn't send him back to Niagara Falls. Instead, he was off to hockey's version of Siberia. Bob Ring was on his way to Springfield, Massachusetts, to play for Eddie Shore's Springfield Indians. Needless to say, he picked up his fair share of stories while playing for the legendary Shore. Shore owned the team and he owned the players. And if you didn't like his penny-pinching ways or the way he ran his team then it was too bad for you. "He basically gave you a contract and you either signed for what they were offering or you didn't play."

As an example, Ring points to Bill Sweeney. Sweeney led the American Hockey League in scoring for three straight seasons in the early 1960s. "The year that I was there, he went to Shore, who was in his mid-'80s [actually 60s but it may have seemed like he was in his 80s] at that time and was really getting whacked. Sweeney was making $10,000 at the time and he wanted a $2,000 increase in his contract. Shore wouldn't give it to him and he held out for two weeks at camp. Shore finally called him in and relented and gave him the $2,000 increase. So Sweeney went and started camp and then Shore fined him $1,000 a week for the next two consecutive weeks for lack of hustle in practice."

I'm sure you're familiar with the hockey term "Black Aces." It is always thrown around at playoff time. Teams load up on extra players in the postseason. These players practise with the team but rarely get into games. You can thank Shore for the term, says Ring. "He had to carry eight players that were known as the Black Aces on their team because there was no player in the American Hockey League that would want to jeopardize their career by going on loan to Shore to fill in and backfill for fear that Shore might make a deal for them. So he had to carry a group by the name of the Black Aces who did nothing but practise and fill in for spots."

Ring continues, "If Shore decided to reprimand a player and suspend him for lack of performance or hustle, in order for a player to collect his

5

paycheque, and players in those days were starved, he was relegated to go into the stands to sell concessions. I mean, those days are just unbelievable. I was there for three months."

Once the season was over, Bob Ring had to think about the next stop on his hockey journey. It was a summer of indecision. And he had a monumental choice to make. This wasn't simply about hockey. This was about his life. The Vietnam War raged and the draft beckoned. And we're not talking about the hockey draft — Ring was worried about military conscription. Top college students might get a deferment, but a 19-year-old hockey player was out of luck. "There were no options for me," Ring says. "I had to take advantage of going back to university. Which of course meant you had to walk away from the professional career and hope that in four years the opportunity to come back to the league would still be there for you." It was pro hockey and the Vietnam draft or college and possibly an end to his professional hockey career. That's pressure for a 19-year-old kid.

Bob Ring started writing to big American schools like Boston University and the University of Michigan. He soon found out that he was out of luck: he was not considered to be an amateur under NCAA rules. He then focused on Canadian universities. He wrote to Acadia University, wondering if he was eligible to play in Canada. "I was very naive and I was hoping that maybe my background, not my scholastic achievement in high school by any means, would get me into Acadia."

September came, and Ring had a choice to make: he had received his draft notice and he had got the call from Acadia — he was accepted into the small Nova Scotia university. He had thought about this moment for the entire summer; now it was decision time. "It was really tough. In those days the war was just horrific."

Ring chose to go to school and not to war, even though it likely meant his chances for another crack at the NHL were slim. "Given the limited opportunity that you had in the league, you really suspected that after being out for four years, you wouldn't get another opportunity."

Less than a year after playing for the Bruins, Bob Ring showed up at Acadia University in Wolfville, Nova Scotia, three weeks after classes had begun. He did not get off to a good start. "I'm walking down the hall on the Monday I registered, and I needed to enroll into a business school or whatever. I had just met with head of the school of commerce, who had looked at my transcripts from high school and had told me that the best advice he could give me is to pack my bags and go home — because I'd never be able to get through his school of business. So now I'm thinking, 'Draft Board. I'm totally screwed.'" But as one door closed, another opened for Ring, literally, just a few steps away.

"There is a fellow down there by the name of Ralph Winters. He was the head of the school of economics. Like most of the faculty, he was a hockey fan. I was about to go pack my bags when he called me into this office. And I met him for the first time and he asked me how I was doing and I told him, 'Not so well.' And he said, 'What's the problem?' I said, 'I'm not going to be accepted into the school of business and I really don't know what I should do.' He said, 'Well, have you ever considered the school of economics?' And I'm thinking, 'Hmm . . . economics. Home economics. I can cook. Sure, why not.'"

Just like that, Ring was in Acadia's school of economics, but there wasn't a lot of cooking going on. He studied and he played hockey. He was surprised to learn that Maritime universities were loaded with a lot of former junior and pro players. The play was top-notch. "The hockey was great and it was really very natural, and one of the best things about being in Canada is that the Canadian system allows you to get your amateur status back. And I was able to take advantage of that."

In his freshman year, Ring was named his conference's All-Star netminder and Acadia's MVP. The books were another story. "The first summer after my freshman year I had to stay and take two courses to make up for what I had failed."

The word "failed" would not sit well with the American military. Luckily for Ring, that particular word never came up when the Draft Board called Acadia or any other Canadian school to check up on American students. "The Draft Board was always going to the universities to determine whether you were in the top half of your class. And if you weren't you'd lose your deferment. The Canadian universities would tell the Draft Boards only that you were a student in good standing. They really were supportive of their students — they helped me out tremendously. Without the support of the faculty I never would have made it."

By the end of his senior year at Acadia, the freshman student who had to take summer classes was on the dean's list. Bob Ring graduated in 1970 with a degree in economics. "One of the most memorable experiences that I've ever had was when I had the opportunity to go back to Acadia some six or seven years later to be inducted into their Hall of Fame, and I was able to thank the people in the audience who had changed my life, who had done everything for me. Acadia had just 1,200 students at the time and if I had been accepted into a major university I would have just been a number and there would have been no one there to act as my support system. The faculty gave me such tremendous support and basically gave me the opportunity to catch up on all the education I didn't get in high school. And it made all the difference in the world."

After graduation, Bob moved back to New England. He worked for a telephone company and played senior hockey in Concord, New Hampshire. The senior team paid $100 a game — in those days that was good money for a young guy in the working world. After a few years, he hung up the blades. He now lives in South Carolina and he still has a hint of a New England accent, but it's been over 50 years since he played that one night at the Boston Garden for his hometown Bruins. "A lot of it happens so fast that you don't have an opportunity to truly appreciate the moment. But it gets to be more important to you as time goes on. Looking back, it is obviously one of the wonderful things in my hockey career, but at the time it was just a natural progression. You don't think that it's the end of it. You think that it's going to continue."

But then other things occur — things you'd never expect. Like playing for Eddie Shore and the Vietnam draft, and having to make a decision that no 19-year-old kid should ever have to make.

Bob Ring chose to give up a professional career and head to a small Canadian school to pursue an education and avoid a war. "It changed my life," he says, "and it was probably the best thing that I ever did."

SID VEYSEY *Mr. Comeback*

In the summer of 1978, Sid Veysey was back at home in New Brunswick. One day he found himself on first base in a New Brunswick Intermediate A baseball game. But Veysey didn't want to stay on first base, he wanted to get to second base. He quickly made up his mind; he was going on a 90-foot trip to second. Veysey didn't think of his plan to steal the second bag on the diamond as any sort of gamble. After all, Veysey, a pro hockey player in the winter, didn't have anything in his contract about not playing baseball in the summer. "The only stipulation back then was no motorcycles. You weren't supposed to drive motorcycles. But there wasn't anything about baseball."

That's too bad, because Veysey's decision to steal second went horribly wrong for a guy who had missed the second half of the previous hockey season with a dislocated shoulder. "The second baseman was standing in front of the bag. It wasn't very smart of me. I thought I would slide and take him out of the play. Well it didn't work out so well — caught right above my ankle and snapped the bone back." Veysey's foot was dangling from his leg. His leg was broken in two places. "It was a pretty traumatic experience."

The timing could not have been any worse. The previous winter, Sid Veysey played in 54 games for the Tulsa Oilers and one game for their parent club, the Vancouver Canucks. But now, here he was, lying on his back on a baseball field in New Brunswick, with a broken leg and no contract. Veysey was a free agent that summer; he had yet to sign a deal with the Canucks when his leg snapped. "I did have the opportunity to keep playing, but I knew I couldn't play so I had to let my agent know that I broke my leg," Veysey remembers. "A broken leg — of course Vancouver wouldn't re-sign me."

Just a few months before it all went wrong on the diamond, it was all going right on the ice. He started the 1977–78 season with the Vancouver Canucks. Veysey spent the first two years of his pro career averaging over a point per game with the Fort Wayne Komets and the Tulsa Oilers. The NHL was his for the taking. "The regular season started and we went on a three-game road trip. The first night I sat out — I think it was New York. The second game was in Colorado and I played. I remember I had a good chance to score. Missed a couple of passes — I'm normally a pretty good playmaker. I remember I missed my winger. I fed him a little too far and we got a couple of icing calls. It was a little faster paced than the exhibition games. Maybe I felt a little more pressure than in the exhibition games."

Veysey wasn't overwhelmed by making his NHL debut. It was almost a been-there-done-that feeling. He had played in several pre-season games with the Canucks, so he wasn't floored by suiting up for his first regular-season tilt. A lot of us may think of a player's NHL debut as some sort of magical moment, but that wasn't the case for Veysey. "I'd played about 10 exhibition games the year before, and I think they played about 15 or 18 exhibition games that year and I'd played in all of them."

Veysey's tenure in the NHL didn't have a Hollywood ending. It wasn't all feel good and sappy. As soon as the Canucks' road trip was over, the 22-year-old got the news: he was going back to Tulsa. "I felt like I could play at that level, but we came back from the road trip and they said, 'Well, we want you to get more ice time so we're going to send you down to the farm.'"

Veysey went down to Tulsa, determined to put on a good show and get back to Vancouver as soon as possible. "I was disappointed that they were sending me down, but they had made a trade. At the time, I was the third centreman on the team, and the team had four lines but we only had three centremen. So it was kind of like we have one guy double-shifting and playing on the second and fourth line, and I was kind of in there on the third line." That trade that Veysey mentioned was on November 4, 1977. The Canucks picked up veteran centre Pit Martin from Chicago for futures. Suddenly Veysey moved down a spot on the Canucks' depth chart. They never called him up again. Then things got even worse for Veysey.

"I kind of had a streak of bad luck with injuries where I dislocated my shoulder. That was midway through the season — January, I guess. And then I missed the rest of the season because I needed surgery."

Combine that with a broken leg a few months later and Sid Veysey was in a world of hurt. Luckily though, he was just fine between the ears. Veysey had already been taking classes at the University of New Brunswick that summer, so with the help of a set of crutches, the man who had played for the Vancouver Canucks on October 14, 1977, was a full-time student at the University of New Brunswick in September 1978. Hockey, for now, was out of the question; it was time to hit the books. However, it wasn't long before Veysey was itching to ditch the crutches and get back on the ice. "I had a good doctor. I was going to UNB and recuperating. It was painful, but Donnie MacAdam was the coach at UNB and he let me practise with the team."

The comeback didn't last long. Remember, this was the late '70s — it's not like today, where rehab is serious business. Veysey's leg was feeling better and he was doing fine on the ice. So one day he hit the slopes. "I decided to go skiing and re-fractured my leg. Went to the hospital to get it x-rayed and they said, 'Well, you've got a broken leg,' and I said, 'I know. I broke it three or four months ago.' They said, 'Oh.' But then I learned that I had re-fractured it. So I had to get another cast on." This seems really funny to Veysey all these years later. Of course it wasn't so funny in the winter of 1978.

If there's one thing I'm getting from Sid Veysey's story it's this: the man is a quick healer. The next fall, just a few months removed from re-breaking his leg, Sid Veysey was on the comeback trail again. He didn't start the semester at UNB. Instead, he was at the Toronto Maple Leafs training camp, looking to crack a roster that featured Darryl Sittler, Walt McKechnie, Pat Boutette and Garry Monahan. "My agent said, 'We have an opportunity for you to go to the Leafs camp.' So I did that, but after sitting out a year I probably wasn't in the best shape to make the Leafs. Actually, the Leafs were going to send me to the American Hockey League team and I said, 'No that's ok. I'm going to go back to the university.'"

So it was back to school. Thanks to the three years of pro hockey that Veysey had played, he only had two years of university eligibility left. But his UNB hockey career could not have gone any better. He was back home racking up the points for UNB. He had 53 points in 27 games during his first year and another 37 points in 20 games during his second. Veysey was tearing up the league, and opponents definitely knew there was an NHLer in their midst. "Even though I had only played two years there, I was captain of the team and I was an AUAA [Atlantic Universities Athletic Association] All-Star. Actually I just saw something the other day. I was the third leading scorer in the CIAU [Canadian Interuniversity Athletic Union]." Veysey was named to UNB's all-decade team for the 1980s. Not bad for a guy who only played for one year in the '80s.

After two years at UNB, Veysey's eligibility was up. He was on his way to earning a business degree, so he was back at UNB in the fall of 1981 to finish up his fourth year. He was playing a little bit of senior hockey but nothing too serious. That's when yet another Sid Veysey comeback story took place. Veysey's next hockey adventure begins in one of the strangest places you could imagine. He didn't have his agent call anyone. He didn't go knocking on any doors looking for a tryout. Sid Veysey was simply acting like a university student, studying at the UNB library. "The Fredericton Express, the farm team of the Quebec Nordiques, needed help at centre. Actually I was just studying in the library one night and the trainer, who used to be our trainer at UNB, came running over and said, 'Sid, Jacques Demers wants you to play tonight.' And I said, 'Oh, shoot.' I'm such a guy for routine, eh, like the pre-game meals and the pre-game nap. I said, 'Oh, shoot. It's 5:30. The game's at 7:30 and he wants me to play tonight?' So I went over and played and he said he wanted me to keep playing. It was fun."

And Veysey kept playing. The full-time student was a part-time AHLer. That's a pretty good job for a college kid. But like any good student, Veysey didn't let his part-time gig get in the way of school. "Actually they wanted me to go on a road trip for two weeks at Christmas time and I was in the middle of exams. And I said, 'Well, if you want to sign me to a pro contract then I'll go.' But I already had the pro experience, so I wasn't just going to leave my university exams to go on a road trip."

Soon enough, Veysey was the faceoff specialist for the AHL franchise — think of him as the David Steckel of the 1981–82 Fredericton Express. "It was funny. Jacques used to put me out for every faceoff. That was almost a little embarrassing. Because he didn't have too many natural centremen. He'd say, 'Okay, you go out and take the draw and then come right off.' So he put me on every faceoff in the offensive and defensive zones."

Eventually, Veysey Comeback 3.0 was put on hold. Coach Demers had to deliver some news. "After I'd played 15 games or so, Jacques said, 'Sid, listen. We've got our injured guys back and the Nordiques have sent a couple of guys down, so we don't think we'll need you anymore.' I said, 'Okay, that's fine. Thanks, I enjoyed it.'"

The news from Demers was anything but a big deal for Veysey. He put his head back in the books; one day he even went skiing. Luckily this time around he didn't have an accident on the slopes. He got home after a long day at the hill feeling just fine. Now it's time for Vesey Comeback 4.0, if my accounting is correct. "I went skiing one Sunday and we got back at suppertime and there was a message from Jacques. 'Sid, I need you in the lineup tonight. I'm shorthanded.' So after being on the ski hill all day I had to rush to the Aitken Centre again." That's a long day.

Veysey played in a total of 17 games for the Express in 1981–82. The following year he entered the working world, played senior hockey in

New Brunswick and started a family. Before he knew it, his pro hockey career was over and the one night he played for the Vancouver Canucks seemed a lifetime away. It's not that suiting up in an NHL regular-season game wasn't anything special, it's just that the one game doesn't really stand out from the rest of the time Veysey spent with the Canucks. "I'd scored a goal in an exhibition game, so that was more of a thrill. I scored a goal on Rogie Vachon playing for the L.A. Kings. It's a funny story. I think I'm an answer to a trivia question. I scored the first-ever NHL goal in Tucson, Arizona. You know how the teams move around and play exhibition games at different locations? We played the Los Angeles Kings in Tucson, Arizona, and I got the first goal of the game. Anyway, everybody asks me if I kept the puck and I say, 'No, no. I thought there would be a lot more of those.'"

These days Vesey works as a business development manager in the consumer goods industry. He also spends a lot of time in rinks around Atlantic Canada. He is the Atlantic Canada head scout for the Saint John Sea Dogs of the Quebec Major Junior Hockey League. Veysey won a QMJHL President's Cup with the Sherbrooke Castors in 1974–75 and two more as a scout with the Sea Dogs. "I was joking around with our old coach Turk — Gerrard Gallant — and he said, 'I set a record now. I've won the President's Cup more than anybody else.' Gallant won it twice as a player and twice as a coach. I said, 'Yeah, I'm right behind you, Turk. I won it once as a player and twice as a scout.' He says, 'Yeah, you're second. I'm first.'"

Sid Veysey's one regular season game is just part of his hockey story. No more or no less than the rest. Sid Veysey loves looking back on his UNB days, his Sherbrooke days, his Tulsa days and his Vancouver days. "I tell the boys a few stories once in a while in the dressing room. You know, I put my winger in Tulsa in the NHL. I played with him for the first 20 games. He got 20 goals in the first 20 games and I assisted on every one of his goals. So they called him up to the Atlanta Flames and he got Rookie of the Year in the NHL. So I put him in the NHL." That winger was Willi Plett. He played in 834 NHL games. His old centre in Tulsa played in one. For Sid Veysey, that one game was just part of a much bigger picture.

"I can't really say it was a huge thrill or anything because I felt like I was on the team for more than the one game. I had gone through three NHL training camps and played 25 exhibition games or so, so it was just being part of that whole process. I mean, it was great to be there and that was the thrill, the overall thrill, just playing at the level."

GLENN TOMALTY *House League Hero*

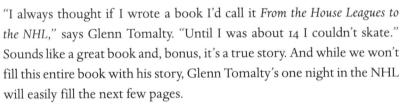

"I always thought if I wrote a book I'd call it *From the House Leagues to the NHL*," says Glenn Tomalty. "Until I was about 14 I couldn't skate." Sounds like a great book and, bonus, it's a true story. And while we won't fill this entire book with his story, Glenn Tomalty's one night in the NHL will easily fill the next few pages.

These days we'd call Glenn Tomalty a late bloomer. Actually, these days we call anyone who starts hockey after age 10 a late bloomer. Glenn Tomalty's story is a testament to hard work and perseverance. It also shows you just how much the game, and in particular the development of young players, has changed since Tomalty was a young boy.

"I wasn't a kid star," he says. "I struggled to even make a rep team until I was about 17. That was the first time I really was a first liner on a team."

Glenn Tomalty took the long way to the world's greatest hockey league, missing an entire season with an injury when he was 19 years old and playing Canadian university hockey at Concordia. It wasn't a high-profile league for an up-and-comer, but it did provide one huge bonus. "I didn't skate more than once a week until I was about 13. Going to college was good for me because it allowed me to practise every day to develop my skills. So when I got out of college at 22, I was somewhat ready."

Tomalty landed a tryout with the Toronto Maple Leafs after his final year at Concordia. In the fall of 1977, the kid who could hardly skate less than a decade earlier found himself surrounded by some of the biggest names in the game. "That's in the days when the Leafs had a hockey team — Börje Salming, Lanny McDonald, Ian Turnbull, Errol Thompson, Tiger Williams. It was a strong team. I wasn't in awe so much because I wasn't 20 years old, I was 22. But I just knew there was no way I was making this team, this year or next."

The Leafs were so stacked that Tomalty couldn't even cut it with Dallas, their top farm team. He hardly played any pro hockey at all that year but the following season he found himself in the old Eastern League. He had 47 points in 41 games. His play was good enough to catch the attention of the Winnipeg Jets. He signed on to play centre with the "new" NHL team.

After hanging around for all three weeks of Jets training camp in 1979, the Jets sent Tomalty down to the Dayton Gems of the International Hockey League. He was a point-a-game guy. Meantime, the Jets were doing their thing in the NHL, but they were not doing it well. They were losing, a lot. Luckily for Tomalty, one night during the season, Winnipeg rookie Jimmy Mann did something that caught the attention of the league. "Jimmy Mann was kind of the enforcer for the Jets the first year, or he was supposed to be the enforcer. He was suspended for a couple of games, so I got called up to replace Jimmy."

Tomalty got the news in Dayton. He was going up to the Show. There was just one problem. He had to get to the Show *now*. He got the news in the morning and had to be in Washington that night for the Jets game against the Capitals. "They'd already made the flights. It was going to be tight. So I stopped at home and grabbed my shaving kit. I knew it would be at least overnight. The only equipment I took were sticks and my skates and I took a cab to the airport."

Tomalty literally grabbed just the essentials — he had no luggage when he arrived at the airport, no bag at all. He went through security and onto the plane with his skates and sticks in his hands. I can't see that happening these days. But it happened in 1979. Even then, though, a guy with a large pair of blades in his hands was enough to catch the attention of one of the flight attendants. She got the captain. "The captain came out of the door. He asked, 'Where are you going?' I said, 'Well, I'm just going to Washington to play a hockey game.' And he said, 'Okay, fine. I was going to keep the skates up here with me, but it's fine. You can just take them on.' So I was fortunate enough to get on the plane."

With his unique carry-ons, Tomalty tried to relax as much as he could. But that wasn't easy. He was running late and was wondering if he was going to make it to the game on time. The plane finally arrived in D.C. and Tomalty told the cab to get him to the arena as quick as possible. The cabbie made his way to Landover, Maryland, the home of the Caps. Tomalty showed up with absolutely no time to spare. "When I walked into the rink I knew it was kind of late. The players were all still sitting in the room and they were all pretty much dressed and the other team was out for the warm-up. Tommy McVie [the Jets head coach] said, 'Get dressed as quick as you can because we're all going out together.' So they waited. I think it took me maybe six or seven minutes to get dressed. Also, when I was walking to my stall I noticed the trainer was sewing my name onto the back of a sweater. I thought that was pretty cool."

So, deep breath, Tomalty was in the lineup. He knew all of the Jets from training camp, but he was looking around for the *Golden* Jet. After all, who wouldn't want to play with Bobby Hull. "I guess my biggest disappointment was Bobby Hull wasn't on that road trip. He wasn't even in training camp because I was at training camp the full three weeks or whatever it was. He'd only joined the team in late October and I never did meet him. I thought he might be on the road trip but he wasn't on the road trip for some reason."

After putting aside his brief disappointment at a non–Bobby Hull sighting, it was time for Tomalty to focus on playing his first NHL game. Like most rookies, he took his usual spot when the game rolled around — on the bench. "From what I remember I would have been on the fourth line. You're kind of watching the game and you're sitting in an NHL rink. I'd played some exhibition games, but I hadn't played a regular-season game. I was just wired and as full of energy as you could be getting in there for your first game. It's something you've been working at, especially in the last four or five years in college and the minor leagues, getting ready to try to make it to the NHL, and all of a sudden you're there."

Soon enough, though, it was time for Tomalty to hit the ice. This was real. The kid who played in the house leagues all those years was now in the NHL. "On my first shift I remember shooting the puck from outside the blue line in to the end. I shot it at the goalie, which you're not supposed to do. You're supposed to shoot it so he can't handle it. But I was just wired. I just wanted to get the puck to the net and go. So probably skating around at 100 miles an hour, and what I got from the game is just this desire. I played with all these guys in training camp and exhibition games and I guess everyone feels like they belong and wants to contribute and you're just hoping and working toward that chance."

That one shot that Glenn Tomalty dumped at the Capitals net is the only shot on goal he recorded in his NHL career. The Jets sent him back to Dayton the very next day. Tomalty continued to hum along in Dayton at a point-per-game pace, while the Jets stumbled their way to just 20 wins. If the Jets were looking for help, they were not looking to get it from Tomalty. He never got called up again. "I was hoping I would. I don't know where I was on the depth chart. Fergie [Jets GM John Ferguson] had recognized me as a good, solid two-way player and defensive minded. I talked to him in training camp and I knew he liked me, so I thought if they needed someone they would call me up, but obviously they never did. In view of their plus-minus record that year, I don't think I could have hurt them," laughs Tomalty. He has a point. The Jets finished the season with a minus 100 goal differential.

Tomalty spent the next season in the IHL and the CHL. After the 1980–81 campaign, it was decision time: give the NHL another crack, continue to live life in the minors or start a new adventure. "I didn't get called up and didn't really get any encouragement that I would be. At that time I was 25 or 26, so I kind of knew that I was probably done as far as being able to get back to the NHL. I was at the age where I'm not high on their depth chart coming into another training camp, so I took the opportunity to go to Europe."

Tomalty and his wife headed across the Atlantic. He spent his first European season in Belgium, followed by a year in France. The solid two-way North American forward was a European scoring star. Forget about being a point-per-game guy: in Belgium he was a four-point-per-game guy. "When you can produce in that mode, you're treated like a king. That was an excellent way to finish off: we're going through college, I played pro for four years, it was a good option and a good alternative to see Europe for a couple of years."

By the summer of 1983, Glenn Tomalty's hockey career was over. A few years earlier he was skating in the NHL, but once he retired, the game took a back seat in his life for a long time. "It had to be 10 years where I really didn't want to pay attention to hockey or think about pro hockey. I guess I wished I was still doing it. That kind of thing."

Eventually Tomalty came back to the game. He played beer league until his late 40s. These days he works for GE and is a Calgary Flames season ticket holder. He doesn't dwell on his one game as a Jet. His NHL experience just seems to be part of his overall professional experience. "I don't look at my time in the minor leagues as something you just had to go through to play an NHL game. I enjoyed playing hockey. And for a lot of guys who played in the minors, it was a way to keep doing something they loved to do long into their 20s versus having to get a job at 20 years old.

"For me it was worth it to play in the minor leagues even if I hadn't played a game in the NHL. I would have still done it. It certainly was worth it. It was a bonus for me to get the one game, to play at least one game in the NHL."

A remarkable bonus when you consider that Glenn Tomalty, a teenage house-leaguer, made it to the best league on the planet.

KEN DUGGAN *Retired Times Two*

KPE Archives / University of Toronto

Ken Duggan's story isn't just about one game. It's hardly about one game at all. It sounds romantic: a rookie skating out onto the ice, in front of thousands of screaming fans for his first NHL game. It sounds romantic because it is. It is for me, anyway, but it isn't all that romantic for Ken Duggan. And if you expect Ken Duggan, who played his only NHL game for the 1987–88 Minnesota North Stars, to thrill you with the details of his big night, think again. In fact, dream on. "I want to say it was in Minneapolis." And who was it against? "I couldn't tell you, to be honest."

Ken continues, "The reason it's a little blurry is that I dressed for warm-up for three or four games. It's not one of those things where I can remember putting on the North Stars uniform for the first time and going out. I did that in Hartford, but I didn't play. But I did that in Philadelphia. Maybe it was in Philadelphia." For the record, Ken Duggan's only NHL game happened at the Spectrum in Philadelphia on January 24, 1988. The Flyers won 5–3. Duggan finished with an even plus-minus on the night.

21

Duggan can't fill you in on any huge hits, any of the goals or any other intimate details of that night. But his one night in the Show came as a result of a long and less travelled path to the NHL. It's just part of his story that ended in an early retirement from both the game and the nine to five grind. If you've ever been inspired by those old Freedom 55 ads, well they have nothing on Ken Duggan. We're talking about Freedom 40ish here. Ken Duggan hung up the skates in his mid-20s. He retired from the business world in his early 40s.

Ken Duggan's hockey journey started out like a lot of other Canadian teenagers. He had his sights set on Major Junior and began playing with the Sault Ste. Marie Greyhounds in the OHL. But he didn't stick with it for long, and when he was 17 years old he went back to Toronto to play tier II hockey. The following year he passed on Major Junior again for another year of Junior A, hoping for an NCAA scholarship. However, his second year of junior didn't go as planned — he didn't think he was getting enough ice time and quit his team. The scholarship offers went away. After a brief cameo for his high school hockey team, he ended up playing Junior B for the rest of the season. On paper, Junior B is a long way from anywhere, but it was here that Duggan rediscovered his love for the game.

"It was the best thing I ever did. It was a pretty good team, not a great team. But all of a sudden it was fun. Hockey was fun again. There wasn't a huge difference between tier II and Junior B, so it wasn't like you were going down there and you were a star. You get a little more success with the hard work maybe, but it was just the situation itself — from the coach to my teammates. It was a lot more fun. Part of it was that some of the pressure was off internally. It was like, 'Okay, let's just go play hockey.'"

Instead of playing U.S. college hockey, Duggan ended up playing at the University of Toronto. He walked on to the team as a freshman — a big freshman. He was 6-foot-3 and 230 pounds. The kid who walked away from the game just started getting better and better over the course of each year at U of T. No wonder, just listen to the future coaching stars he got to lace them up for while he was with the Varsity Blues. "I had Gord Davies, who was a heck of a university player, as a coach my first year,

Mike Keenan my second year, Tom Watt my third year and Paul Titanic my fourth year. And if you want to work hard the opportunity is there.

"I was an out of shape, lazy player when I showed up, and I was the opposite of that when I left."

Mike Keenan obviously took note of his improving monster-sized defenceman. Keenan left U of T after the 1983–84 season to become the head coach of the Philadelphia Flyers. Apparently one year without Duggan was enough for Iron Mike. After Duggan's third year as a Varsity Blue, he was invited to Flyers camp. Duggan impressed the Philly brass enough to be offered a 25-game AHL tryout. But Duggan, a future stockbroker, stepped back and did the math. Things just didn't add up. Duggan figured finishing up at university far outweighed a 25-game AHL tryout. Duggan passed on playing for the Philly organization and instead returned for a fourth year at U of T to finish his degree.

After his fourth year, the pros came calling again. Two teams wanted his services: the Vancouver Canucks and the New York Rangers. Duggan chose Broadway. All these years later he says it was the wrong move. "In hindsight, I would have been better off with the Canucks because it wasn't six weeks or two months after I signed with Craig Patrick that he got fired and Phil Esposito came in as general manager." It was bad news for Duggan. Patrick had scouted him right out of U of T, but now he had a new boss who hadn't seen him play at all.

"Esposito proceeded to trade or try to trade every university-educated player that he had. I swear he was targeting the kids with university education because they weren't good hockey players — his idea of what a hockey player was. I have a very low opinion of Phil. The exposure I had wasn't a great deal but there was enough to realize that he was out of his depth. He was probably 25 years too late in the hockey world. It was a professional business at the time that he took over. His assistant general manager was a guy by the name of Joe Bucchino who had been his limo driver. I kid you not."

Duggan played in some exhibition games with the Rangers and ended up in the AHL with New Haven. The Rangers and L.A. Kings split the affiliate, so you had a team comprised of future Kings and future Rangers. After just a few games in New Haven, Duggan ended up with the Flint Generals in the IHL. If Duggan didn't like Phil, he sure liked his boss in Flint: Rick Dudley. "I have nothing but nice things to say about Rick Dudley. A very intense man, but he's the kind of guy you wanted to play for — smart guy. At this point, we're talking 1986–87, he was learning the game as a coach-manager and stuff like that. So he was interested in learning how to do things better."

After year one, the Rangers bought out the second and final year of Duggan's contract. He was a free man. In the fall of 1987, Duggan decided to pass on the NHL and chase another dream: the Olympics. He spent the early part of the hockey season with Canada's national team. He played for Canada at the Spengler Cup in December 1987 and returned with the national team to Canada. "I got to play against the Big Red Machine a number of times. That was something to see in that day and age."

The Calgary Olympics were just a few weeks away, but Duggan could see how the next few weeks were going to unfold. "The writing was on the wall that I probably wasn't going to play in the Olympics. There was talk about it, and it turned out to be true that they were going to bring in some ex-NHLers and that was sort of the first step to the NHL participating in the Olympics."

When Duggan's Olympic dreams ended it was back to the dream of a life in the NHL. Once again Duggan had a choice to make between two teams: the Minnesota North Stars, who had run into some injury troubles on their blue line, or the Chicago Blackhawks. He chose the North Stars. "I ended up down in Minneapolis, St. Paul, for a couple of weeks. I think I met them in Hartford, that's how long ago it was, when the Whalers were still in business, when the North Stars were still in business. So that's how it sort of ended up."

But if you're looking for details from Duggan's one game with the Stars there basically aren't any. "Then they had a couple of guys come back [from injuries] and that was sort of it." And this is where his story takes *the twist*. It was the Freedom 40ish twist. Duggan could have gone back to Flint and slugged it out in the minors. He didn't. The future stockbroker started thinking. "The money in hockey wasn't great. I remember doing the math at 25 years old and sitting there and saying,

'If I play another couple of years in the minors and then I play five years in the NHL and I live and I live okay and I pay taxes, I'm going to have enough money to buy a house in Toronto.' So that's if I played five years in the NHL. So you sit there and you say, 'Okay, I'm not doing this for the money. If I'm playing in the minor leagues, I could have had a job waiting for me in Toronto that would pay me twice what I was making in the minor leagues.' So you're sitting there saying, 'Well, what do you want to do? Hockey's been a huge part of your life.'"

An agent found him a gig in Europe. He ended up on the worst team in the Dutch First Division for a season. The team wanted him to return the next year as a player-coach and manage the team. And that's when Duggan made up his mind. "From my upbringing, hockey was fun, it's a game. Now do I want to make it my life? Do I want it to be my job? And the answer is no."

Duggan walked away from the game, but he didn't walk away from competition. He took a job on the floor of the Toronto Stock Exchange for $16,000 a year. It was a gutsy move and it panned out. "It was an interesting cut in pay from playing hockey.

"I started in the stock market and that is a place where, in 1989 when I started, if you wanted to work and you wanted to work hard, the opportunities were literally limitless. I was a trader. I was a risk manager, a derivatives trader. That sort of thing — they pay you well."

For most players these days, their playing days are their chance to make the big bucks. That was not the case for Duggan, but he still retired early anyway thanks to all the hard work he put in before he turned 40. "I ended up in a mathematically driven business, but I was a political science student. So I had to learn math and economics after I finished hockey."

What did Duggan take with him from the ice to the trading floor? A strong work ethic. "I was a very good college player. I was good minor-league player. I was as fringe NHLer maybe, whatever. But underlying it all is just the basic assumption that you're going to have to work hard. And I'm not alone in this. A number of guys I played with in university who also did well in hockey have noticed that hard work is mistaken for excellence in the business world. Just by working hard you are already well ahead of the vast majority of people who punch a nine-to-five clock. I guess I had an aptitude for risk taking, but I just had a better work ethic than everybody I worked with. And I learned that in hockey because I was a lazy kid. Hockey prepared me for the trading world because you're expected to work hard and prepare — to have that ability to handle pressure."

You can see why Ken Duggan doesn't remember many of the details of his lone NHL game. You and I may look at playing in the NHL as some sort of dream come true. Duggan, a pretty analytical and practical guy, didn't really have stars in his eyes during his playing days.

"There is something very alluring about being a pro athlete, especially a pro hockey player in Toronto. If you say you're a pro hockey player when you're 25 years old, it's like, wow. But if you get the ego out of the way, it's like, let's make the right decision for the future."

Ken Duggan still plays with his old university buddies. He says the years he spent as a Varsity Blue were the best times he ever had in the game. But even though he retired from the game and his business life worked out as well as one could imagine, you still have to ask. You were 25. Did you walk away too soon? I mean with the cash that's being made by players today, would you walk away at 25? "Probably not, I probably would have given it two more years. It's hard because I have a much different view of money and economics now, having worked and having been involved in the stock market. I'm much more analytical now at 51. I look at it in a way I wouldn't have looked at it then: what's the net front value of those earnings?

"You could sit there and say, 'You know what? The carrot at the end of the stick is a five-million-dollar contract.' I don't know what Gretzky was making when I was playing but if someone was making 300 grand or 350 grand when I was playing, they were making large money."

Duggan did the math and left pro hockey. It paid off.

BROCK TREDWAY *Hockey's Moonlight Graham*

Brock Tredway will never forget first stepping onto the ice for a National Hockey League game. Sixteen thousand Los Angeles Kings fans were losing their minds. The Kings and Canucks were meeting in Game 4 of the second round of the 1982 Stanley Cup playoffs. The Canucks held a 2–1 series lead in a tight series. All three games had been decided by one goal. "I'm walking out on the ice, [Kings] fans are cheering and I can hear them say, 'Come on, Taylor. Come on, Dionne. Let's go, guys. Come on, J. P. Kelly. Come on, Tred —? Tredway? Who's Tredway?' That was a funny moment."

Brock Tredway stopped Kings fans in their tracks. They hadn't seen this Tredway guy all season long and here he was making his NHL debut in the Stanley Cup playoffs. The Great Western Forum faithful were asking how in the hell this happened. "We had just finished our [AHL playoff] series against the Rochester Americans and had some success in that. So what happened was in those days — boy, things have changed a lot — they generally called up one player per position as a backup. So up I go with very little notice," says Cornell grad Brock Tredway.

Just like that, Tredway took his place with the rest of the Kings extras to watch the series. That is when fate intervened during Game 3. "Jim Fox goes down with a hamstring or leg injury of some sort. I didn't really think too much about it, but right after the game I was told, 'You're going to be starting the next game.'"

It sounds simple enough. Tredway entered the Kings lineup during a wild spring in Hollywood. L.A. was hot off a 3–2 first-round series win over the Edmonton Oilers. That series was highlighted by the Miracle on Manchester. The Kings pulled off an amazing Game 3 comeback. They erased a 5–0 deficit with five third-period goals and scored the winner in overtime. Daryl Evans, who played alongside Tredway for most of the year with the New Haven Nighthawks in the AHL, scored the overtime winner. The image of Evans running on the ice is etched in hockey lore, but when Tredway got the call up to the Kings they were deep into their series against the Canucks and there wasn't a lot of time to reminisce about the Miracle. "I don't recall talking to Daryl specifically about that. As the series went on I was just so focused on what I was doing that we didn't really have much of a discussion, if any. I was so focused on getting into the game and doing what I needed to do to help out the team at that point."

Tredway spent most of 1981–82 on a line with Evans and Bernie Nicholls in New Haven. They put up some solid numbers. Nicholls scored 41 goals in just 55 games before he joined the Kings. Evans got called up as well. Tredway ended up with 59 points in 80 games for the Nighthawks. "Back in those days, scoring goals was quite a bit easier than it is today. We put up some pretty good totals down there and those guys got the call up earlier on and then it was my turn later."

Tredway's turn finally came on April 19, 1982. And here's the thing, he describes his memories of the night as "sporadic." He was lined up against the Vancouver Canucks, who would make it all the way to the finals in 1982 before losing to the eventual champion New York Islanders. "So I started the game, it was just so surreal. The fans were going nuts. I'm standing there with Bernie Nicholls and J. P. Kelly was the left winger and off we go. The game was quite a blur, but I do remember thinking Harold Snepsts was about 6-foot-9 without skates on. He's like the Zdeno Chára of today."

Tredway had a long way to look up to Snepsts. He may have seemed Chára-like, but in reality he was *only* 6-feet-3. Still, that was a long way up for Tredway, who was listed at an even 6-foot and slightly less than 170 pounds, giving up about 45 pounds to Big Harold. On April 19, 1982, though, it didn't matter. "I remember feeling absolutely fearless. It didn't matter whether I got my head cut off. I was going into the corners. I was the lightest guy and that was really the downfall of my career. I really couldn't put any weight on. I was a minnow, but I could score goals. But I just remember that fearless feeling of going into the corners just so energized."

One thing that does help Tredway make sense of that night is the game sheet. At that time, it wasn't like you could just go to NHL.com and go over your stats. But Tredway has them now. He tracked down a game sheet from that night, and it's one of his prized possessions. The Kings outshot the Canucks 37–15 but lost 5–4. "What really happened was that we got out-goaltended. Richard Brodeur was the goaltender and he just sort of stood on his head and he had a great run. They were calling him 'King Richard.'

"I had three shots on net, which also surprised me because I don't remember any of them. The whole thing is just a blur. They don't have a plus-minus on here so that's quite comical as well."

Like a lot of hockey memories, it's not the on-ice stuff that stands out. Talk to any retired player and they will likely tell you that they miss the dressing room and the guys in it as much as they miss the game. The L.A. Kings in those days were led by Marcel Dionne. When Dionne retired at the end of the 1988–89 season, he was the second highest scorer in NHL history. In 1981–82 he racked up 117 points for the Kings. For one night anyway, Brock Tredway could call him a teammate. "Marcel was an incredible leader and the guys really, really looked up to him. It was a new coaching staff. And we get in the dressing room, I think it was between the second and third periods, and he says, 'Guys, I don't know how many times I've told you. On the power play just give me the puck and get the fuck out of my way,'" laughs Tredway. "What he meant was I'll get the puck back to you, just give me the puck, get out of the way, get in front and I'll get you the pass. You'll be fine."

However, the Kings were not fine on that night. As Tredway says, they got out goaltended. King Richard made 33 saves and the Canucks headed back home with a 3–1 series lead in a best-of-seven series. After the game, the Kings dressing room looked like a 1982 version of *Entourage*. "Jamie Farr comes in and the guy from *Welcome Back, Kotter*, Gabe Kaplan, comes in. I'm thinking, 'Wow, this is Hollywood.' I think Jane Fonda was at the game. In fact I'm sure she was. So then I'm thinking about the next game, naturally, and the next game is going to be back in Vancouver."

Tredway had the full intention of extending his NHL career beyond one game. Jim Fox, however, had other plans. The Kings flew to Vancouver — a huge upgrade for Tredway, who was used to the buses of the AHL. There was a day off in between games, which meant a little extra rest for Jim Fox. On game night, Fox took the pre-game warm-up and so did Brock Tredway. Since Brock is featured in this book, I'm sure you can figure out how things went down. "Jim was the proverbial game-time decision. So I took the warm-up and I saw him skating around and I knew. It was Bernie Nicholls's tradition to be the last guy out at the end of the warm-up, and I kind of went off at the very end with him because I had the sense that I wasn't going to be playing. So I stayed on as long as I possibly could. I shot pucks in the crowd and passed them out. And as strange events would have it, that was the last touch of NHL ice I would ever have. I never got a sniff again. In the dressing room, the coach informed me that I wasn't going to be playing."

Brock Tredway could only watch as the Vancouver Canucks skated to a 5–2 win over his L.A. Kings. Bernie Nicholls opened the scoring just 90 seconds into the game, but once again King Richard and the Canucks were too much. The L.A. Kings were finished and so was Brock Tredway. "The following year I probably had my best camp, camp number two. I even grew a beard so I could look tougher. It was pretty funny. Again I may have weighed 170 pounds, but my heart was into it for sure. I did everything I possibly could to turn my body around, got in tussles and all that sort of stuff. I played with Bernie the whole camp. It was just 'you're going here, you're going there' and I was back down to New Haven, and that was all she wrote."

Tredway played three more years in the AHL and then a bit in Europe. But he never got close to the NHL again. A lot goes into that — timing, luck and injuries. Tredway had a gruesome incident one night. "I got my eye cut in Maine one New Year's Eve. My contact lens split in my eye. They had to take it out with forceps." Eventually Tredway knew it was time to pack it in and call it a career, with a single NHL game on his résumé. "The last bus trips I would say, 'Brocky, you did the best you possibly could. You did everything you possibly could do and it just didn't happen.' And even telling myself that didn't help. It was very, very difficult to come back to start a real life or a normal life. It is kind of a real la-la land. You're in a different time zone. If I had to talk to players starting out today, I would just remind them to be so grateful for that lifestyle. It is tough in terms of the bus trips and that physical toll, which I'm still paying the price for now, but boy oh boy, not having to go to work from nine to five and having the summers off and all that stuff. It's quite a lifestyle.

"I lived with it for quite a while and there was really a lull period there. I was down and upset and disappointed and disillusioned and I felt like I'd failed myself. There was a long time there, four or five years afterwards, where you hear lots of stories about guys [struggling with retirement] and it's so true because you can imagine focusing on something from the time you're six or seven years old and really wanting to do it and putting everything into it and then it's all over. It was very traumatic."

Tredway had trouble to adjusting to life without the game, even if he did have a degree from Cornell. Hockey had been part of his life since he was just a kid growing up on a backyard rink, and now it was gone. That's not easy to take. We always hear about that *ah ha* moment. You know, it's a moment of clarity, perhaps of finding yourself or of being content with your situation in life. Brock Tredway can more than put his hockey career in perspective now, but it was gradual process. There was no *ah ha* moment for the former hockey player.

"It's more like an incremental release, I guess . . . there was no moment, really. You tend to have a little more perspective when you get to be 55 like I am now, and you realize like Moonlight Graham that it wasn't meant to be and maybe you can be more successful in other areas."

In *Field of Dreams*, Burt Lancaster plays Moonlight Graham, a professional baseball player who played in just one Major League Baseball game in his life. He went on to become a doctor. Tredway has a great sense of humour about his career now and even signs fan mail with the inscription "Hockey's Moonlight Graham." However, just like Moonlight Graham did in the movie, Tredway often takes a trip back in time to his playing days. "There are times when I still have dreams. I'm back at Cornell or I'm playing with the Kings or different scenarios. I'm watching from the stands. It's just quite interesting, the mark that it does make when you've invested so much of your heart and soul into it."

Tredway ended up in financial services and insurance after his playing days. He describes himself as an "entrepreneur at heart" and is currently working on a product called ImedgeBoards that will "change the way snowboarders capture video while they are out on the slopes." It's a long way from the NHL, but that's life.

"I would not trade my life for anything. I mean, I got injured from toe to head between the professional game and the college game and all the games before that . . . I swallowed my tongue at Cornell and almost died, and if it weren't for a trainer and a doctor that jumped on the ice to pull my tongue out, I'd be dead. And you just keep going and you just go and go. I guess my disappointment has turned to gratitude. There are so many guys who would give their eyetooth for just one little game. One game in Washington on a Tuesday night — who cares what it is, even one shift."

TREVOR FAHEY *Coach International*

When you're a kid you often don't see what's right in front of you. In this case it was *who* was right in front of me. For a couple of falls during my minor-hockey days at the Hector Arena in Pictou, Nova Scotia, young wannabe NHLers were instructed by an outfit called Coach International. I enjoyed the drills but I was really impressed that they had a player named Bobby Heighton from the Junior C Pictou Mariners as one of their instructors. It turns out I should have been more or equally impressed with the School's head instructor, Trevor Fahey. "They were packed. We had great camps there," Fahey recalls of his time in my hometown in the mid-1980s.

Go back a couple of decades to the mid-1960s, and that hockey instructor was himself one heck of a player. New Waterford, Nova Scotia's Trevor Fahey was a 20-year-old first-year pro living the big life in New York City. Along with a slew of other young players, he was trying to make a name for himself with the New York Rangers farm club, the New York Rovers, in the Eastern League. "The Eastern League was a really dirty league. Oh my God almighty, you risked your life to go on the ice."

33

Fahey survived his first few months playing with the Rovers at Madison Square Garden as he cut his teeth as a first-year pro, literally just inches away from the NHL. On weekends, the Rovers would play their games at 2 p.m. and then the Rangers would play their games at 7:30 that night. It was a double header for New York hockey fans, and one day it was a double header for Trevor as well.

On January 10, 1965, Trevor was doing his thing for the New York Rovers, playing an afternoon game at MSG — nothing out of the ordinary. However, while Fahey was playing for the Rovers, the Rangers suddenly realized they were short a man. "They had called up a guy from the St. Paul Rangers for that night's game and, lo and behold, the flight was cancelled because of a snowstorm."

The Rangers needed a man as soon as possible. Fahey, who had turned 21 just a few days earlier, was about to get a belated birthday present. Once the Rovers game wrapped up, someone from the Rangers stormed into their dressing room. "They said, 'Trevor you're playing tonight for the Rangers. Go grab something to eat and come back for the game and get dressed.'"

Fahey, who led the Rovers with 30 goals in his first year as a pro, was about to get his shot at the NHL. On the downside he had no time to prepare — but on the upside . . . he had no time to prepare. Could you imagine the scenario today? Headlines would scream, "Double Duty for Rangers Rookie!" But in 1965, it wasn't that big of a deal. Fahey just did what he was told and started prepping for an NHL game that was going to happen in just a few hours. "I went down and got a quick little bite to eat there and of course I was shaking like a leaf. But I came back and got dressed and they gave me a number and a jersey and I was ready."

Fahey took care of the business side of things as well. And, no, there were no agents involved. "I signed a $100 contract for that one game, so they gave me $100 and I played the game."

When Fahey talks about the fact that he played two games in one day he's not as impressed as I am. He just matter-of-factly states that he suited up in two different uniforms for two different teams in two different leagues in one arena within a six- to seven-hour time span. It's all in a day's work, I guess. "I was right there. I was lucky," Fahey says of his sudden call-up.

"I got about six shifts, which wasn't bad. Once the score was three or four to nothing, they let me over the boards. In fact, what happened was I played with Earl Ingarfield and Bobby Nevin on a line. They were longtime Rangers. I think Earl played centre and Bobby played the right wing and I played left. We got a few shifts together and actually I got a couple of shots on Johnny Bower."

The Rangers lost 6–0 in front of 14,991 at Madison Square Garden. Fahey was impressed with the fact that he got a couple of shots on goal, but one of his biggest thrills came after the game. "Steve Brklacich, who coached me during my last year of junior in Kitchener, was coaching us on the Rovers, and after the game he took me to a diner because I hadn't eaten much. We walk in and, lo and behold, Johnny Bower is in there all by himself. And Johnny Bower and Steve were friends from Toronto. Johnny said, 'Hey, come on over, Steve.' And Steve introduced me and Johnny said, 'I remember you, kid. You had two pretty good shots tonight. You almost scored on me.' I said, 'Well, you got some great legs there. You made some good saves.' So that was a real thrill for me.

"Johnny Bower, what a humble guy. He sat there and talked to me and everything. He wished me luck."

After Fahey's one game with the Rangers and his meal with Johnny Bower, it was back to the Rovers and the Eastern League. He skated with the big club from time to time. "I practised on the same line as Rod Gilbert and Jean Ratelle three or four times during the season." But he never got in another game.

Fahey spent the next five years in the minors. He put up some impressive numbers including 76 points in 57 games for the International League's Des Moines Oak Leafs in 1967–68. Then after six seasons of pro, Trevor Fahey got a rather intriguing call from his brother Gus. A former star at St. Francis Xavier University in Antigonish, Nova Scotia, Gus Fahey wanted to know if his brother wanted to give up the pro game, pick up the books and play some university hockey. "Gus said, 'You're 25, 26 now. Why don't you come back and go to college?' So Gus went down and talked to them a little bit. Would they take me in and give me a shot?"

Trevor Fahey had one big problem, though. Like a lot of men from his era, he threw away his books in order to pursue his hockey dreams. Fahey had quit school in grade 10. When he was home that summer, he met with the folks at St. Francis Xavier University. Thankfully, he passed a mature student exam and was accepted into the school. He was granted a partial scholarship and the next thing the old pro knew, he, his wife and young son were on their way to Antigonish. Fahey's pro career was over. Actually, for the time being his entire hockey career was on hold. "They said, 'Trevor, you can't play the first half of the season until we see what kind of a student you are. You go to school and keep your marks up, then you can play.' I couldn't even practise with them. So my wife helped me study and I was getting along pretty well and I passed my tests and everything, so after Christmas they let me play."

Fahey scored 144 points in 79 regular-season games during his four years at St. FX. And it was good hockey; a lot of Maritime university squads were littered with former pros who Fahey was more than familiar with. "St. Mary's University brought a bunch of guys in. Guys I played against in the International Hockey League, actually. A lot of those guys played in the International League and Eastern League. They didn't play in the NHL, but they did play pro. And I remembered a lot of them.

"I ended up graduating with honours. That was the funny part."

The student would then become the teacher. In the fall of 1972, the Summit Series opened up a lot of eyes in Canada. It showed us that we were not the only hockey super-power on the planet. It opened Trevor Fahey's eyes as well. He was 28 and watching Soviet hockey for the first time. Even today when he describes what he saw and what he heard from the play-by-play announcers in the fall of '72, you can feel the passion in his voice. "When you heard Game 1 in that first series it was, 'They're coming over the line. They're coming down the ice. The Russians.' And he's going, 'Drop pass, another drop pass, another drop pass, another drop pass, shot. Goal.' That was the Russian offence."

The game of hockey had taken the kid from the small town of New Waterford, Nova Scotia, all the way to the bright lights of New York City, but Fahey had never seen anything like this. Within a couple of years, the kid from Cape Breton found himself in the Soviet Union. In 1974, Fahey's wife borrowed $500 from friends so Trevor could join a group of students from Concordia University to head to Russia and study the Russian game. He was among the first Canadians to ever head to the USSR for the sole purpose of studying Soviet hockey.

"I was in the first group to go. It was an unbelievable experience. I learned so much over there. I learned more about teaching the game, teaching skills and coaching. They broke it down step by step.

"What surprised me the most about how they played was how they taught the game. They taught every skill. They broke it down in steps, in two or three different phases. There was the beginning phase, then the middle phase and then the final phase. So they took you through all the steps of what your body should be doing — called biomechanics. What the biomechanics of your body should be doing to make this thing happen. That was in shooting and passing and skating."

The next year, in 1975, Trevor Fahey returned to Russia — this time as one of the program's coordinators. He was the head coach at Manitoba's Brandon University at the time, and he brought eight of his players and their parents along with him. He could not get enough of the Russian game. "We watched their Midget team practise and they did the same drill for an hour, focusing on breaking out, getting in, setting up, moving the puck — over and over again. So repetition became a very big thing in how I taught and how I coached my teams here. We taught repetition. When I coached, the drills became the game. I didn't teach systems, I taught drills — game drills that became the game with various options off those drills. It was fantastic. I learned all that from over there."

Before he knew it, Trevor Fahey was on the cutting edge. He penned two books on how the Soviets played the game. *All About Hockey* in 1974 and *Hockey: Canadian/Soviet* in 1977. He was now a top-notch student and teacher. Then he started up Coach International. That's what brought him to my neck of the woods in the mid-1980s, and he could not get enough of teaching.

Trevor Fahey is in his 70s now and he's still coaching. He teaches in Florida at the Tampa Bay Skating Academy. And he still preaches the same thing: skill, skill, skill. His genuine love of hockey still shines through. "I grew up in Canada. It's just a love of the game. I think the most important part of all is when you teach the little kids and they listen and they go out and do it. Watching them actually do it, executing the skill or the play and seeing that look on their faces and then the parents' faces, that's the real sort of happiness of it all. Watching the kids develop. And all of a sudden, man, they are just off to the races and holy cow.

"We play a Russian style of hockey: puck control, drop pass, moving the puck, open net goals . . . Bang." It was like Fahey was going to jump through the phone with excitement.

After hearing all this, I suggest that his single game with the Rangers is really just a small part of his hockey life. But he is quick to jump in. It was that one game with the Rangers in January 1965 that opened the doors to everything. "It led to all of the stuff I'm doing. When I first came down to Florida and advertised that I was going to coach little kids, my first advertisement said, 'Trevor Fahey once played in the NHL.'"

Fahey would tell any client that he only played one game in the NHL. He would tell them that he played junior as well, spent years in the minors and that he was the captain of his university team. But it was that one game in the NHL that's always impressed everyone. And it still means a lot to Fahey as well. "There were only six teams in those days. Remember, there were only 18 left wingers in the whole world . . . and for one game I was one of those guys."

JAMIE DOORNBOSCH *What Are You Doing Tomorrow Night?*

Nick Pearce, Saint Mary's University

On February 11, 2011, the Pittsburgh Penguins defeated the New York Islanders 3–0. The real story of the game, however, wasn't the score; it was what happened with 17 seconds to go in the third. Matt Cooke and Rick DiPietro collided with 17 seconds left and then the gloves came off. The only fighting majors went to the goalies — a scrap between DiPietro and Penguin Brent Johnson. It ended in one punch. Johnson delivered a left that knocked DiPietro down to the ice. The Pens and Islanders wouldn't meet again until April 8. It was the Islanders' second-last game of the season, and payback was on their mind. As the one-time Islander Jamie Doornbosch remembers, "I was stickhandling out by the blue line [during warm-up] and Islander Trevor Gillies was out there without a helmet on. He knew he was fighting that day. He had his Mohawk and his handlebar. He was looking as mean as nails. He was backing up and I ended up tripping him. I didn't see him. His skate hit my skate and he ended up spilling over backwards. I just looked at the ceiling, thinking, 'Tell me that didn't just happen.'" Doornbosch's NHL career was off to a horrible start before it even officially began.

He did what any rookie would do, especially one that was suiting up for his first NHL game. He got off the ice as quickly as possible and headed for the dressing room, hoping that no one noticed his trip on his teammate Gillies. "I got back in the room and one of the guys was like, 'Did you see Gills spill out there?' I just buried my head. 'That was me.' When Gillies came in one of the guys said, 'Gills, who spilled you?' And he goes, 'The fucking new guy.'"

Just a day earlier, playing in the NHL and tripping your tough-guy teammate in the pre-game skate was nowhere near Jamie Doornbosch's radar. He was in Kitchener, Ontario, licking his wounds from the OHL playoffs. His heavily favoured Kitchener Rangers were upset by the Plymouth Whalers in the first round. Doornbosch was nursing a shoulder injury from the series and thinking about what to do now that his junior career was over. "After we got kicked out, I was just distraught because I thought we were going all the way to the finals. A couple of days later, my agent asked me if I wanted to go play pro down south and I was like, 'For sure, what's available?'" What's available as in maybe a cameo in the East Coast League or the AHL? It turned out Doornbosch's agent was in talks with the AHL's Bridgeport Sound Tigers but a trip to Connecticut wasn't in the plans for his client.

"I guess the Islanders had a bunch of injuries and a couple of guys from Bridgeport had got called up already and then they needed another guy. Andy MacDonald had got hurt the night before. So my agent called me — it was on a Thursday night — and he says, 'Jamie, how do you feel about playing in the NHL tomorrow?' And I started laughing. I was like, 'What are you talking about?' And he goes, 'Well, New York just had another injury and I got you a spot for tomorrow night's game.' I was like, 'What do you mean you want me to play tomorrow night? I haven't been on the ice in almost a week.'"

Doornbosch had another problem aside from some rusty legs — the shoulder injury. He got hurt in Game 7. But who would say no to this chance? So Doornbosch told his agent what any other kid on the planet would tell his agent: *yes*. He was on his way to Long Island. "My room-mate drove me from Kitchener to my parents' house in Richmond Hill. I flew out at 5:30 the next morning from Pearson and I was in New York by 7:30 and a guy was sitting there with my name. He took me to a sports physiotherapy clinic and they did some testing. I was just gritting my teeth while they tested my shoulder. I just got through it. I ended up pre-game skating with them in the morning and then, since I hadn't really slept at all, I slept pretty much that whole afternoon."

Doornbosch jammed in his nap at a hotel across the parking lot from the Nassau Coliseum. He woke up and made his way across the parking lot for his first NHL game — your typical day for a 21-year-old. Now, remember, this was the return match against the Penguins. When Doornbosch made his way into the Islanders dressing room, a few of his new teammates thought there may be some new muscle in the lineup. "A couple of guys asked me, 'You just got called up. Are you a fighter?' And I just started laughing, 'No. I'll play the power play or something.'"

It didn't take long for Doornbosch to get a taste of just how talented NHLers are. Sure there was no Sidney Crosby or Evgeni Malkin in the Pens lineup, but before Doornbosch could even say, 'Wow, I'm in the NHL,' he was a minus one. "I got scored against during my first shift on the ice. Just the exact opposite of what you want."

Soon enough though the kid settled down and found his comfort zone. You hear this from a lot of one-gamers; at times the NHL can almost be easier than the lower leagues. That's because guys in the NHL always know just where to be, just where to position themselves to help out a teammate. It happened when his defence partner sent him a pass deep in the Islanders zone. "He passed the puck off the boards to me and I saw Max Talbot screaming down on me. It was a D-to-D pass behind the net and I just tapped the puck as I was getting crushed. I didn't even know if the centre was really there and it ended up being perfect, right on his stick. That was the difference between the NHL and junior: guys were always in the right position. That was when I felt comfortable and I was like, 'I'm okay. I know where everyone should be,' and it kind of went well from there."

Doornbosch finished the night with one shot on goal in five minutes and 21 seconds of ice time, and he was a minus one. If you're wondering if he got rich, the answer is no. Doornbosch was on an emergency call-up contract. "It was just per diem. I remember signing something before I played. It said 'emergency' right where I was signing. I asked my agent, 'Am I going to get paid?' My agent just started laughing. He said, 'Don't ask me about that. I'll talk to you after the game.'"

Doornbosch met his parents back at the hotel, changed into his civvies and headed for the hotel restaurant. That's when he got a taste of NHL life on Long Island. "There were a whole bunch of Islanders fans. I guess that's where the fans go after the game. And I asked the hostess for a spot for four and as soon as I went in the restaurant the whole place went nuts. 'Oh, that's Jamie Doornbosch.'" I was like, 'What are you talking about?' I just came here from playing junior. They had to put me in the back."

Doornbosch got a thank you very much from the Islanders and soon enough he was back home in Richmond Hill, wondering where his hockey life would take him next. He was looking for some decent pro offers: "I was hoping for some sort of free-agent deal . . . a good one-way contract, but I didn't find one I wanted." So Doornbosch did what a lot of kids who got a taste of the NHL would *not* do — he went to school. Jamie Doornbosch decided to take advantage of his OHL scholarship and he went east to St. Mary's University in Halifax, Nova Scotia, to play for former NHLer Trevor Stienburg. As of this writing, he is still at SMU. He's completed an undergrad degree and is working on an MBA. When he showed up at SMU in the fall of 2011, he told anyone who asked that he was a former Kitchener Ranger, not a New York Islander. "When I showed up most of them were like, 'Oh, this guy's going to be a big shot. His last game was in the Show.' And then after a couple of weeks they realized I wasn't very loud about it. I really let people find out about it themselves rather than me telling them."

Aside from brushing off a few trash talkers who thought he was too cool for school, Doornbosch had to adjust to reality. He was in Halifax, Nova Scotia, playing in front of hundreds, not thousands. "Yeah, it was kind of tough. I think for every single junior player, let alone a guy whose last game was in front of 20,000 people, it's a big adjustment. It took me until Christmas to realize I underestimated the hockey, big time. It's just as hard, if not harder, to play in the AUS than junior. But it's without all the glitz and glamour. There won't be 5,000 people at every game. You're not going to get the same treatment, the same glitz in the dressing room and all that kind of stuff. But it's a hard, skilled league to play in. There are guys who come from pro who can't put up a point a game like they think they are going to.

"When people come and get a chance to watch, it's a different experience. I think they would be surprised at how physical it is. Brad Marchand's brother Jeff plays on our team and Brad flies down every once in a while to watch a game. And he tells Jeff how surprised he is at how much hitting there is. Like, 'You guys hit way more than we do. It's crazy.' It's physical. And I guess that's because a lot of the skill guys find spots in pro to go to. And a lot of the good second-, third-, fourth-line guys end up coming to CIS."

Doornbosch says when he showed up at SMU the knock on his game was his lack of toughness. That, he says, has changed and he looks forward to bringing his tougher style of play back to the pros once he finishes school. And if it all goes according to plan, maybe you'll have to rip these pages out of this book one day.

"That's the plan. Obviously I am getting older, but I think this time in the AUS has been beneficial toward my game and making me more well rounded. That's kind of what I needed going into pro anyways. Hopefully after this season I'll be able to find a spot in either the Coast or the American League and work my way up from there. I think I have the work ethic and the state of mind to be ready for it."

Maybe one day Jamie Doornbosch can pull another NHL sweater over his head. The Islanders jersey he wore on April 8, 2011, left his hands right after the game. Remember, he suited up for the Isles' last home game of the season. The team's sweaters were auctioned off that night and Doornbosch had to hand over his jersey to a lucky fan. The rookie and the rest of the Islanders returned to their room clad only in shoulder and elbow pads. It was no big deal for longtime NHLers, but who wouldn't want their jersey for their first NHL game? That sentiment was not lost on Big Bad Trevor Gillies, the tough guy that Doornbosch tripped up during warm-up. "After the game, we were all stretching and I went up to Gillies and apologized. He was like, 'Don't worry.' And he said, 'Did you get to keep your jersey?' And I told him, 'I didn't, actually.'

He said, 'Okay, I'm going to buy you your first jersey.' He ended up buying me a jersey and shipping it to my house. He told me, 'No one ever did that for me. So I'm going to go ahead and do that for you.'

"That was a very nice gesture. The jersey that he sent over is hanging in my dad's office right now."

CHAPTER TWO
OLD SCHOOL

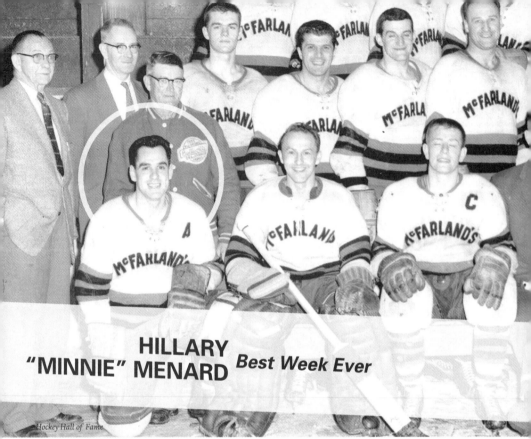

HILLARY "MINNIE" MENARD

Best Week Ever

"Here was my week. Do you want to know my week?" laughs Minnie Menard as he takes me all the way back to February 1954. It all begins on Tuesday, February 2, with a junior game in Guelph. "We played on Tuesday night in Guelph, I got on the train Tuesday night, got to Chicago early Wednesday morning. I practised with the Chicago Blackhawks Wednesday, played that game on Thursday night against the New York Rangers, got on another train after the game and made it back to Guelph in time to play another junior game. I happened to score two goals that night." Now that is one wild week for a 20-year-old. A game in Guelph, a trip up to the NHL for his first game and then a quick train back to Guelph for a Friday night game. But here comes the kicker. "Here's what nobody knew all this time: I got married on Saturday after the game Friday. That was a tough, tough week. I got married in Toronto."

You ask about a single hockey game and just like that you get filled in on a week that shaped the rest of his life. The game was one thing, but the wedding back in Toronto was a top-secret affair. "I didn't dare tell them I was getting married because in those days they didn't like junior hockey players to get married."

One of Minnie's brothers, Howie, who also played in the NHL, got married when he was in junior as well. When the Toronto Marlies found out about his nuptials they traded him to Hamilton. Now it worked out for Minnie's brother — he was named captain in Hamilton and they won a Memorial Cup. But that was years later. In 1954, this was a lot to take for Minnie Menard.

Minnie hopped on that train to Chicago with the full intention to play his best for the Blackhawks. But he also had a plan in place to make it back to Toronto for his Saturday wedding, just in case Chicago wanted to keep him up in the NHL. "I'll tell you how stupid young people are. I purposely didn't take any extra clothes with me, thinking if they decide to keep me — they don't know about the wedding, right — 'I'll tell them that I didn't bring any clothes or anything and I have to go back.' I was too afraid to tell them I was getting married. But if I needed to I would have."

There was no need to fill the Chicago brass in on the wedding. Menard was sent right back to Guelph after that one night against the Rangers. "Going up to Chicago happened so fast. I wasn't overly impressed with it. I just didn't have time to absorb it all, to be honest with you. New York beat us 2–1. And, I mean in all sincerity, I generally played a very good game. Sid Abel was the coach at the time and he played me on power plays. He let me kill penalties. I did everything."

Menard wasn't all that worried about being sent back to Guelph. He was still only a kid, a soon to be married kid, but he figured there would be plenty of stops in Chicago in his very near future. Abel liked him. But following a sixth place finish in a six-team league, Abel left Chicago after the 1953–54 season. But it wasn't just Abel that was let go; the Blackhawks turned over their entire front office. It was a front office that had been keeping an eye on Menard since he signed a C-Form with Chicago when he was only 15.

In the 1950s, you needed a few things to make the NHL. You needed skill and you needed the right people to give you a chance. There were only a few spots in the league and if a coach or GM didn't take a shining to you it was tough luck. "If they didn't like the way you combed your hair they didn't keep you, literally. You weren't allowed to have beards. There were so many hockey players that could have played but didn't for one reason or another.

"I was able to go to the National Hockey League when it was the Original Six — that means a lot. There were 120 guys playing in the league whereas now there's probably 700."

Menard kept playing. He eventually found himself in Belleville, Ontario, and that is where things really took off for Hillary "Minnie" Menard. He was putting up huge numbers on the ice. Then, suddenly around Christmas 1956, he started to take in some huge numbers off the ice. Menard signed with the Belleville McFarlands in the fall of 1956. He told the team he could get them 30 goals that year. Menard had 30 by Christmas. That's when he found himself in the GM's office. Before he knew it, he suddenly turned into perhaps the first ever player-agent the game had ever seen. "I was joking with him and I said, 'This will be the last cheque I'll be picking up.' He says, 'What do you mean?' I said, 'I'm going to take the rest of the year off because I'm going down to Florida for the winter.'"

Minnie Menard was joking. However, the GM thought his leading scorer was deadly serious. "He says, 'You can't do that.' I said, 'Well, I promised you 30 goals and I've got you 30 goals.' And all of a sudden I realized that this turned from a joke to a serious conversation." It was time for Minnie Menard to make his move. First he asked for his wages to be doubled, then Menard threw something else out there, something that no player had ever received before.

"And I said, 'Year round.' And he said, 'Okay, I will.' And that's a true story and that's the way I ended up getting the deal. I was the highest paid hockey player in Canada at the time. I was making more than most NHLers." At a time when plenty of men in the big leagues were making well below $10,000 a year, Minnie Menard got himself a deal that paid him $18,000 a year to play senior hockey.

"I knew Bobby Hull real good because he was from Belleville. And I saw him after that and they all knew I was making a lot of money but they didn't know how much. Nobody ever knew because in those days hockey players didn't share. Even my linemates didn't know the kind of money I was making."

Minnie Menard had found his hockey home. His Belleville McFarlands won the Allan Cup in the fall of 1958 and the World Championship the following spring in 1959. Menard says the Allan Cup win in 1958 is the highlight of his hockey career. The entire Allan Cup series was played out west against Kelowna. "I had a very good playoff series. I scored some winning goals. We were down 3–1 in games and came back and beat them, and all on the road.

"Probably one of the goals I remember the most happened during the sixth game. We were tied 3–3 and if we lost, we'd be done, and I scored the wining goal in the third period. And that allowed us to go to the seventh game where I got two goals, so I had a very good series. I would say those were the highlights that I remember."

Menard and the McFarlands got back on the train and headed back to Belleville. They made plenty of stops on the way back with the Allan Cup in tow for everyone to see. "The Allan Cup was considered second to the Stanley Cup. I remember we had stopped in Calgary and there were a few thousand people to meet us and cheer us on. They gave us big Stetson hats. It was nice. It was great."

Eventually the NHL came calling again. Menard had drawn the interest of the Detroit Red Wings. They wanted the Belleville McFarlands star in their lineup. Once again Minnie Menard went into negotiations. He was at training camp with the Wings when their GM Jack Adams offered him a deal. "He offered me a contract to turn pro with them, but he offered me $2,500 to sign and $4,500 to go out to Edmonton for the season. Edmonton was their number one farm team. Well, I had a little problem with that because I was making $18,000 a year playing for Belleville. I'm not saying this to brag, I'm giving you information, and I don't do this very often. And I said, 'Mr. Adams, $4,500 and $2,500 — that's $7,000. It sounds very good' — because the minimum salary back in those days in the National Hockey League was $6,600 — 'but I've got a problem with that. I'd be taking a pay cut.'"

Menard had two kids at the time, and the family would eventually add a third, and just like any other family man he wasn't interested in a cut that would pay him less than half of his current salary. Adams inquired further, trying to figure out just how much Minnie Menard was making playing senior hockey. "He said to me, 'How much are you making?' I said, 'I'm making $18,000 a year. So how do I go home and tell my wife I'm going to take that?' He said, 'Well, I'll guarantee you at least five games with Detroit.' I said, 'Yeah, but still I'll only be making $7,000 a year.'" It was basically a 66 percent pay cut for Menard. But that was hockey at the time. Adams then pulled out the Gordie Howe card.

"He says, 'The Big Guy [Gordie Howe] only makes $25,000 a year.'" That did not move Menard on his stance. Menard offered this quip to the Wings GM. "I said, 'It sounds to me as if Gordie's got a problem then, doesn't it.' He said, 'The league won't last a minute.' And I said, 'That might be true but how can I take that kind of a cut?' He understood. He didn't like it but he understood. It wasn't long before they gave Gordie his raise."

So a life in the NHL was not meant to be for Minnie Menard. His younger brother Howie played 151 regular-season games and Minnie played one. He doesn't regret a second of it. "Whatever little bit we got I owe it to hockey."

Hockey eventually cost him vision in one eye but even that didn't diminish his love for the game. You can still hear the passion in Minnie's voice. He eventually settled in Iowa. The game brought Menard and his family to Des Moines in the early 1960s. Once he was done playing, he opened up a cocktail club. "After a few years, I found out that was not a good business for a married guy with kids to be in."

Menard started a lighting business that he still owns with his three kids. It's his days with the Belleville McFarlands that he really treasures. Not that he isn't proud that he played with the Chicago Blackhawks, but you can tell Belleville is where his finest hockey memories lie. He made solid money while he was in Belleville, while most of his teammates "were making about $150 a week. Now bear in mind, if you went to work at a factory or something you would have only made about $40 a week in those days."

Eventually, the rest of the McFarlands found out what their old sniper was hauling in. But it took a while. "I think it was our 50th anniversary.

We got together and we had a party and they all started talking about their salaries. And then finally they said to me, 'Okay, Menard, it's your turn. And don't give us any bullshit because we know you were making a lot of money.' And I did let it out at that time."

I asked Minnie if he picked up the tab that night; he laughed and said he picked up a lot over the years. It's amazing where a simple phone call can take you. I had called Minnie Menard to talk about his one game with the Chicago Blackhawks, and he offered me up a story that had so much more. I couldn't resist. Going back to the story of the wild week when he made his Blackhawks debut *and* got married, I asked: What was the highlight? Playing for Chicago or getting married? Before Minnie could even take a breath I could hear his wife, Loretta, in the background shout, "Getting married."

Minnie, of course, a man who has been married for over 60 years, gave the right answer as well. "It was a pretty darn good week. But the highlight, no question, was getting married. That's the truth."

LEN BRODERICK *It's in the Cards*

Back in my minor-hockey days — and I'm sure many of you share the same experience — I'd drive to a game with my dad and beg him to step on the gas. "We're going to be late," I would say. The old man would always get me there on time, though, just like Len Broderick's dad did when he drove Broderick to Maple Leaf Gardens on October 30, 1957.

"I was supposed to be at the game an hour early and my dad had been offered tickets from his boss. He had not been to a Leafs game for probably 10 or 15 years so I had to go with my dad, pick up his boss and drive to the game. I got to the arena at 7:15 and the game started at 8:00," says one-time Montreal Canadien Len Broderick.

Being a little late was usually no big deal. Broderick played goal for the Toronto Junior Marlies, and in his spare time he made $25 a game serving as the visiting team's backup goaltender for Toronto Maple Leafs games. "I usually sat in Conn Smythe's box up in the greens. You just had to be there and if anything happened then you were in."

On this night, however, for the first and only time in Broderick's career, something happened. The Canadiens star goaltender Jacques

Plante suffered an asthma attack and couldn't play. The Habs were scrambling to find 19-year-old Len Broderick, but he was nowhere to be found. When he walked through the player's gate at 7:15, Broderick was told that the Habs were looking for him and he was going to be their goaltender that night. "So I was like, 'Where's my equipment?'" laughs Broderick. "At that time that was probably one of the greatest teams Montreal ever had, with Jean Béliveau, the two Richards and Doug Harvey."

The kid made his way through the bowels of Maple Leaf Gardens and down to the visitor's room. He walked in, just a kid amongst some of the greatest players the game has ever seen. The Rocket was the first one to come and say hello. "Rocket Richard, who was the captain of the team, came over and sat down and introduced himself and talked to me. I guess he was trying to settle me down." The Rocket didn't need to worry about calming down his newest teammate. "I didn't get upset about playing games. In fact, I enjoyed playing pressure games more than I enjoyed non-pressure games."

As Len Broderick's NHL career was about to begin, his dad was up in the stands peering over at Conn Smythe's seats, looking for his son. He didn't see him. When he finally did see him he was wearing the bleu, blanc et rouge of the Montreal Canadiens. And how did the old man feel about seeing his son on the ice? "He never told me, but I'm sure he was very surprised."

When the game began, 14,091 fans, including Broderick's dad and his dad's boss, watched the Leafs and Canadiens in their second head-to-head clash of the season. Absolute legends were doing their thing — there was the Rocket, the Pocket Rocket, Béliveau, Mahovlich, Geoffrion . . . and a 19-year-old named Len Broderick. Soon enough, Broderick got his first NHL test. He looked up and Frank Mahovlich was all alone. "Pretty early in the game, Frank Mahovlich got a breakaway. And I had gone to Leafs camp that year and Mahovlich, in shooting practice, had come down and dipsy-doodled and put it between my legs, and he did it every time to the point where both of us were laughing about it. And when he got the breakaway I thought, 'He is not going to put it between my legs.' So I kept them closed and he tried to put it through my legs and it didn't go in. And as he was skating around I saw him look back and I could see on his face he couldn't believe it wasn't in the net."

Broderick continued to stymie the Leafs. He stopped every shot he faced in the first and every shot he faced in the second. He had 13 saves and the Canadiens had a 4–0 lead after two periods. The Leafs were trying everything to get one by the kid, but they could not beat him. During a scrum around his net, one of his foes on the Leafs was basically begging for him to let up. "I do remember Bob Pulford saying, 'Lenny, what are you doing to us?'"

Broderick had a shutout going until nine minutes and 39 seconds into the third. Barry Cullen got the Leafs on the board with a power play goal. Broderick and the Habs left the Gardens that night with a 6–2 win. After the game, Broderick had to return the Jacques Plante sweater he was wearing back to the Habs. But he did end up with a few extra bucks from the Canadiens, a little bit more than the $25 he would have made watching from the stands. "There was a letter from Frank Selke thanking me for playing against my home team. They had to pay me a hundred and they gave me $150."

The classy Habs had tipped him. Why not? He got the win.

After the game, Broderick drove home with his dad. Actually they didn't go straight home: "I went to see my girlfriend," he said. I guess you have to make the most of being an NHLer.

Broderick went back to playing junior hockey with the Marlies. Toward the end of his junior career he tore some ligaments in his knee. The Leafs wanted him, but Broderick had other plans. As strange as this seems nowadays, Broderick passed on a pro hockey contract because the money wasn't good enough. "When I finished junior, Smythe phoned me up at home and wanted me to come out, and I said I was finished because at that time they were only paying first-year players in the NHL $8,000. And I wasn't willing to go get battered and banged up for $8,000 a year. I was a chartered accountant at the time, so I just decided that I was going to make more money being a chartered accountant than I was from being in the NHL."

Broderick's career took him to the United States and he now lives in Greenville, South Carolina. He has a picture of him and the Richard boys to remind him of his one night in the NHL, and every once in a while little cardboard reminders of his one night in the show arrive in his mailbox. How perfect was Broderick's timing back in 1957? He got to play in net for the legendary Montreal Canadiens, his dad attended his first game in 15 years and got to watch his son play in the Show, and, on the night Broderick played, a photographer for a hockey card company just happened to be at the game snapping pictures. "I'm on three hockey cards and I still get requests a couple times a month for autographs and stuff."

PAUL KNOX *The Night Horton Got Hit*

"Do you know that game at all? Well, the most significant thing wasn't me," laughs Paul Knox.

The game he's referring to is his one and only in the NHL. When I picked up the phone to call Paul Knox, all I knew was that he suited up for the Toronto Maple Leafs during the 1954–55 season. That's when he fills me in on the details. On a night that still lives on in hockey folklore, Paul Knox had a front row seat for one of the most infamous hits in the history of Maple Leaf Gardens.

"It was the night that Bill Gadsby hit Tim Horton at centre ice and broke his jaw and leg. He had the concussion, damaged ribs and he ended up in hospital for quite a while. And that is really what I remember most from that game. And it was a clean hit, right at centre ice. Tim Horton was winding up for a rush from one end to the other. He had the puck and when he got to centre ice for whatever reason, and it sticks in my mind, he looked down to see if the puck was still there and at that crucial moment Gadsby hit him. So he wasn't prepared for it at all. He just crumbled. I was on the bench watching."

That hit occurred on March 12, 1955. Tim Horton missed the rest of the season and the first half of the following year. In the aftermath, Leafs owner Conn Smythe chased Gadsby in the hallways of the Gardens. It was quite a night for Knox to make his NHL debut. "I certainly remember it, and I think anyone who was at the Gardens that night will remember that game for that reason."

Just a day earlier, Paul Knox was minding his own business, studying at the University of Toronto. His junior career at St. Michael's College had wrapped up the previous spring. He attended Maple Leafs training camp in 1954 but he didn't catch on. He decided to hit the books and enrolled at the University of Toronto, where he played with the Varsity Blues. One day before Gadsby hit Horton, the Leafs tracked down Knox. One of Toronto's players was under the weather and wouldn't be able to play the following night against the Rangers. The Leafs wanted Knox to suit up. Knox had played plenty of games at the Gardens before, but this time it was in the NHL. The Leafs put him on a line with Sid Smith and future Hall of Famer Ted Kennedy. "I needed all the help I could get."

The significance of the game, at Maple Leafs Gardens on a Saturday night, and with Foster Hewitt calling the action from the gondola, got the best of the 21-year-old Knox. "I think it was the only time I remember stopping to take two or three really deep breaths just to get control of myself. I guess I felt the pressure. I was relatively naive and immature at that time. But I loved playing hockey so it was something I felt natural doing. But that night, instead of seizing the moment I think I said, 'Hey, don't make a mistake. Don't make a mistake.' And that's when you start to hesitate. You've gotta play hockey all out, you've got to play the game."

If the nervous youngster was looking to his future Hall of Famer linemate for a little advice, he wasn't getting any. "To be quite honest I don't think Teeder Kennedy said a word to me. But Sid Smith was terrific. He warned me about Bill Ezinicki, who used to play for Toronto and was with New York at the time. Bill Ezinicki could really bodycheck, and he loved to get at guys as they came around the net. Because when you come around the net there isn't too much room to get out of the way if anyone's coming after you dead on. So he warned me of that.

"Other than Sid Smith I don't think there were too many people who said anything to me, which is too bad in a way."

Tim Horton, like Knox, was a product of St. Michael's College. Horton's legacy at St. Mike's trickled down through the years. "He was said to be a really strong person. If he went into the goalpost — the goalpost bent. And that was sort of it, I guess. During that game in Toronto he just wasn't prepared at all."

And all these years later, Knox figures the Gadsby hit got the big defenceman thinking. "I think that's when the light went on in Tim Horton's mind saying, 'Hey, I gotta do something after hockey is over so I better start thinking about it.' And I think that is when the idea of the doughnut place came into being."

By the following Monday morning, Paul Knox was a former NHLer. The Leafs said thank you very much for coming out, and Knox headed back to U of T. The next spring Knox had another crack at the Leafs but ended up joining the Kitchener-Waterloo Dutchmen of the OHA. The Dutchmen also just happened to represent Canada at the 1956 Winter Olympics in Cortina d'Ampezzo, Italy. One year after playing at the Gardens, Knox was playing outdoors in the Southern Alps. "In those days you played every team once and whoever went through the series of games and was at the top was the winner. And I can remember playing Sweden; it was an afternoon game, and it was snowing. Crazy, but we all had to play under the same conditions."

Knox and the Dutchmen, with Martin Brodeur's father, Dennis, in goal, won bronze for Canada. So what stands out more, his one NHL game or his time at the Olympics? That's a tough question for the soft-spoken Knox to answer. He leans a little toward the Olympics. "I would say yes, although both are experiences that I'm glad I have."

After the Olympics, Knox continued to play a little hockey on the side, but he basically concentrated on school. He became a teacher. He says he is sure a few of his students knew of his old athletic days but he never made a big deal of it. He's a grandfather, and he says that not even all of his grandkids are aware that Grandpa was once a hockey star.

And he still thinks of that infamous night at the Gardens, more than 60 years ago, when he suited up for the Leafs: "A terrific experience. One that I was very fortunate to get."

The Minor Midgets

JACK MARTIN *The Friends You Make*

St. Michael's Tower, 1956

The Minor Midgets, boasting great power on all fronts, had a most successful season. When the regular schedule was completed the Irish lads found themselves sitting on top of the heap. The playoffs are now in

bull, Hall and Hunt... The "kid line" of Mealing, Belliveau and Tindale, presented a strong reserve unit. Brian Neilson took over the goalie spot at the close of the season and showed well

When I tell Jack Martin I'm writing a book on men who played just a single game in the NHL, it doesn't take long for the name of another one-game wonder to pop up. "I met Don Cherry at Maple Leafs camp and then I played against him in the Eastern Professional Hockey League. We kind of got along all right. We went out and had a few pops together after a game one time. I think it was in Sudbury."

The EPHL's Sudbury Wolves were Jack Martin's first pro team. He signed on with the Wolves after playing with St. Michael's College during school and then two years of junior with the Toronto Marlboros. Martin found himself in Sudbury when he was just 19. "In those days you used to call it a three-way contract: the National League, the American League and either the Western League or the Central Pro League — so let's say three divisions. Sudbury offered me $4,000 for the season. If I was in the American League I would have gotten $6,000. And in the NHL I would have gotten $10,000. Well, of course they could have offered me $50,000 because I wasn't going to be playing there anyway."

Or so he thought. On November 27, in the second of back-to-back games against the Detroit Red Wings, Jack Martin got the chance to take to the ice for the Toronto Maple Leafs. It was a Sunday game in Detroit. But the game in Motown could have been the second of his NHL career. "From what I understand, Detroit played in Toronto on Saturday night and they actually called me but I wasn't in. They wanted me to play that night in Toronto. They must have been missing a person. I think Ron Stewart was hurt or something. Anyway, the next day, they got a hold of me and they wanted me to come and play in Detroit."

Martin made his way to Union Station in downtown Toronto. The Leafs 1960–61 schedule is littered with back-to-back Saturday and Sunday games against the Wings. It was usually a game in Toronto on a Saturday followed up by a game in Detroit on a Sunday. As per usual, the team jumped on an early morning train and headed for Detroit. "There were sleepers there so I just went and lay down. I remember Red Kelly was below me. I was on top and he was below. Everybody was sort of stretching out. It wasn't a long trip."

When Martin arrived in Detroit he had an issue. "I remember that I didn't have my skates so they gave me another pair." This may have been a problem for Martin, but it wasn't really a problem for the Leafs. So what if he didn't like his new blades — it wasn't like he was going to use them that much anyway. After all, if Martin didn't hit the ice at the old Olympia, the Leafs could save a few bucks. "Basically the rule was if you just sat on the bench for the game you got, I think, either $50 or $75, and if you stepped on the ice you got $100." Martin did get into the game, so he got his full $100. But he didn't play a ton and the memories of that day in Detroit don't exactly come flooding back. He was, however, witness to hockey history.

"Gordie Howe got two assists that night and that gave him 1,000 points." How's that for timing? Martin played one game and saw Mr. Hockey achieve a milestone. "Yes. Him and me," laughs Martin.

Martin and the Leafs took the train back to Toronto after the game. The Leafs tried to sign him to a deal, but it didn't happen and he ended up back in Sudbury for the rest of the year. He had 21 points in 44 games during his first full year as a pro. Of course, the plan was to crack the

Leafs lineup the following year. Martin was a high-scoring centre during his time in junior and if he was going to make it in the Original Six that's what he would need to continue to do. But he never got the chance. He was in a battle for a spot on the Leafs with one of his old buddies from St. Mike's College. "Bob Davidson was the head scout of the Leafs, and I ran into him coming out of Maple Leaf Gardens at the end of the season. And he kind of said to me, 'It was between you and Keon.'" That would be Dave Keon. Keon, of course, stuck with Leafs and went on to a Hall of Fame career. For the record, he and Martin are still great friends and they still exchange Christmas cards every year. But as Keon went on with the Leafs, Martin found himself in San Francisco, of all places, playing for the Seals of the Western League in 1961–62. "When I got off the plane in San Francisco I said, 'Where the hell am I?'"

Like a lot of players from his era, Jack Martin had fun on and off the ice. He split the 1961–62 season between three teams in three leagues. The following year he had 65 points in 67 games with the Charlotte Checkers of the EHL. Racking up points in the Eastern League was never a problem for Martin, but he was a long way from the NHL.

"I had no problem scoring goals. But the Eastern Pro League was a tough league. You had to watch what you were doing." Martin survived and thrived in a league that was notorious for its toughness. In 1963–64, he led the Nashville Dixie Flyers with 107 points. The next year he suited up for the Knoxville Knights and was on top of the team's scoring race with 108 points. But after those 108 points, Jack Martin retired from pro hockey at just 23.

Martin, like some of the other men in this book, made it all the way to the best league in the world when there were only six teams. You get the sense, however, that he knows he could have had more than just that one night with the Leafs. "You're looking to play in there regularly, but it just didn't work out. I didn't behave myself, you know? I just went on talent. I didn't put out too much."

Following his hockey career, Martin worked as a firefighter for about four years. Then he found himself in the Barrie, Ontario, area working for Bombardier. He was in the Ski-Doo business, mainly in the clothing end. "I was the supervisor just near the end." Then it was back to his hometown of St. Catharines where he worked for the city for 28 years. His brother Frank, who played in 282 NHL regular-season games, also worked for the city.

If the details of his hockey career don't come charging out of Jack Martin, the friendships he made during his time in the game certainly do. Some of us treasure pucks, or sticks, or uniforms. But when you talk to a lot of former players, you realize it's the friendships they made with their teammates, and in some cases their opponents, that they truly treasure. Martin played at St. Mike's with guys like Keon and Gerry Cheevers. He is still tight with both of them. Cheevers winters in Florida but spends his summers in St. Catherines. Martin and Cheevers still get together quite often. It was that friendship with Cheevers that gave Martin something that still lights him up to this day. Cheevers didn't do anything for Martin, instead he allowed Martin to do something for a young boy from St. Catherines way back in the 1970s. "I had a little guy I was looking after. Winter was coming and I said to him one day, 'John, do you have a favourite hockey player?' And he looked at me and he said, 'Yes, I do. Gerry Cheevers.'"

You can feel the warmth in Jack Martin's voice as he tells this story. He's not bragging about a goal. He's not bragging about a hit or a fight. He's not bragging at all. He's simply telling a story about what a privilege it was to be a pro hockey player, even if for a second. And how that privilege of being a pro player, and knowing other pro players, was able to make a little kid's day. Two weeks later the Boston Bruins were in Toronto to play the Leafs. Martin phoned up John's mom to ask if it was okay to take the little guy down to the Gardens to meet his hero. His mom said it was okay to go, so the two made the trek to Toronto and found their way into Maple Leaf Gardens. They were walking along the perimeter of the rink, when they ran into Wayne Cashman, who was standing outside the visitors' dressing room. "And I stopped and I said, 'Wayne, could you tell me if Gerry Cheevers is in the dressing room? I'm looking for him.' He said, 'Just a minute.' So he went in the dressing room."

Jack and John patiently waited outside the visitors' locker room. A few minutes later, Jack's old friend, and John's favourite player, Gerry

Cheevers walked out. "I introduced Gerry to John and I said, 'Gerry, you're John's favourite hockey player.' Well, how many guys pick a goaltender, you know? And Gerry talked with John for a few minutes and then he said, 'Come with me.' So we walked to the dressing room, and Gerry introduced him to all the players. Bobby Orr was there, all those guys. So he introduced them and then he gave John his stick and he got everybody to sign it. So here was this little kid with his hockey stick and it was just the thrill of his life."

I tell Jack Martin that it's amazing he was able to provide a little guy with the experience of a lifetime. But like a true hockey player, he won't take the credit. Instead, he hands it off to the men he met when he played the game. "It was fortunate that I knew people who I could do this with."

CHAPTER THREE
LET'S GO, PRETTY BOY

CAM BROWN *A Hall of Fame Career*

On March 3, 1991, left winger Cam Brown stepped on the ice at Chicago Stadium for his first NHL regular season pre-game warm-up. His NHL debut was just 30 minutes away but he was ready to go to work. He was not going to give Canucks head coach Pat Quinn any excuse to take him out of the lineup. Just a couple of months earlier, one of Brown's teammates on the Milwaukee Admirals of the IHL told him of a call-up he'd had with Chicago a year earlier that turned out to be every young player's worst nightmare. All seemed well as he took the warm-up under the watchful eye of head coach Mike Keenan. "He called the guy in after warm-up," Brown says, "and said, 'If you call that a warm-up I don't need you on my team.'"

That was enough to convince Cam Brown to bust his guts, and that night his pre-game routine was about more than just checking his bucket-less lid in the reflection of the Plexiglas as he got set to take on Chicago in front of 17,595 fans. "I thought, 'You know what? I'm going out here for warm-up and I'm going to bust my ass,' as I always did.

I really concentrated on picking the corners of the net instead of just firing it, different things like that.

"I remember being awfully jacked up and flying around . . . I was doing everything as quickly as I could. In hindsight it's kind of funny to think about guys who were maybe six- or seven- or eight-year pros at that point looking at me going, 'Look at this kid. He's raring to go, but seriously?'"

The intensity worked. No one gave Brown the tap when he came off the ice. He was just 15 minutes away from this first NHL game.

Just a day earlier, Brown, a first-year pro, was pulled off his team bus in Milwaukee by Admirals coach Mike Murphy. The Admirals were set to bus to Fort Wayne, Indiana, but the coach wanted to chat before the bus hit the highway. Like any other young kid, the first thought that went through his head was, "What did I do?"

"He said, 'I got good news and I got bad news. The bad news is you're not making the trip tonight.' I said, 'Oh, what's the good news?' And he said, 'You and Andrew McBain are going up tomorrow. They'll call you with travel arrangements but you're going to Chicago tomorrow to play for the Canucks.'"

The Canucks wanted a little more muscle in their lineup. They were without the services of Gino Odjick, who had broken his cheekbone thanks to an elbow from the Penguins' Jay Caufield just a few days earlier. Brown was no stranger to dropping the gloves. "For them to pick me and ask me to come up blew me out of the water. Talk about being out of left field. I was playing decent but I definitely wasn't the same heavyweight calibre as some of the NHL guys. They told me to go home and pack." Brown called his folks and tried to get some sleep.

The next day Brown and his fellow call-up Andrew McBain got on a train headed for Chicago. Brown remembers being overly curious about what was going to unfold in just a few hours' time. For McBain, a veteran of seven full NHL seasons, it was almost routine. He knew what was coming. Brown was wide-eyed. "I remember Bainer saying, 'Just relax.' I got kind of worked up asking questions. We had a pretty good relationship and he was pretty cool and calm and he was looking at it as an opportunity for him to get back and get established up there. So he probably had his own things to worry about — he didn't need some 21-year-old punk asking him about how this is all going to play out. But I remember thinking, 'Man, I'm on my way to the game. I'm on my way to *the Apple*. The Show is what they call it now, but back in that day the NHL was the Apple. And we were in the Crab in the IHL."

When Brown and McBain arrived, Canucks assistant GM Steve Tambellini was there to meet them. He had a gift. It was cold hard cash. That night's game in Chicago was the first of a five-game road trip for the Canucks, so Brown, who was not making millions in the IHL, was handed his first-ever NHL per diem, and it was for the entire road trip, not just that night's stay in Chicago. "I was pretty excited about that. I thought, 'Holy shit, we're up for this whole trip.'" That seemed to be the plan at the time anyway.

Brown and McBain met their new teammates, most of whom they both knew from their time in the game or from training camps. Still, it was a nice treat for a young kid to have a familiar face break the ice. "Trevor Linden was a guy that I'd played junior against and he'd been with the Canucks for two years at that point. And obviously being the player that he was, the leader that he was, he said, 'Hey, how's it going? Good to see you, Brownie. You ready to go?'

"A lot of those guys were guys I'd looked up to — Garth Butcher and guys like that. Guys that came from the west, specifically guys who I'd watched in junior. The way they treated me made me feel comfortable and ready to go: 'Don't worry about the nerves, just harness them and go out there and have some fun.'"

That night, once his super intense, calorie burning warm-up was out of the way, Cam Brown was good to go. If you're looking for a "welcome to the NHL" moment, Chicago Stadium is the perfect place to find it. Talk to anyone who has played there and they will tell you that the singing of the national anthem in Chicago is a very special thing. "For me to be in Chicago Stadium for my first and only experience was mind-blowing. All that anybody says about the national anthem and the electricity in that arena all bore out. It was definitely what you hear about it. You couldn't hear yourself think. Obviously being my first game it was a big enough thrill on its own, but then to have that coupled with the noise and the electricity of that stadium and that venue was pretty amazing."

Brown did what a lot of rookies do for the early part of the game: he rode the bench. Eventually though he did get his first shift. Now, Cam Brown is no dummy. He knew why he'd been called up. Odjick was out and there were a number of tough guys in Chicago's lineup: Mike Peluso, Bob McGill and a guy Brown knew from back in British Columbia, Dave Manson. Brown got his first shift late in the first with his Canucks already down on the scoreboard. He skated onto the ice, and standing right beside him was Bob McGill. "I lined up beside him and I kind of leaned into him. He said, 'Hey, kid,' and that was it." It was a no-go for Brown. And that's too bad. It would have made for a great reunion just a few years down the road.

"The funny thing about him is he ended up coaching me in Baton Rouge years later. We talked about it. He didn't remember it, obviously, with the number of games he played in the NHL. But I told him that story and he kind of laughed."

McGill wanted to know why Cam Brown didn't come back with any trash talk that night or an offer to drop the gloves. "Were you scared?" McGill asked him.

"I said, 'No, I just didn't know if it was time to say anything. We weren't down yet to the point where I was looking to give my team a shot and there was nothing to be talking to you about because you hadn't done anything to our guys.' And he just laughed."

The Canucks were down 2–0 after the first and 5–0 after the second. It was a bad time to be a Vancouver Canuck. They had lost their previous game 7–1 to Montreal. But it was a good time to be Cam Brown. "It was a bad blowout, which played in my favour for the amount of ice time. I'm a fourth-line guy going up to show what I've got, and by the time the first period ended I think we were down 2–0, so from the second period on I was a regular every third shift. So that was good for the ice time. I was getting more comfortable."

Just under three minutes into the third, Brown finally ran into Mike Peluso. Peluso led the NHL with 26 fighting majors in 1990–91, but it wasn't go time just yet. "I hit him and he kind of gave me a shoulder.

I turned around and gave him a light cross-check just to see if he was going to go. And he's probably thinking, 'There's no reason for me to fight this donkey at this point in the game. We're up 5–0.' He didn't even give me the time of day." Brown ended up with a cross-checking minor. He went straight to the box. "I went back down in the penalty box. I was just glad they didn't score another one on that."

Once Brown got out of the box, he continued to get a regular shift. This might have been a bummer of a night for most of the Canucks, but for Cam Brown this was a chance to make an impression. With 4:59 to go in the third, Brown went driving to the Chicago net. He ran into Peluso again. "I was getting some opportunities obviously. It was 7–0 at that point. I was going to the net and going hard and he was on the ice and he came in after and I kind of gave him a shove. I don't even remember the specifics of it. I've got it on VHS. I can't really remember how it all played out, but it was pretty quick. The gloves were off and we were going and they escorted me off the ice with four minutes left in the game.

"In hindsight I look back and think, 'What if I had gone out there at 3–0 and tried to stir it up and get something going and had success in it? Maybe it would have had an effect on the outcome.' But you can't do too much overthinking."

Brown finished his first NHL game with a very impressive even plus-minus in an 8–0 Vancouver loss. He also racked up seven penalty minutes. That's tied for the highest total for someone who played only a single game in the NHL.

"I got into the locker room by myself before any of the team came off. It was a pretty subdued, quiet bunch. There was no talking. I got a couple of guys saying, 'Good job out there, man. You played well tonight. You didn't look out of place.' I remember hearing that a couple of times so that was pretty cool."

Brown went back to the team hotel that night and woke up the next morning and took a flight to Pittsburgh with the rest of the team. He enjoyed an off day in Pittsburgh and woke up on March 5 ready to head to the old Igloo for the morning skate. Brown was pumped for that night's game against the Penguins and Jay Caufield, who had taken out

Gino Odjick a week earlier. "I was just jacked, thinking, 'I've got one game in. I've got the nerves out and all the rest of it.' I come wheeling into the rink and everyone is all subdued again. And the word breaks that Garth Butcher and Dan Quinn were moved to the Blues for Cliff Ronning, Sergio Momesso and I think it was Robert Dirk." The Canucks also picked up Geoff Courtnall and a fifth-round pick in the deal. Two roster players were going out and four roster players were coming in. Three of the new Canucks were forwards. The math did not look good for Cam Brown. The newest Canucks were on their way to Pittsburgh for that night's game against the Pens. But the reality of the situation didn't set in for the Canucks rookie. "I was focused on the game that night. Jay Caufield hurt Gino Odjick in their previous game, so I was thinking, 'I gotta get out there and fight Caufield.' And I was trying to get myself jacked and ready for that. I took the morning skate but still hadn't connected the dots."

When Brown arrived at the rink that night, the new guys were already there. Brown was told he was not going to be in the lineup. "I didn't even know the rules. I was on an emergency recall because of numbers but as soon as that roster changes, as soon as two guys leave and you get two extras coming back, it's not going to work."

Brown took a spot in the stands with Andrew McBain, who was also scratched, and got a lesson in NHL reality from the old vet as they watched the Penguins hand the Canucks a 4–1 loss. Geoff Courtnall scored Vancouver's only goal. "Me and Bainer sat in the stands and he was pissed because obviously he had made the connection already that with these guys coming in and dressing for that night's game there was no chance that we were going to be around. He basically got me ready for that. 'Trust me, you'll be hearing whether we make the trip tomorrow or we get sent back tonight.'" Brown was sent back to Milwaukee right after the game.

"Pat called me in and told me, 'Great job in the game in Chicago. You were the one thing I was happy about in that game' and then blah blah blah. 'And make sure you go back and work on this and that and I look forward to seeing you maybe later this year and, if not, then at camp next year.'"

Brown worked his butt off that summer. He was determined to return to the Canucks. He worked on his foot speed and he put on about 15 pounds. The weight was put on to help survive against bigger, tougher men in the NHL. But at the Canucks training camp, Brown realized the extra bulk came at a cost. "My foot speed was never part of that game. I put that muscle on to help me in the corners and fight the bigger guys in the NHL, but I actually lost a step."

Brown was sent back to Milwaukee. If his first pro season was a dream, his second pro season was a nightmare. He had a hard time getting in the Admirals lineup. The team had brought in a number of independent players, and Brown just couldn't get a regular spot in the forward corps. "I was a healthy scratch 28 or 30 times during the year. My attitude went to shit and I actually asked at one point if I could go down to Columbus, Ohio, in the East Coast Hockey League for a few games just to get the fun back in the game." He joined the Columbus Chill of the ECHL and earned 17 points in 10 games.

Brown started the next season with Vancouver's new AHL affiliate in Hamilton. It was the same old situation. He asked to go to the Coast again. He got his wish again, but he also got released by Vancouver. This time around his play caught the interest of the Buffalo Sabres. He played for their ECHL affiliate in Erie and got a few games in with their AHL team in Rochester. He had an invite to go to Sabres camp the following season but instead decided to pull a total 180 and head overseas. "In Rochester I was the 10th forward. I didn't do anything but get on the ice to fight. I realized I had to expand my game and came back down to Erie, finished the year out and accepted a contract from a team in the Czech Republic. I went to work on my skating and my skill set, and I figured if I could come back and make an impression somewhere and get a tryout then I might get back up to the NHL somehow."

After one year in the Czech Republic, Brown retuned to North America. Things did not go as planned. He broke his jaw at a training camp in Vegas and ended up back in Erie. He had a few games in the AHL with Adirondack. It was another up and down year. He was offered a tryout in Detroit and Adirondack the following season. By this time, however, reality had set in. "I was 25 years old and had bounced around a little. And Erie offered me the player-assistant coach job and I thought, 'Do I want to go back up and be a 10th forward or healthy scratch to fight in the American League on the off chance of an NHL call-up?'" Brown knew what his answer was. He took the player-assistant coach gig in Erie.

"I never accepted another call-up."

Brown began an 11-season run in the East Coast Hockey League and ended up in the ECHL Hall of Fame. Now, no one will ever mistake the ECHL for the NHL, but the league gave Cam Brown something the NHL never could — stability and a life beyond the game. "What didn't it do? It offered me the chance to continue playing the game that I loved. At that point I realized I wasn't going to make the NHL and I was fully okay with that. I wanted to start working on channelling my game toward being a coach and learning what I could from whoever became the head coach. I spent two more years in Pennsylvania and then we moved the whole franchise down to Baton Rouge and that's where life took a whole different path. I spent six years as a player, met my wife, had both of our children down there and that's when life becomes more important off the ice. I was 30 years old and started seeing that there was something else that I needed to put ahead of becoming the best hockey player I could be."

Brown lives in Georgia now and works in the computer industry. He's a mechanical technician for a data facility in metro Atlanta. And he rarely thinks about that one game in Chicago. In fact, the initial email I sent him took him down memory lane for the first time in years. "It's not something I've given much thought to. Since you contacted me I've spent more time thinking about that game in the last month and a half than I probably have in the previous 19 or 20 years. I know for a little while there when I still had a VHS player, my boy used to watch it and he was probably three years old. I remember sitting there, watching it, thinking, 'That was a long time ago. I was a different person' and stuff like that. But career accomplishment? I don't want to say infamous, but it's kind of the notoriety of being a guy that played only one game — but I did get that one game. I've got a lot of friends I played with and against throughout the minors and junior who always say, 'Yeah, but you still got that one game.' And you know what, I would probably never tell anybody. It's just not something that ranks up there. I spend more time thinking about what I'm doing today for my job or what I'm doing today for my wife and kids. I guess looking back on it one day I'll think, 'You know, I did get a game at the highest level of the sport . . .'"

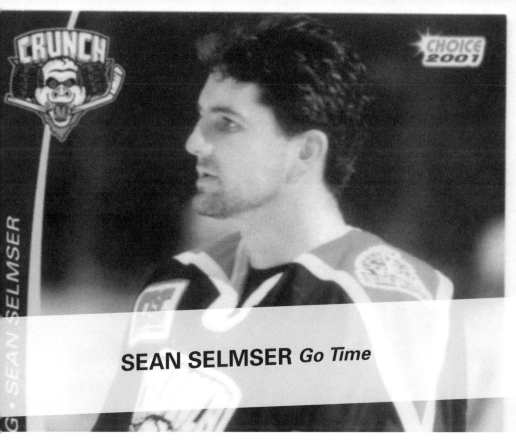

SEAN SELMSER *Go Time*

Have you ever challenged yourself to do the most with what you've got? Sean Selmser isn't exactly Rocky Balboa, but for a very long time he kept on getting paid to play hockey. "I played 17 years with minimal skill because I was stubborn enough to keep going."

On March 26, 2001, the Columbus Blue Jackets were in Edmonton when forward Alexander Selivanov injured his knee against the Oilers. He could not play the next night in Calgary. The Blue Jackets made Sean Selmser an emergency call-up. "It was a dream come true, really. I was sitting in Syracuse with my wife. It was about 10:30 at night and I got the phone call from my coach there and he said, 'You're getting called up.'"

The 26-year-old couldn't afford to waste time. The next thing he knew he was out the door on a cross-continental flight to his hometown of Calgary, Alberta. On the plane, when not trying to jam in a little sleep, he was trying to put this out-of-nowhere adventure into perspective. "It's one of those things where it kind of starts out surreal but you've gotta collect your thoughts a bit. It's kind of a balance between nerves and excitement I guess. I was a little bit older than most guys when they get their first game. So I wanted to make the best of it. Mentally you're just trying to get prepared. It wasn't really all that stressful on the flight. But once you get to the rink things change pretty quick."

The Saddledome was the place where Selmser watched the Flames as a kid. But walking into the Dome for your first morning skate with an NHL club is slightly different than cheering on another group of NHLers from the stands. "I'd been in that rink a million times, but on the top level, not the bottom. So it was a little bit frantic. I knew all the guys from camp but now fast-forward four months, and it's a different team. Just trying to recall it, my reaction was just, 'Let's get this done. Let's get in the room and let's get her going.' Because the heart rate is going pretty good by then."

Thanks to the last-minute nature of the trip, Sean didn't have a chance to line up his friends and family with tickets, but they did manage to fill quite a few seats. "I think everybody was there. Everybody except my wife because she couldn't get in on time. But her family was there. My family was there, some friends. It was pretty cool. There's no question about it."

Selmser's posse didn't have to wait long to see him on the ice. Columbus head coach Dave King kept it classy and put the hometown guy playing in his first NHL game into the starting lineup. "I remember standing on the blue line for the national anthem, just trying to soak it in. Trying to remind myself to enjoy this moment. I don't remember the first shift, but I do remember standing on the blue line."

Now remember, Sean Selmser is a guy who says, "I played 17 years with minimal skill." So in other words, he's not a sniper or a playmaker. And in the world of hockey, if you make it to the NHL, you stick with what got you there. If you're a goal scorer, you try to score a goal. If you're a playmaker, you look to set up someone. If you're a checker, you check. And if you're Sean Selmser, you keep on being Sean Selmser. In other words, you stir it up. It didn't take Sean too long to start stirring. Just over 10 minutes into the first period, the call-up from Syracuse found a dance partner. "I was looking for anybody. Calgary didn't have a whole lot of guys. Jason Wiemer was a left winger and I was a left winger so we never lined up against each other. And, to be honest with you, I wasn't so keen on trying to go after him. And I didn't know if Chris Clark would fight or not. I just kind of kept poking him and eventually he decided to go. He was more of a scrappy-type player than I expected, to be honest."

Dropping the gloves was nothing new for Selmser. However, early in this tilt against Chris Clark he knew he was in trouble, and it had nothing to do with his opponent. If you're a fan of hockey fights, you are no doubt familiar with what some call the "Rob Ray Rule." Ray basically used to make his living by letting opponents remove his sweater and all his upper body gear. The next thing you know, a naked-from-the-waist-up Ray is in a scrap with a more than fully clothed opponent. By the time the 2000–01 season rolled around, the NHL had seen enough of semi-nude fighters. Check out the NHL rulebook for rule 56 — Fisticuffs (aka the "Rob Ray Rule"): "A player who engages in fisticuffs and whose sweater is not properly 'tied-down' (sweater properly fastened to pants), and who loses his sweater (completely off his torso) in that altercation, shall receive a game misconduct."

Normally this wasn't a problem for Selmser. "I don't know how many fights I had between junior and pro — there were lots. And not once did I forget the tie down. But sure enough that game I did. It was right by the Flames bench and my jersey started riding up. I don't know if he was really trying to pull it but the bench was yelling at him to pull it over my head because the rule had just changed where if it comes off you get kicked out of the game. And so I spent the first part of the fight with my head pushed back as far as I could to keep my jersey on. I didn't want to get kicked out of the game. I think it was Don Henderson who was the linesman and he yelled at me, 'No. He's okay. Let it go, let it go.' And then we got back into it with a couple punches and we both fell down."

Crisis averted. Selmser spent the next five minutes in the penalty box basking in all the glory of his first NHL scrap. What's not to like? The public-address announcer was saying his name, and he was on the sheet. "I had to get on the scoresheet, that's all I knew. And I didn't want to take a tripping penalty. I would have rather have had a goal, but . . ."

Once his time in the penalty box was up, Selmser skated back to the Blue Jackets bench. Now remember, the newest member of the

Columbus Blue Jackets just spent the previous night getting from Syracuse, New York, to Calgary, Alberta. He was high on adrenaline and low on sleep. He just dropped the gloves. He was tired. Check that — he was tapped. He didn't have much left in the tank and really needed a breather. Just as he took his spot on the bench, fresh off NHL fight number one, his veteran teammate Kevin Dineen hit him with this beauty. "I get back to the bench and I had been in the fight and I was trying to be hard-nosed, as scrappy as possible. And Kevin Dineen grabbed me and said, 'Go out there and make something big happen. We need a player like you to stick around here a little bit longer.' And it made me feel really good, but then I started thinking, 'Holy Christ, I'm exhausted. I don't know if I can.'"

The rookie did his best to impress his sarcastic veteran teammate. "The whole time you go out there for the shift and you get your 20 seconds and then your legs and lungs just start burning. So I did what I could. I don't know if I did what he wanted me to, but I really tried."

Sean Selmser had his tilt, and then he almost had his goal too. Once he got his legs back under him, Selmser found himself on a two-on-one. "I had a gaping net and I never did get the pass. The one guy took it — I'm not going to tell you who it was — and I thought, 'That would have been a nice little tap in for my first game.'"

The Blue Jackets didn't tap anything by the Flames that night. They were shut out 3–0 by Freddie Brathwaite. But Selmser's NHL adventure wasn't over. He and the Kings headed to Los Angeles. Remember, he was an emergency call-up, so as long as Selivanov was out of the Columbus lineup he could play. Selmser took the warm-up against the Kings. So did Selivanov. "He gave his leg a shot and decided it was good to go." And that was it. Sean Selmser's NHL adventure was over.

He didn't really have a "gee, I made the NHL moment" during his stint with Columbus. He wanted more. "Every player has the goal of playing in the NHL, but then once you get it you don't feel accomplished at that point because you want to play more. And then once that dream kind of dies, when you know you're not going back, you can sit back. That's when that accomplishment kind of kicks in and you start feeling a little prouder of yourself."

Selmser says his NHL dream died when he signed on to play in Europe after he spent the 2001–02 season with the Hamilton Bulldogs. By that time, he was 27 and had 387 minor-league games on his résumé. "I became a veteran in the American Hockey League and it was obvious to me. The writing wasn't so much on the wall but it was becoming more obvious to me that it's going to be that much tougher for an NHL team to justify signing me when I'd been a career minor-league guy. And then my agent tells me, 'You better go to Europe. You're not getting another job.'"

Selmser split his first year between Scotland and Austria. The following season was the first of seven straight in the Austrian League, the last four of which he spent in Vienna. Playing four straight seasons in Vienna was a magical time for a guy who had bounced from team to team and league to league for the first part of his career. "It was awesome. My daughter is named Vienna, that's how fondly we thought of the city. I've been to Stockholm and it's about the only other city that can compare to Vienna for me."

Aside from playing hockey in Europe, Selmser also hit the books while he was overseas. "It was no secret I had to scrap, literally and figuratively, through my whole career. So the life after hockey thing was definitely top of mind for me. And I had an opportunity to go over there and do a postgraduate, get a master's degree, and I jumped at the chance to do that. The hockey itself was not all that memorable, nothing to write home about. But the schooling experience at that stage of my life was kind of cool, actually. I really enjoyed it, even though it was lot of work."

Sean Selmser earned a master of science degree in sports business management, and he essentially learned how to run a professional sports franchise. But if you think a return to the pro game is imminent you can hold off, for now at least. Selmser is content to stay in his hometown of Calgary. "I'd love to get back into hockey but I don't want to put my kids through it. You know, I did it for me and like I said I don't have any regrets with it, but I don't necessarily want to put them through it."

Check that — Selmser does have one regret about his hockey career. But it has nothing to do with the pro game. Like many, some of Sean Selmser's best memories came before he started getting paid to play hockey. It's also happens to be the place where his one hockey regret occurred. "I was in Midget AAA for the Calgary Buffalos and I had made the Canada Winter Games Alberta team. So my coach asked me *not* to go. There were four of us who made it. He asked us all not to go. And why I listened to him I don't know. So I didn't go. That's my only regret in all of hockey." If that's your one regret after a lifetime of hockey, you should consider yourself very lucky.

These days, not many people know that Sean Selmser played in the NHL, as he puts it, "because when you've played just one game in the NHL they assume you never did. So it really doesn't come up all that often." But when they do find out, he'll admit it and add a footnote. "I make sure I quickly follow up with 'just the one game.'"

And when Selmser thinks back on his hockey career, he's happy with the way it played out. "Slugging it out in the minors in the East Coast League, it's not overly glamorous but there's a lot worse ways to make a living." But all those scraps in half filled barns in minor league towns did lead Sean Selmser to a terrific homecoming in Calgary for his only NHL game.

"I'm really proud of it."

PAT MAYER *Muscle for Mario*

On March 19, 1988, the Philadelphia Flyers and the Pittsburgh Penguins got nasty at the old Igloo. The two rivals combined for 123 penalty minutes in a lopsided 7–0 Pens win. The events of that night paved the way for minor league tough-guy Pat Mayer's NHL debut the following afternoon in Pittsburgh. "Jimmy Mann, who was the resident tough-guy for Pittsburgh at the time, left the building on crutches," says Mayer. "As Philadelphia was leaving the building they were saying, 'Just wait until tomorrow in our building.'"

With their team down one tough guy after an evil Saturday night at home, Pens management put out a late-night call to Mayer, who was patrolling the blue line for the Muskegon Lumberjacks. Oh, and he was throwing around his weight in the IHL as well. In 1987–88, he racked up 450 PIMs for the Jacks. Mayer answered his phone at 11 p.m. that Saturday night. The Pens wanted him in Philly the next afternoon, and Mayer immediately knew why. With Mann out of the lineup, they needed muscle.

How did Pat Mayer prep for his NHL debut? Well, he didn't sleep a wink that Saturday night. "A lot of things enter your mind, but there were only a couple of weeks left in the season. So I'm thinking I might be going up for a couple of weeks or a month. And at the time I was a minor leaguer — all you thought about was making a couple of extra bucks going to the National League because your wages are five times as much there. So I paced a hole in the floor all night long. I show up for the game with two weeks' worth of clothes and 20 hockey sticks . . . I only needed one."

Mayer caught an early morning flight and the magnitude of the moment hit him on his way to the game. "I got in a taxi and was heading to the Spectrum and all of a sudden I'm on Broad Street. Well, growing up watching hockey it was the Broad Street Bullies and the Big Bad Bruins, but you know, it was the Broad Street Bullies that I remember. So I thought that was pretty cool."

You might assume that when a guy joins a team with Mario Lemieux that he'd be in awe of the Magnificent One. But that wasn't the case for Mayer. He knew Mario pretty well: "I went to training camp with Mario a number of years in a row. He is just a great, great guy. Unbelievable talent and very down to earth." Mayer was also well aware of what Mario and his new teammates were in need of that afternoon. (They didn't have any trouble scoring goals, but in those days everyone needed a little extra muscle at the Spectrum.)

"They were pretty happy to see me, you know what I mean. They'd left the happy confines of Pittsburgh and they're in the Philadelphia Spectrum and Philadelphia is talking shit. Danny Quinn comes up, and Mario, and they're all shaking my hand, 'Hey, good to see you, Pat.'"

For this game only, career stay-at-home defenceman Pat Mayer found himself on the left wing. He also found himself on the Pens bench — a lot. He was on the fourth line with Charlie Simmer and Wayne Van Dorp. For the opening 11 minutes or so, Mayer was the Pens gatekeeper. Then he got a chance at his first shift in the NHL. "I was sitting next to Charlie Simmer. And I'm opening and closing the door. All of a sudden Charlie is shoving me, going, 'The coach wants you out there.' I said, 'Okay.' Left wing in the offensive zone . . . and all I'm thinking about is back-checking. Make sure you don't get scored against. Well, we lost the draw and they wrapped it around. And our defenceman got over there and I was back-checking kind of up the middle of the ice. I got to the blue line and then all of a sudden we got control of the puck at the blue line."

This is when the defenceman, who had scored nine goals in his pro career, channelled his inner Mario. (Something must have rubbed off on Mayer during that pre-game handshake.) "The first thought in my head, like any good defenceman, was go out there and don't get scored against. But now I'm thinking, 'I'm going to score.' So I went to the net . . . It was pretty funny." Mayer didn't score, but he got an instant reminder of why he was called up by the Pens just 14 hours earlier.

"All of a sudden I'm getting shoved from behind by Rick Tocchet. I just turned around and punched him." If Mayer wanted to go, and it's a pretty safe bet to say that he did, it wasn't going to happen this time around. The gloves stayed on. "It was close to a fight. I knocked Tocchet down with my gloves on so he got a deuce and I got four."

Pat Mayer sat in the box for four minutes. Once his time was up, he made his way back to the Pens bench, where Penguins head coach Pierre Creamer was waiting to deliver a message. "I come off the ice and the coach is telling me not to go too fast. And I'm like, 'What are you talking about? Don't go too fast?' 'Yeah, well we're in Philadelphia. We don't want to start any fights. We just kind of want to get out of here without anybody getting injured.'" Mayer was perplexed to say the least. He thought he got the call to provide a little muscle. If he ended up in a tilt, so be it. Wasn't that part of the reason he was in the Pens lineup? Well, he never got a chance. Pat Mayer's one shift midway through the first was the only time he hit the ice that day.

"I had only one shift." But you have to stay positive. "Didn't get my goal — got on the game sheet though."

The Pens lost 4–2. Mayer and the team stayed in Philly that night and returned to Pittsburgh the next day. That's when he got the news. "Assistant coach Ricky Kehoe came in, and he said, 'You're going back.'"

Mayer was back in the minors, but that was nothing to be ashamed of. He and the 1987–88 Muskegon Lumberjacks racked up 58 wins, top in the league. They led the IHL in goals with 415, and they were tough as well. They had four players with over 300 penalty minutes that season, with Mayer leading the team with 450. "It was fun," he says. Though the fun ended for the Lumberjacks in the first round of the playoffs. They were upset 4–2 in their best of seven series against the Flint Spirits.

Mayer split the next season between Muskegon and the AHL's New Haven Nighthawks, and then he retired. He was out of the game just before his 28th birthday. "I was a career minor-leaguer. I could have, should have, maybe gone further and stuck. I was 24 coming out of college, so by the time I was 28 I was fighting with Tony Twist and thinking, 'I'm 28 and these guys are 20. Who's getting the shot to go to the NHL?'

"You could call me a goon or whatever, but I could skate. I locked down the defence; my goaltenders loved me. I got the puck over the blue line and I got off the ice. That was my goal and if anybody screwed around with our small guys, well, you'd have to go through me."

The numbers clearly tell you how Pat Mayer played the pro game. In his four professional seasons, he spent 1,423 minutes in the penalty box. All but four of those minutes were spent in penalty boxes in places like Muskegon and Toledo. It could have been more than four, though. Hockey, you see, is a lot like any other line of work — sometimes it's as much about who you know as what you know. In the pro game, hundreds of players are separated by just the tiniest amount of skill, or toughness. If you know the right guy, you can get that break. If you don't know the right guy, maybe you never will. "My second year or third year, Rick Ley was my coach and Tony Esposito was the GM in Pittsburgh. And Ricky told me, 'If I get the job in Pittsburgh, Pat, you're going with me.' He didn't get the job. He ended up going from Muskegon to Milwaukee."

Mayer stayed in Muskegon.

"There's a lot of politics involved. Look at all the first-rounders that never make it. Why don't they make it? They get hurt, they don't have the attitude, or they don't have the heart. I'm fortunate that I learned a lot going through this — currently I scout for a USHL team. I coached for many years; I've got a son that's playing division one hockey. I'm fortunate. All the things that I got to do and all the people I got to know can still help the young kids, and I can give my son some direction on what to do, what not to do, and how to manage things."

Mayer won a Turner Cup with Muskegon in the spring of 1986. His minor-league memories and teammates come first and foremost when he thinks of his career. He can rattle off names like he is reading them from a team roster. He had the thrill of playing at one time or another with guys like Mark Recchi, Phil Bourque and Wendell Young. And he enjoyed playing in a time when the gloves were quick to come off. It's a lot different from the game his son plays at Ferris State University in Michigan. "He's proud of it. He looks at my penalty minutes and he tells all his buddies. The game has changed so much compared to what it was."

And the achievement of making it to the Show isn't lost on Mayer. "It's always your goal to get to the highest level. I have friends around Detroit, a lot of hockey guys who say, 'Holy shit. You played in the bigs.' And I'm like, 'Whatever.' But it's pretty cool. I mean, I don't even know what the odds of making it are . . ."

SEAN MCMORROW *Fighting for a Spot*

It was just another regular Rochester Americans practice, at the tail end of another skate, on another long day, in another long season. But then-Amerks head coach Randy Cunneyworth pulled aside his young enforcer Sean McMorrow. "Half my thoughts were, 'Is this it?' The other half was maybe he was pissed at me for something and wanted to talk. I didn't really know what was happening. He looked at me for about 10 seconds. And then the words that he used were, 'You got the call. You're going to the Show.' I'll never forget the way that he said it. He probably had a lot of practice, being an AHL coach for a while, but it was pretty cool the way that he did it."

There were hardly any of McMorrow's teammates on the ice at that point, just a few guys at the end of an AHL practice. Sean McMorrow's next practice would be in the NHL. His thoughts turned to his mother. "My parents got divorced when I was young and my mom — I have three other siblings and we were all in hockey including my sister — so my mom did a really good job raising me and my brothers and sister. It was tough for her. She ended up getting remarried when I was 14, but for the majority of our childhood she was raising us as a single mother." McMorrow got off the ice and picked up the phone.

"It was the first call I made. I told her that I was getting called up. She said, 'Against who?' And I said, 'Against Toronto, this Saturday.' It was quite something.

"She was so delighted. I could tell that she was crying."

The call-up was a reward for all the McMorrows. Being a single parent is not easy nor was the style of game that Sean McMorrow decided to play. He says he was a solid stay-at-home defenceman as a kid, and he was a second-round pick in the OHL draft. However, after the Buffalo Sabres took him in the NHL Draft, they reached out to his junior team, the London Knights, and asked them to put the big defenceman on the wing. "They did that and I switched. But growing up as a defenceman, I thought of myself as a skilled player," says McMorrow. "But then when it came time to actually make it to the top level that was the role that I had to go into to give myself that opportunity."

By the time Sean McMorrow made it to the pros, he was a bona fide enforcer. During his first year with the Americans he dropped the gloves a mind-blowing 41 times. *Forty-one* scraps. The Sabres definitely took notice. "At the time, being a tough guy was an important role still. This was back during the 2002–03 season."

The big club needed a tough guy for a game in McMorrow's hometown. (He's a Scarborough guy and grew up loving the Leafs.) First though, a little background. On March 6, 2003, the Leafs visited the Buffalo Sabres. Eleven minutes into the first, a hit at the whistle prompted a scrum at the Maple Leafs blue line. Two men emerged and dropped gloves: Sabre Rob Ray and Leaf Alexei Ponikarovsky. If you're thinking that doesn't sound right — it doesn't. And it didn't look right either. Ponikarovsky held his own for a few moments with the seasoned scrapper before Ray, taking his time, delivered a fight-ending right. As the great Rick Jeanneret screamed from the play-by-play booth, "Ray dropped him with a roundhouse right."

That tilt set off three more later in the first period. The next meeting between the Leafs and the Sabres was set for March 22 at the Air Canada Centre in downtown Toronto. It was a *Hockey Night in*

Canada game. Tensions were high given the last meeting and Buffalo was in need of another tough guy in case things got out of hand. Rob Ray, the seasoned vet heading toward the end of his career, was shipped from the Sabres to Ottawa on March 10 and wouldn't be around for the Sabres and Leafs rematch. Sean McMorrow would. "The Buffalo papers were kind of stirring up that Toronto might want some payback when the Sabres go and visit."

Even though they were just down the highway, McMorrow and his Sabres checked into a Toronto hotel on Friday night. McMorrow got up on Saturday and made his way to the pre-game skate, but he was having a hard time believing it. "It's your life, you're living it, but it's almost like it's half a dream, like you're half dreaming. You're wondering, 'Is this really happening? Am I going to wake up soon? I know this is me. This is the same feeling that I have every day, but this is the major leagues. This is the Show; this is the NHL.'

"I remember a lot of details — certain guys. Daniel Brière, for example, was by far the nicest veteran. He wanted to make sure that I had everything I needed. If I had any questions he was there. That stands out a lot.

"I was so excited just to be there. I knew that I deserved to be there because of how hard I worked but I was still thankful that I had no injuries, was at the right place at the right time, all that kind of stuff."

During the anthems, reality set in. He was in the National Hockey League. He can thank the Toronto fans for that. A few nights earlier in Montreal, Canadiens fans booed "The Star-Spangled Banner" before an Islanders and Habs game. It was a tense time in the world and it had nothing to do with hockey. The USA was leading a war in Iraq and thousands of Canadiens fans were not impressed. Two nights later at the Air Canada Centre, Leafs fans were having none of that. "When the national anthems started, the ACC was so loud and electric that I just couldn't believe what I was a part of. We knew that it was going to be a little bit special because of what had happened in Montreal, but the amount of noise for both the Canadian and American national anthems right before the game — I knew it was real once I felt that energy. You don't experience energy like that playing in the minors and in junior. That's major league, 19,000 people being extra excited because this is a big deal."

McMorrow was pumped, and, remember, he knew why he was in the Sabres lineup. Leading up to the game, McMorrow and Eric Boulton, another Sabres tough guy, went over Toronto's lineup. McMorrow was asking questions like, "What kind of stuff does Tie Domi do? What kind of stuff does Wade Belak do? And he's telling me, 'Domi likes to do the spin. Belak likes to use his reach.' And I'm hearing all this stuff and it was just so awesome because we're talking about guys who I idolized."

Fortunately, or perhaps unfortunately if you're Sean McMorrow, the night of March 22, 2003, did not live up to the pre-game hype. There was not a single tilt. The gloves stayed on — but that wasn't due to a lack of effort on McMorrow's part. Again, if goal scoring got you to the NHL, you should try to score a goal. If you're a checker, you check. And when you're a fighter, you fight. McMorrow played just 1:27 that night, but on one of his shifts he was lined up against one of his boyhood idols, Tie Domi. It seemed too good to be true. "We lined up together. I asked him if he'd give me a shot. He pretty much — as a big veteran like him is able to do — laughed it off. He goes, 'You gotta make the team first, kid. You gotta start the year. I'm not fighting call-ups,' and he just kind of laughed it off.

"That's kind of something that I might say to a rookie in my league, so I completely understood, although I was disappointed."

McMorrow was a big fan of Wade Belak too. And by big fan I mean he admired his game and would have loved to drop the gloves with him. But they never ended up on the ice against one another. McMorrow didn't get the chance to fight, and he admits that as strange as it may sound it was a bummer. "Even if a psychic told me that I was going to break my nose if I got into a hockey fight, I probably wouldn't have cared. And I would have dropped the gloves with Domi just because he was my idol. There would have been nothing cooler to me because I was such a big Leafs fan growing up in Toronto. As weird as that sounds, that's what it was. It was disappointing that I didn't get a fighting major."

The Leafs, who were bound for the playoffs, kept it clean and won the game 3–2 in overtime. McMorrow finished with no points, no PIMs and an even plus-minus. But it still felt good. McMorrow played his first game in his hometown in front of friends and family and, of course, in front of his mom. "After the game when I came out to see my family . . . just the look on her face. I'll never forget that look of how proud she was because she knew that she was a big part of that process and she was obviously very proud of her son."

An emergency call-up, McMorrow stayed with the Sabres for three days, and he cherishes the experience. "It's everything that goes with it. It's pretty much a completely different world, to be honest. It's not even the fact that the guys are making so much more money. It's the attitude. It's the confidence. It's them knowing that they're at the highest level. That kind of gives them that extra . . . not ego, just confidence.

"When it all comes down to it, I think the most important thing was just knowing that you reached your dream and gaining the confidence that comes with that."

And that was it. At 21, his NHL career had started and ended in a span of three days. He spent a few more years in the Sabres organization playing with the AHL Americans. McMorrow did what got him to the league in the first place: he kept piling up the PIMs. Over the next three AHL seasons he piled up 705 PIMs in 156 regular-season games. By the end of his tenure in the Sabres organization, he had been in 130 regular season and playoff fights. By the time 2006 rolled around, demand for McMorrow's skill set was already beginning to wane. After the first NHL lockout, the tough guys were fading. Players like Peter Worrell, who made a living for years as NHL heavyweights, were suddenly out of work. There was a trickle-down effect. This led McMorrow to one of the most notorious leagues in hockey, Quebec's LNAH (Ligue Nord-Américaine de Hockey). If you were a fan of tilts in 2006, then the LNAH was the league for you — in fact, it still is. McMorrow found himself in a league that boasted, among other tough guys, Jon "Nasty" Mirasty, Jacques Dubé and Steve "The Boss" Bossé. After two years of slugging it out in Quebec, McMorrow ended up back in the AHL with the Rockford Ice Hogs. After playing 25 games that season, reality set in. Even though he was only one league away, the NHL was still a long way off. He had a decision to make. "I was a fourth-liner. I made close to the league minimum, maybe not getting that much ice time, but I was sticking to it because I know that there's a chance that I could get called up. I'm just one level away. Or I could try to do something different. And when players do something different that means they go to Europe. Maybe make a little more money, maybe get the experience of your life . . . be able to travel the world while still playing professional hockey."

Knowing his chances of getting back to the NHL were very slim, he headed overseas and signed with the Belfast Giants of the British Elite Hockey League. McMorrow embraced Belfast and Belfast embraced McMorrow. Makes sense with a name like McMorrow. "All I had to do was prove that one of my grandparents was born over there. I went to the British embassy and they granted me an ancestry visa, so I was able to go over with the full support and confidence of my family. It was a really cool opportunity with the role they wanted me to play on the team and in the community. So that helped with transition of me kind of giving up the AHL-NHL dream."

As he was in Rochester, McMorrow became actively involved in the community. Fans in Ireland called the tough guys "hard men" and McMorrow was a hit. It was a unique situation. Historically, Belfast has been a very troubled city and is divided by the number of soccer teams in the area, but when it comes to the Giants, the fans are united. "They wanted a hard man who was a community guy that could kind of be like the face of the team. They felt that I fit all those criteria. So it was very humbling to have them tell me all this."

He was enjoying himself and loving his life in Belfast when things came to a crashing halt. McMorrow, who was three times voted his team's "Man of the Year" in the AHL for contributions and volunteering in his community, was charged with drug trafficking. An FBI investigation accused him of smuggling marijuana across the Canada-U.S. border during his days in Rochester. The case took years to eventually resolve.

In May 2012, things finally came to a close. McMorrow, who pleaded guilty to drug conspiracy charges, was sentenced to two years in a low-security American prison. He thought he was going to get probation. When you speak with Sean McMorrow it's shocking. He is a charming, smart, witty guy. "That whole thing was either going to make me or break me. I learned a lot from it. I got a lot stronger from it. It was very drawn out. When everything was all said and done it was nine years after when they were saying everything occurred. It was based on when I was 21 years old and I was 30 years old when I got sentenced. Everyone always says that the U.S. is the only country where that could have happened. But regardless, guilt by association goes a long way and you just have to learn your lessons from that."

McMorrow served 20 months. Eventually, he was a free man and free to play hockey once more. He ended up back in the LNAH. For the past few years he's patrolled the blue line in one of the craziest leagues in the game. He's well into his 30s and still scrapping. Now more than a decade removed from his one night in the NHL, the style of hockey that Sean McMorrow plays is almost extinct in most professional leagues. "I'm making more money than I would be in the East Coast Hockey League because I have a very good deal with my team." The team pays for his housing as well as his schooling. So for Sean McMorrow there is still a place to ply his trade even if the league has calmed down a bit since the early 2000s.

"They're trying to make the league very legitimate. There are a lot of good hockey players that come through the Quebec system."

Now life is about more than just hockey for McMorrow. What he's been through can really put the game in perspective. He still loves it, but it is not everything. He's taking business courses at St. Lawrence College in Quebec City and prepping for life after the game. He and his much taller younger brother — 7-foot-2 pro basketball player Liam — would love to open up a training facility for athletes. "We have always talked about opening a sports training facility, but make it very unique and different and geared toward hockey and basketball players because we're both playing pro and we're specialized in those sports. And we also want to make it for the body and mind. We want to do a lot of classroom stuff, a lot of team building stuff, and we want to tie it all together. I've already done a business plan and me and Liam are going to be partners. The idea is that I'll be able to bring in the hockey clientele and he'll bring in the basketball."

Once upon a time, Sean thrilled his mom with a game in Toronto. Now he's trying to give his mom a thrill by pursuing an education and setting himself up for life after the game. "I'm doing it for both of us. I made the promise for her, but I obviously know life after hockey can be difficult if you have no education."

Based on his history, don't bet against McMorrow.

"I can say that I made it. That all the hard work was worth it, even though it was just the one regular-season NHL game. I can say that I was able to reach my dream. Anything's possible."

CHAPTER FOUR
THE WHA CONNECTION

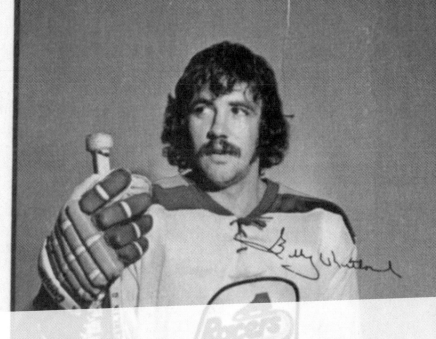

BOB WHITLOCK *The WHA Connection*

Growing up in Nova Scotia, I used to hear stories about the golden days of Maritime senior hockey. In my hometown, I always heard about Mark Babineau. In Halifax, I'd hear stories about the legendary Dugger McNeil (by the way, if you're ever in Halifax you can't miss his son Ross — he's the best-dressed guy in town.) As I got older, another name would always pop up: Buck Whitlock. The man is a Maritime hockey legend.

As Hugh Townsend put it in a column in the *Pictou Advocate* on October 1, 2014: "Sound like he piled up a lot of goals? He sure did. According to Corey Hartling, he totalled 788 goals along with 985 assists for 1,773 points in nearly 1,000 games. You can't top that. He was widely recognized as the best scorer ever in Maritime hockey."

So, you can imagine how pumped I was when I looked through a list of one-game NHL wonders, and a Whitlock popped up: centreman Bob Whitlock — the son of Buck. I absolutely had to track Bob down. The P.E.I. Sports Hall of Famer is a B.C. boy now. He's lived in Trail for almost 40 years.

"My dad could've gone on to play with the Montreal Canadiens. He had a contract to go play with them with Béliveau and that crew, but my mother wouldn't marry my dad if he left," says Bob Whitlock. And here's the kicker — something that's still hard to believe all these years later. "And my dad was making just as much money playing senior hockey in Charlottetown."

While his dad was spending his winters during the 1950s playing for teams like the Saint John Beavers, the Charlottetown Islanders and the Fredericton Capitals, young Bob was working on his game on the frozen ponds of P.E.I. and everywhere in between.

"I'd practise with my dad and all the senior hockey players as a young kid and that's where I developed, playing with my dad and all the older people. I left home when I was 15 to play junior. I was playing Midget, junior and juvenile all at the same time. And that's all I really wanted to do: move on and play professional hockey."

Whitlock's first junior stop was Halifax, and stints in Edmonton and Kitchener followed. In Kitchener he caught the eyes of Minnesota scouts who offered him a tryout. "I got invited by Wren Blair to Haliburton, Ontario, for the Minnesota North Stars training camp. I was only about 158 pounds in them days, looking at guys like Tom Reid, J. P. Parisé and all those guys up there, Danny Grant and Claude Larose. I had a hell of a camp."

All 158 pounds of Bob Whitlock were impressive enough to earn an invite to the North Stars main camp in Minneapolis. Whitlock continued to shine and earned a spot with the Stars' top farm team, the Central Hockey League's Iowa Stars.

Whitlock's Stars were having a great year during the 1969–70 season when he got *the call*. The 20-year-old son of a Maritime hockey legend was on his way to a league he'd always dreamed about — one his father never managed to play in. The first thing he did, of course, was call his dad. "It was pretty cheerful, to tell you the truth, because all I wanted to do was to make sure I got to the NHL one way or the other. He was so proud of me when I did. We just chatted about hockey and he said, 'Hold your head up and play the best you can.' And that's just what I did."

Whitlock and his Iowa team were in Omaha when he got the call.

He hopped on a plane the next day and joined his new Minnesota team-mates in Los Angeles for a game against the Kings. "I played on a line with Danny Grant and Claude Larose. I had many opportunities. I just didn't score the goals."

Whitlock says he fit in well and he even got a little physical against a much bigger opponent. "We had a big ruckus in the corner with Dennis Hextall — I didn't stand a chance with some of these big guys. I think I got a penalty — five minutes for receiving and he got five minutes for fighting."

After the game, the North Stars asked Whitlock to stick around. But get this — he didn't. He was 20 years old, and his Iowa team was ready for a deep playoff run, so he passed on staying up in the NHL for a return trip to the minors. "After the game Wren Blair said, 'We're going on a road trip. Do you want to come or do you want to go back to Waterloo, Iowa, for the playoff run?' And I said, 'Well, I'm going to get more ice time back there.' So I went back there. One of the major decisions I got wrong. I should've just stuck with the team and got my chance to play more."

He didn't realize it at the time, but that would be the last time Bob Whitlock ever played in the NHL. When you're 20, anything seems possible. Like taking a quick trip back to minors to join your buddies for a playoff run. Perhaps Bob was thinking the NHL would always be there next year. But it wasn't.

Whitlock spent his second pro season in the AHL. In 1971–72 he joined the Phoenix Roadrunners of the Western Hockey League. He put up some decent numbers, 79 points in 65 games, good enough for seventh in the league's scoring race. And Whitlock's season in Phoenix caught the attention of hockey's other major league, the soon to be World Hockey Association. The Rebel League was set to make its debut in the fall of 1972. And they wanted Bob Whitlock. To be more precise, the Los Angeles Sharks wanted Bob Whitlock. "Los Angeles, they flew me out, the boy from P.E.I., with a $20,000 cheque. They signed me for $100 and some thousand over three years. It was great money. They said 'You're going to be the cornerstone of the team, so work hard.' So I fly back to P.E.I. and tell my dad and buy my dad a car and all this other stuff like a kid does, and within three weeks I was traded to Chicago."

That sudden trade to Chicago kind of sums up the WHA; it was a league that always seemed to be on the move. Some would say it was full of turmoil. But it was also a league that let a lot of players show off their skills on a major stage. And as Bob Whitlock will tell you, the Cougars did not take a back seat to the Blackhawks in the Windy City.

"I remember the first three years I played in Chicago, or two and half years in Chicago, we had the bright yellow shirts, the jerseys, and we had Pat Stapleton and Rosie Paiement and we had Reggie Fleming, Eric Nesterenko and we were competing with the Blackhawks. It brought out everybody in Chicago and all of a sudden the city's got two teams. And we were drawing well too. It really benefitted the whole NHL and the WHA."

And then there was the money. Whitlock was suddenly rolling in dough. It was a far cry from his early days with Minnesota when he was just scraping by: "I signed for a $2,000 bonus and $5,000 a year. That was about $301 every two weeks, so we didn't make much money." In the WHA, though, Whitlock had more than a few coins to spare.

"Nobody was getting paid until the World Hockey came in. Then all of a sudden Bobby Hull signs for a million. Derek Sanderson, he blew all of his money. Pat Price, I remember him, and he blew all his money. A lot of guys didn't know what the hell to do with all that money. In them days nobody was telling us what to do with the money. When I first signed with L.A., a boy from P.E.I. doesn't know what to do with that type of money, you know."

If the money was overwhelming, the hockey was, according to Whitlock, just as good. When the Cougars hit the road, Whitlock shared a room with former Montreal Canadien Ralph Backstrom. Backstrom won six Stanley Cups with the Habs. "We were sitting on a road trip and Bob says, 'This is great hockey. This is just as good as when I played in the NHL.'"

After a few seasons in the WHA, Whitlock was on the move. That's when he found himself in one of the most notorious leagues in hockey history — the North American League. For any movie aficionados out there, yes, this is the league that inspired *Slap Shot*. And yes, Whitlock even played for the Johnstown Jets, the team that was the inspiration for *Slap Shot's* Charlestown Chiefs. When Paul Newman and company showed up to make the film, Whitlock missed out on his chance at stardom. He had a broken ankle. A lot of his teammates got a role in the film, though. It was a movie that meant to make '70s minor-league hockey look as vile as possible, and Whitlock says the fictional Federal Hockey League was pretty close to the real deal. "Yeah it wasn't too far off. Beer league. If you had to have a pee you just go to the front of the bus. They had a urinal at the door."

After 20 games with the Jets, Whitlock was ready for a more refined life. He decided to hang up the blades. "I said, 'Enough. I'm almost 30 years old.' I was going to go back to school and get my phys-ed degree."

Whitlock headed back to P.E.I. for the summer. One day the phone rang. The call changed his life. On the line was another Islander who was now playing hockey in British Columbia. He asked Whitlock to pack up his blades one more time and move all the way across Canada to Trail, B.C., home of the legendary Trail Smoke Eaters. "I said, 'I don't want to come out there. I went through that town once and I didn't like it.' He said, 'Bob, they'll send everything. They will ship your furniture, and your wife can come on out, take the train, whatever you want to do. And if you don't like it you can leave.'"

Whitlock took up his buddy's offer. He headed for Trail in the fall of 1977. Thirty years after his father was a senior-hockey star in the Maritimes, Bob Whitlock was a senior-hockey star in the wild west.

Bob Whitlock played in the NHL. And he suited up for 244 WHA regular-season games. He made a living as a pro hockey player. It was all he ever wanted to do. That's something he shared with a young man during one of his frequent trips back to P.E.I. for a hockey banquet. "One of the kids said, 'What was your greatest accomplishment? I said, 'My greatest accomplishment was just being a hockey player.'"

Bob Whitlock followed in his father's footsteps. And his dad, a fellow P.E.I. Sports Hall of Famer, is never too far away from his mind. "I'm here in my office right now, and I got his picture and my picture in the [P.E.I.] Sports Hall of Fame. And that's what was so special about that night. It was my dad and me being together."

JACK STANFIELD *Coming to a TV Near You*

If you ever watched a hockey game on a regional American television station back in the '80s, chances are you have Jack Stanfield to thank. The same can be said if you've ever watched coverage of the Masters in Latin America, Australia or any other far-off part of the planet. Back in the 1960s, Jack Stanfield was a hockey player. By the mid-1970s, he was a hockey executive. By the 1980s, he was bringing regional sports networks to different parts of America. "Still," says Stanfield on the phone from New York City, "as much as I've done, to this day, I'm a hockey player."

Jack Stanfield shared the ice and the dressing room with legends like Gordie Howe, Stan Mikita, Don Cherry and one of the toughest characters to ever play the game, John Brophy. He comes from a hockey family, and his brothers Fred and Jim also played pro. Jack's professional career began in 1962 and lasted for more than a decade. He played in seven pro leagues, and one night in 1966, he even managed to play a game in the NHL. "Every year I would be called up for the playoffs. You'd be a standby in the playoffs."

On April 14, 1966, 23-year-old Jack Stanfield went from standby to legit NHLer. An injury forced one of the Blackhawks out of the lineup and Stanfield found himself on the ice for Game 5 of Chicago's first-round series against Detroit. "I played on Stan Mikita's line. Ken Wharram was the right winger and I was the left winger."

When Jack looked across the ice, among the men he saw was Gordie Howe, who would one day become one of his teammates. And in that moment, in his first game, Stanfield found himself a little bit awestruck when he saw his opponents and his surroundings. "It was such a big deal you were nervous. You were tentative."

The details of his one night on NHL ice don't come pouring out of Jack Stanfield. The overall experience, however, did leave him with something. It was the feeling that he belonged. He may have been a little nervous, but it wasn't like he couldn't handle himself out on the ice. By the time he made his NHL debut in the 1966 playoffs, he had 209 professional games on his résumé. "There were so many good hockey players in the American League. I played in Buffalo with guys who should have been in the NHL. There were lots of guys who were as good, so it wasn't like you were out of place. You were comparable as a player. You knew you could play there. I wasn't uncomfortable."

At this point Stanfield starts to chuckle. It's not the game that stands out. Or the players. And it's certainly not the money. When he thinks about his NHL cameo, or the other times he got a call-up and never got into action, it's the *sticks* he thinks of first. Yes, *the sticks*. In the NHL the food was better. The hotels were better. Everything was better. "The sticks were so much better. That sounds silly but when you went to the big club that's where you got the good wood. I used to use Billy Hay's sticks. Red Hay had a beautiful stick and every time I got called up I'd make sure I got a dozen of the sticks he used and I'd take them back down with me." Stanfield went down after the 1966 season. The Wings, by the way, beat the Blackhawks in six in 1966.

Down was where Stanfield ultimately found himself when he started his pro career. He was 20 years old in 1962. He made an impression at the Hawks camp. It's just too bad Chicago didn't impress Stanfield with their offer for his services. "In those days, Tommy Ivan was running the

Blackhawks. At our first training camp he said, 'Jack, we want you to be a Blackhawk.' And they offered me $3,500 for the season and $500 to sign and $7,500 if you made the big club." He told the Hawks no thanks and took a chance on a move to another big American city.

"I went to Philadelphia and I played in the Eastern Hockey League. I got 33 goals and 34 assists." That's impressive. But what's even more impressive is what Stanfield adds.

"I roomed with John Brophy. I roomed with John Brophy." Stanfield says it twice for emphasis. But it hits me right away. Jack Stanfield was 20 years old in a tough town and he was living with one of the toughest men to ever play the game. The old Eastern League was known as a rough circuit. And on that circuit the late John Brophy was the toughest of them all. In the hockey world Brophy stories are legendary. So of course I ask Stanfield, who lived not only with Brophy but also Bob Bailey while in Philly, to share one.

"We're in Nashville. Bob Bailey was my right winger, a great hockey player, and after the game we're drinking. I'm with these guys like normal hockey players and we're drinking beer. We're walking back to the hotel, and four hoods came at us down the street. We come face to face and nobody's moving. Bailey pitches a right-hand swing and dislocates his shoulder. Everybody, including us and the other guys, starts laughing their asses off because Bailey is hanging there. We go back to the hotel and Brophy's there. And Bailey was one of our best players and we were getting close to the playoffs, needing him and stuff like that. We come in and Bailey's got his arm hanging. And Brophy's so pissed. He picks up a flowerpot, a big flowerpot in the lobby of the hotel, and throws it through the fucking window."

John Brophy: 1. Hotel window: 0.

"He would get so intense . . . just trigger intensity."

Brophy, the future head coach of the Toronto Maple Leafs, led the Philadelphia Ramblers with 140 PIMs that year. We can assume he led the league in broken hotel windows as well.

The next year, Stanfield again showed up at Chicago's camp. He put on another solid show. This time Tommy Ivan upped his offer. "Ivan says, 'Jack, you had a great year in the Eastern League. We want you to be a Blackhawk. We'll give you $1,000 to sign and $4,000 for the season and $8,500 for the big club.' I said, 'I'll take it.'" Stanfield said goodbye to John Brophy and the Philadelphia Ramblers and hello to Phil Esposito and the St. Louis Braves of the Central Professional Hockey League. "Phil Esposito was my first centreman in St. Louis. This was before Phil went to the Blackhawks. I played on a line with Phil and a guy by the name of 'Boom Boom' Caron. Boomer got 78 goals. Esposito went to the Blackhawks halfway through the season." By the time Phil got the call, he had 80 points in just 43 games. And after he left the Central League, he never went back. Phil went on to NHL greatness while Stanfield finished the year in St. Louis. He ended up with 56 points in 63 games.

Stanfield spent the next two seasons in the AHL with Buffalo as he tried to crack the six-team NHL. He got his chance in the 1966 playoffs. At the time it seemed certain he'd get another opportunity, but he never did. Stanfield showed up at Chicago's camp the next year, roaring and raring to go. He had a sense that a spot on the big club was his for the taking. "You know when you go to training camp whether you're going to be on the club or not. And I got the stick right. I got my uniform right. I got my new skates. All these signs that tell you you're going to be on the club. So I'm playing preseason and I was dancing. I was as good as I had ever felt at training camp. I had a game program that has a picture in it: *The Newest Blackhawks* — maybe four or five guys — so I'm in the program that way. I got a breakaway and I pulled my right groin. I just tore it. I bet it took me three years to get over that injury."

Stanfield's days as a Hawk were done.

"It's an interesting thing about how you're only as strong as your weakest link. It really is true. But still I knew I could play."

Stanfield spent the next six seasons playing in L.A., Dallas, San Diego and Rochester. He finally got the chance to play major league hockey again in 1972. He joined the all-new World Hockey Association. He signed on with the Houston Aeros. That guy that he was so in awe of in 1966, Gordie Howe, was one of his new teammates. By this time Stanfield was 30 years old, and of course he was thinking about life after hockey. He always spent his summers working at golf courses back home in Toronto. He had a dream to continue his education after hockey and to coach golf and hockey at a post-secondary institute. He almost got his wish after his first season in Houston. "Colgate University in New York sent me a letter offering me [the opportunity] to take over the golf program and be assistant coach in hockey with the prospect of being the head coach once the existing coach retired. And they offered me $18,000, and the hockey club offered me $33,000 to stay in Houston."

The $33,000 was a hell of a lot more than what Tommy Ivan had offered Stanfield a decade earlier. He took the cash and stayed in Houston. It's a good thing that he did. That decision ultimately led Jack Stanfield to his second career. And although it wasn't in golf, it did ultimately lead him to playing at Augusta National.

The 1973–74 season was Jack Stanfield's last as a player, but it wasn't his last in hockey. He retired from the game and joined the Houston Aeros broadcast crew. Soon enough he became the vice-president of the team. "I got into packaging and selling and ended up doing all the marketing and sales for the team."

When the Aeros left Houston, Stanfield moved on to soccer. "I took over and ran a North American Soccer League team, the Houston Hurricanes, in 1979, and all during that time I was doing television." Television is the key word of Stanfield's post-playing career. It was a time when cable was still in its infancy. It was popping up everywhere, but what could a cable station possibly show that viewers couldn't get on the networks? The answer was sports.

"I started producing, and a friend of mine got a job to build the cable in the city of Houston. And he and I got together and came up with the plan to launch one of the — this is in the early '80s — very first regional channels in the United States: Madison Square Garden TV."

After that launch, Stanfield went on to launch regional sports networks all across the United States. "Pittsburgh . . . And I launched Sunshine Network in Florida . . . And I launched Prime Sports in Colorado." The list goes on and on. The player who crisscrossed America in seven different pro leagues was now crisscrossing America in a new capacity. But this time around, instead of racking up goals, he was racking up new television stations. "It's about having an inquisitive mind. I don't think people understand the learning curve that athletes have in front of them.

And you see it because even in some of the guys who are good commentators on hockey and football and other sports — some of those athletes you see the depth of understanding and knowledge that they collect simply because of the exposure."

Does he believe travelling by bus through the minor leagues was what educated him for a career as a television executive?

"I think it was . . . and it gave me a healthy lack of fear."

In the early 1980s, Jack Stanfield even played a role in bringing one of his old teammates to the airwaves. In 1971–72, Jack Stanfield met an aging minor league defenceman who was looking to make a comeback. He had played 19 games with Jack Stanfield on the Americans before calling it quits to become the team's head coach. By the early 1980s, that defenceman was a star on *Hockey Night in Canada* and he had his own syndicated TV show called *Grapevine*. Stanfield's old teammate was none other than the legendary Don Cherry. Stanfield, a man named Jody Shapiro who worked for the NHL for years, and a couple of others persuaded the regional channels in the U.S. to work together. "I convinced the regional guys to get together once a quarter and trade programming with each other. And I talked to Grapes and we used to bring *Grapevine* down and put it on the regional networks in the U.S."

It wasn't just hockey that Stanfield helped bring to the masses. His other passion in life was golf. Eventually his TV life led him to Augusta National, the home of the Masters. "I made the deal with the Masters to take them to Latin America. Then I made the deal with the Masters to take them to Asia. Then I made a deal with the Masters to take them to Australia and then the Middle East. So I went to the Masters 21 years in a row. In my 15th year, I got the number-one international broadcaster badge. I was so excited that they made a commitment to me, that as long as I was coming I'd get the number-one badge. I had eight consecutive years of getting the number-one international broadcaster badge. When I retired two or three years ago, they retired the badge." You can hear the pride in the old hockey player's voice.

And if you're wondering, yes, Jack Stanfield did get to play Augusta as well.

"It was fabulous," he says.

It's funny, you call someone to talk to them about a single hockey game and the conversation takes you in a totally different direction. It was just one game, but it was a game that proved to Jack Stanfield that he belonged and that he could skate with the greatest hockey players on the planet. The real story, though, is Jack Stanfield's experiences during his entire pro career. That's what led him to his life as a sports TV pioneer. "I would say the principles and things I learned in hockey still live in my heart and are probably an important part of my success in business."

Just then Jack Stanfield's phone buzzes. He has another call coming in and he's running late for a TV meeting in New York City. He's not officially retired yet. He's off to another meeting. He's off to play again.

CHAPTER FIVE
ALL IN THE FAMILY

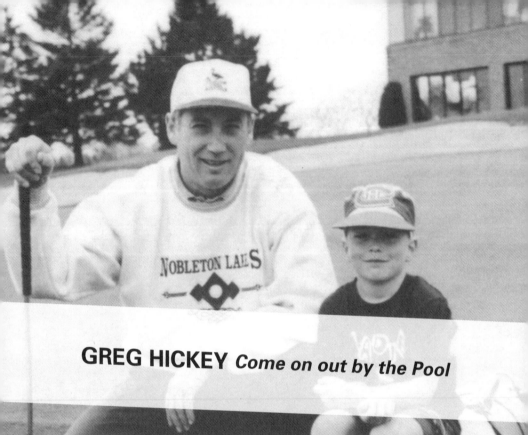

GREG HICKEY *Come on out by the Pool*

Hockey these days is big business. Multimillion dollar contracts await those who put their blood, sweat and year-round workouts into the game. It's serious business. Greg Hickey would not exactly be a poster boy for the game we see today, and that's just fine with him. "I only played hockey because I wanted to be a boy for as long as I possibly could. It didn't have anything to do with the business or anything else. That's probably why I didn't make it to where I might have been able to make it."

Where Hickey made it was all the way to the NHL — at least for one night. Near the tail end of the 1977–78 season, he got to suit up with his older brother Pat and the New York Rangers for a game against the Islanders. "My brother and I played on the same line with Walter Tkaczuk. It was pretty special to play with your brother. I played with Pat in his final year of junior. His final year was my first year of junior for the Hamilton Red Wings, so we played together through training camp and the whole nine yards. Pat was really the consummate professional. He knew what he wanted to do — where he was going. He was more focused and into the game and planning properly and running his business . . . and his little brother was a little wilder and more interested in some other things. Not many guys get to play their first and only game in the NHL with their brother. I don't know that that ever happens."

Hickey got the call after a season with the New Haven Nighthawks. But there was a bit of a problem. Once word spread through the Nighthawks that Hickey was going up to join the big club, his teammates thought they would send him off in style. New Haven's roster was riddled with a number of old pros and former NHLers like Ken Hodge, Bill Inglis and Bill Goldsworthy, and they wanted to give the 23-year-old a nice little going-away fiesta. "We all went out to dinner together. It was pretty standard, had a few cocktails and, well, someone said, 'Let's stop at the pool, I know a place, and we'll go swimming.' Fair enough. I dove out of the hot tub into the pool and wrenched my neck and couldn't play the next day."

The next day, the Nighthawks were set to play the Nova Scotia Voyageurs. Rangers general manager John Ferguson had even made the trip up to Nova Scotia to give Hickey one more look before he joined the big club. The GM didn't get a look at Hickey. "Fergie had flown to Halifax to see an injured pool boy," laughs Hickey. "I don't think he was very happy with me, but I think John got over it."

Eventually Hickey and his wrenched neck made their way to the Big Apple. On April 8, 1978, he suited up. The assignment for the smooth skating youngster: shadow young Islanders sniper Mike Bossy. "Because I was a pretty good skater I could pretty much cover anybody, so I just skated around the ice with Mike Bossy. I couldn't really do much because of my neck and I was doing pretty good, but they caught on. Bossy was pretty smart, so he had me skating to centre ice with him, and Dennis Potvin was moving in every time. I finally turned to Walter Tkaczuk on the bench and said, 'It's crazy.' We were down, I don't know, it was 5–0 or something stupid like that. It was one of three nationally televised games on NBC with Peter Puck back in the day, an afternoon game with everybody watching. And I said, 'This is foolish.' Walter turns to me and says, 'Hey, just take Bossy back to the net. Drop him off in front of the net. Play your game. Get back to the point.' And off we went. I get

Bossy and drop him back in front of the net with Carol Vadnais and I get back to the point to cover Potvin and all of a sudden it was Bingo-Bango-Bongo and fucking Bossy, he scores. And Vadnais is nowhere in sight to cover Bossy. And that's my story and I'm sticking to it."

The Islanders scored seven straight goals to open the game. The Rangers made it look marginally better with two late ones. It was a 7–2 Islanders final. That was it for Greg Hickey in New York. He was sent back to New Haven.

That spring, Hickey and his Nighthawks made it all the way to the Calder Cup final against the Maine Mariners, Philadelphia's top farm team. "If you thought the Philadelphia Flyers were a friggin' goon team, you should've seen their minor-league teams in Portland, Maine. It was a pretty interesting series. We got beat. We didn't win the Calder Cup and off I went home in June to skate and train because Fergie had told my agent, 'Hick, you're going to get your shot.' I was pumped."

Of course he was. He'd had a great playoff run with Nighthawks and thought he'd proved something during his brief cameo with the Rangers. However, shortly after he got the news that he was going to get his shot at camp, the Rangers made a move, "About a week to two weeks after that, Fergie gets fired and Freddie Shero moves into town."

Hickey was back to square one. Shero would be his third boss during his time in the organization. He started with Emile Francis, then saw out John Ferguson and was now playing for the ex-Flyer, Cup-winning coach. Hickey started training camp playing on what he says was a very successful line with Anders Hedberg and Ron Duguay. By the end of camp, he was on a line with two college players.

"There are all kinds of stories I could tell you about how it all went down. In the end it was looking really good for me, then Fergie moved on and Shero moved in and then Shero said, 'You remind me of a guy named Bobby Clarke and I think you're a centreman.' And I said, 'Well, thanks. You know, that's a nice compliment. I guess I'm going back to New Haven.' And that's where I went, back to New Haven. The old 'last cut' story. And I got back to New Haven and I was a centreman for about three games and Nighthawks head coach Parker MacDonald turned to me and said, 'Holy cow, are you ever a shitty centreman.' And I said,

'Well, I think so too. I can play either right or left wing but I'm not a very good centreman.' Back to the wing it was. And I wasn't even considered for a call-up after that."

From that point on, it was life in the minors. And soon enough Hickey started thinking about life beyond the rink. He had always been a golf fanatic. He'd caddied as a kid and had dreams of becoming a club pro one day. Hickey says when he was riding the minor league buses, a golf magazine was never too far out of his reach. Before he was drafted he almost worked in a pro shop, but one vocation got in the way of the other. In 1981, while he was playing for the Springfield Indians, the two professions finally came together. "I get a call from a golf pro who had run into some problems, and he got back into the business and needed an assistant at a club down in Simcoe, Ontario. He phoned me and said, 'Would you be interested? Your name came up that you'd be a good assistant.' I said, 'Sure.' So everything came full circle and I started that in '81."

Hickey kept playing hockey in the winter to fund his golf pursuits. Being on the ice in the winter meant he could learn on the greens in the summers. Eventually he became a head pro. Another dream had come true. He still works in the golf industry. He coaches at Georgian College and he is restoring the Orillia Golf and Country Club in Orillia, Ontario. The track has gone through some tough times, and the club brought in Hickey to bring it back to its former glory.

Greg Hickey doesn't spend too much time reminiscing about his pro hockey days. He and his brother Pat rarely, if ever, talk about the one night they played together for the Rangers. Hickey says there's simply too many other things going on in their lives. "We have kids and families and all kinds of other things to talk about that are much more important than hockey. Very rarely do we talk about the business. We talk about how the game's played and different things like that, but about us? No."

If Hickey does focus on one thing during his sole NHL appearance, it was that he was injured. Who knows what would have happened if he and the boys didn't go hot tubbing before he made his way to join the Rangers. "All in all, had I not had that dinner and gone swimming I might've had a nice little NHL career, but then again I might not have had a great golf career. I played games my entire life. It's either been hockey or golf. I'm 60 years old and I've done things that other people haven't done, and I've got a lot of things I still want to do that other people have done. That's the way I want to live my life."

JORDAN SIGALET **Less than a Minute of Magic/The Sigalet Boys (Part One)**

Clint Trahan

Forty-three seconds — not even a minute. That is the amount of time Jordan Sigalet played in the NHL. But those 43 seconds represent a lifetime full of hockey dreams and so much more. Jordan Sigalet wasn't supposed to play those 43 seconds. Just a couple of years earlier, playing 43 seconds of any hockey seemed almost impossible.

In 2004, Jordan Sigalet was like a lot of other NCAA players. He was at Bowling Green State University in Ohio, attending classes and playing hockey while dreaming of a life in the pros. Then suddenly, those dreams were put into jeopardy. When he was 23 years old, Jordan Sigalet was diagnosed with multiple sclerosis. The MS Society of Canada describes the disease as "an unpredictable, often disabling disease of the central nervous system, which is composed of the brain and spinal cord."

"Right after I was diagnosed, the doctor said there was a really good chance I wouldn't be able to play again because getting overheated is a big factor in people with MS. Overexerting yourself, vision, balance — so many symptoms of MS can affect your game, especially goalies. So I kind of used that as motivation to prove to people that I could still play and to prove to myself that I could play," says the B.C.-born Sigalet.

During his days at Bowling Green, Sigalet kept his condition under wraps. The MS hadn't started to affect his on-ice performance. He was a Hobey Baker finalist in 2005, and then the pro game came calling. The question for Sigalet was what to do next. Should he let the hockey world know about his condition? The answer was yes. "I kept it to myself for about a year and I finally just got sick about hiding behind lies, so my agent and I talked about it a lot. We said, 'You know what? Let's just do it and see what happens.'"

Of course, Sigalet was concerned that no one would take a chance on a goaltender that has MS. But the Boston Bruins, who took Sigalet 209th overall in the 2011 Draft, stepped up and signed him to his first deal. "They said as long as you can play, we really don't care. The only thing it really affected is they really only gave me one-year deals at a time instead of multi-year deals, in case my health deteriorated. But I couldn't have been more thankful for how supportive they were my whole time there."

Sigalet started his professional career with the AHL's Providence Bruins. In January, the big club ran into some goaltending injuries. Sigalet was actually watching the big club on the tube when his future unfolded before his eyes. "It was in January 2006. I remember watching. It was Hannu Toivonen at that time who got hurt. So I got called up and it was me and Andrew Raycroft. At that time, I never would have thought it would have been me going up because it was me and Tim Thomas in Providence."

This is one of those shining moments that a lot of one-game wonders run into. You hear it all the time. One of the biggest factors in a player's career is timing. This time, though, time was on Jordan Sigalet's side. "At that point in the CBA, there was a rule that Thomas would have had to clear waivers to go up because of how much money he made. They didn't want to take the risk so I got the call. I'll never forget that."

Sigalet got in his car and headed north to Boston and the NHL. "Getting up there you're just in awe. It's your first call-up and you're nervous. It was a pretty exciting time."

Sigalet's immediate assignment was to serve as Andrew Raycroft's backup. He was as close as you could possibly get to playing on NHL ice, in a real game situation, but all he could do was watch. "I remember one game backing up against Pittsburgh. Lemieux was still playing, and Crosby. So that's something that will always be special."

On January 7, 2006, late in a game against the Tampa Bay Lightning, Sigalet got the chance to make a better memory. "I was sitting on the bench and the game is almost over and you're freezing cold. We were up 6–3 with 43 seconds left. Andrew Raycroft just comes and keels over the bench, hunched over. So I knew something wasn't right and my heart started racing. Didn't even really think about it. Next thing the trainer passes me my gloves and my mask and I'm hopping the boards, hopping into the net."

At that moment, the odds were officially defied. It didn't look like much, a backup goaltender entering an NHL game with 43 seconds to go, but it meant the world to Jordan Sigalet and to those who knew his story. That night, though, his story was still being written, and it wasn't totally Hollywood at the moment. When Sigalet stepped into the Bruins crease, the first thought that raced through his head was not that his journey to the NHL was complete. "I think the one thing in my mind was that if I get one shot and it goes in, I'm going to have the worst numbers in NHL history — save percentage and goals against. It was more just nervous energy. I didn't have much time to think about it, getting thrown in like that. I didn't even face a shot."

The 43 seconds seemed to last, well, not forever, but a whole lot longer than just 43 seconds. "It felt a lot longer than I thought. There were a few stoppages. There was one shot attempt on net. I remember Andrew Alberts stuck out his stick and the puck went up in to the netting. I don't know if I was thankful that he blocked it or if I would have liked to have had that one save. It was a guy trying to dump it in from outside the blue line, so obviously he was trying to catch a cold goalie."

When the horn finally rang, the Bruins crowded around their rookie goaltender, congratulating each other on a 6–3 win over the Lightning, in typical hockey fashion. "They were all bugging me and making fun of me. I think it was Patrice Bergeron, Glen Murray, they're saying great job. I just laughed and shook it off. They were giving me a hard time."

Three nights later, the Boston Bruins were set to host the San Jose Sharks. And this was no regular January NHL night in Beantown. Just a few weeks earlier, on November 30, 2005, the Bruins altered the face of their franchise when they traded Joe Thornton to the San Jose Sharks. On January 10, Thornton was set to return to Boston for the first time as a member of the Sharks. It was a big deal for the Bruins and the city. "At this point I'm thinking Toivonen is not healthy enough to play but he's healthy enough to backup. I'm thinking I'm going to get this game. I was nervous but excited."

Remember when Sigalet got called up, how the timing was on his side? This time it was not. The Bruins made a call down to Providence. "The next day they ended up taking a chance of putting Thomas on waivers and clearing him and then they reassigned me back down to Providence."

The Thomas recall set an incredible chain of events into motion that started with Thomas finally finding his NHL groove well beyond his 30th birthday and ended with a Stanley Cup for the Bruins in 2011. "It was just part of the game at that time. I was early in my career. I was just happy that they gave me the chance. That was my first year and I didn't have a lot of pro experience at all, so I learned a lot when I was up there just by being around pros like that. During my career in Boston, I was probably up there for about a month and backed up, I'm not sure of the exact number, but probably 10 games. So it was a great experience."

Unfortunately, the next time Jordan Sigalet was back in the news it was not for a heartwarming story. The following season, Sigalet was back in Providence. It was November 16, a regular Friday night game in Rhode Island against the Worcester Sharks. In the third period, without warning, Sigalet collapsed to the ice. He lay motionless, face down on the frozen surface. As the play-by-play announcer said on the broadcast, "The building has gone quiet." Sigalet was out cold. "I remember feeling a little weird or off a couple of days up to that collapse. I didn't really think anything was going to happen. I had just been feeling extra tired, maybe a little bit weak. What ended up happening was just getting overheated and dehydrated and those cord lesions in my spine kind of flared out and caused my legs to give out and collapse."

As the 26-year-old was stretchered off the ice, his health, not hockey, was the main concern. Sigalet had to go through extensive rehab where he basically had to learn to walk again. He eventually returned to the Providence lineup and played in 25 more games that season. He put up some very solid numbers: a 2.39 GAA and a .915 save percentage. After 19 more games in the AHL the following season, Sigalet's North American career was over. He split the next year between Russia and Austria.

Sigalet got married in the summer of 2009 and decided to call it a career and pass on going back overseas. He eventually entered the coaching world. First up was a stint as a goalie coach with the Everett Silvertips of the Western Hockey League. That was followed by three years in the AHL with the Abbotsford Heat. Now Jordan Sigalet is back in the NHL, and it's for a lot more than just 43 seconds. He's the goaltending coach for the Calgary Flames. Sigalet, who holds a degree in computer animation from Bowling Green, is part of a new breed of NHL coaches. During his long hours, his computer is never far from his side as he strives to find new ways for his goalies and his team to get just a little bit better. "I love to do a lot of video on our goalies and opposition goalies, just to help our goalies and prepare our players for the other team too.

"I say it's a little bit different at the NHL level. I kind of work with what's made them successful, whereas in the AHL and WHL sometimes you get younger guys who can make more adjustments to their games. You can still do that at the NHL level, it's just not as drastic, but it's still rewarding. It's great to see them have success, so it's been good."

Sigalet is now, sadly, not the only NHL goaltender to have ever played in the NHL with MS. Former Minnesota Wild tender Josh Harding was diagnosed with the disease in November 2012. Sigalet immediately reached out. "I spoke to him a few weeks after he got diagnosed and formed a little bit of a relationship there. He was really thankful for my advice."

Josh Harding defied the odds and played for another year after his diagnosis. Jordan Sigalet defied the odds and made it all the way to the NHL after he was told he would likely never play again. "The most rewarding aspect? I think it was just you work your whole life to get there, and dream about being there, and then you're young and 23 years old and you think your career is coming to an end with an MS diagnosis, and you bounce back, get back on your feet, get out there and prove to yourself you can do it. For anyone without MS, being out there is a huge accomplishment, but having gone through what I went through, to be able to keep battling out there was an unbelievable feeling.

"I remember when I got off the ice after the game, Ray Bourque was in the room . . . I remember he came up to me and said, 'Congratulations.' And I kind of joked, I said, 'I got 43 seconds, no shots.' And he said, 'Well, you know what? You can say you played the game now.' And you know, looking back at it now, I can. It's funny, no one can take that away from me even though it was less than a minute."

Oh and here's another thing, no one can take one night in the NHL away from Jordan's brother, Jonathan, either . . .

JONATHAN SIGALET *The Sigalet Boys (Part Two)*

"We joke," says Jordan Sigalet's younger brother Jonathan, "that we must combine for the fewest minutes played by two brothers ever in the NHL."

The official tally for the Sigalet's combined NHL ice time comes in at 15:24. You do the math, take away Jordan's 43 seconds and Jonathan Sigalet has 14:41 on his NHL résumé. Like his brother Jordan, all of Jonathan's experience came in one NHL game. "It was a road game in Ottawa. My coach in Providence, Scott Gordon, called me from the rink. I went to get my gear and he gave me the news."

Just like Jordan, Jonathan Sigalet is a soft-spoken guy. But if you want the Sigalet brothers to really open up, get them talking about one another. You get a real taste for the bond that they have. Of course, most brothers have a bond, but the Sigalets take things to another level. They played at Bowling Green together and they played together in the AHL with the Providence Bruins. On January 9, 2007, Jonathan became the second Sigalet to suit up for the Bruins, but looking back on his one night now, the details are vague.

"Honestly there was so much happening so fast I never really got to settle down. You're on the plane, you're letting your family know, then you're trying to get some rest, get your pre-game skate and get your nap in. It was kind of a whirlwind. You never really get to settle in and take a look around."

So let's get his brother to fill us in — after all, who doesn't like to rip on their little brother every once in a while? (I know my brother, Peter, and I love to go at each other.) So, here's older brother Jordan on younger brother Jonathan's NHL debut: "He rips on me because I only played 43 seconds, but I rip on him because he played one game and had, I think, four minutes in penalties and was minus one. During one of his first shifts he shot the puck, it went over the glass and he got a penalty. Then he was skating backwards in a one-on-one situation and he caught an edge and fell down. They went by him and I think they scored on that."

A quick review of the game sheet tells us that, yes, Jonathan fell victim to a fairly new rule in the NHL during the 2006–07 season and he picked up two minutes for delay of game for shooting the puck over the glass from behind his own blue line. However, it didn't happen in the first, it happened at the 10:55 mark of the second period. It was his second penalty of the game. He'd already taken two for holding. A delay of game for shooting the puck over the glass is tough stuff for a rookie. "I don't even think we had that rule in the American League that year. I did it and I was just like, 'Oh —' I can't even say the word I'm thinking. It was my second penalty," laughs Jonathan. "I actually played pretty well but my stats were terrible." His stats for the night were actually a bit worse than his brother remembers: minus two with four penalty minutes in a very respectable 14:41 in a 5–2 Bruins loss. "Jason York, who was an older guy at the time, got hurt 10 minutes into the game. So we actually played with five defence most of the game."

It was quick, it was fast, and it was almost over before it started. Sigalet actually had the Stuart family to thank in part for his call-up. Defenceman Brad Stuart was not available to play for the Bruins that night in Ottawa — the Stuarts were having a baby. But soon enough

Sigalet was back down in Providence. "I wish I had a clearer memory," he says. "At the time it was just such a blur. I mean, you're spending every day of your career preparing for that, but when you never know when it's actually going to happen it's hard to be prepared. It's all the little things that throw you off, like the travel and who you're rooming with. Your meals are different and all that kind of stuff."

And the NHL game is different as well. Though only a few moments from the actual contest stand out, it's the overall quality of play in the show that truly resonates with Jonathan. "Guys are where they are supposed to be. If you give a guy a not-great pass at the NHL level, a lot of times he'll just pick it up anyway."

Back with his brother in Providence, he doesn't really remember discussing the call-up, but he is pretty sure he did. Like Jordan, Jonathan's time on North American ice eventually came to a close, but not before a long tenure in the AHL.

Jonathan spent the next four seasons in the AHL. He moved from the Bruins organization to the Columbus Blue Jackets, but he never made it into another NHL game. At the end of the 2010–11 season, he thought he was in pretty good shape after a 22-point and plus-12 season with the Springfield Falcons. "It was tough. I'd had my best season in the AHL. Maybe not stat-wise, but definitely playing the best I had ever played. I really thought I'd get a decent contract the next year. It was about the middle of July and I had noting yet." Jonathan had to make a choice. His answer was in Russia: "I took the job offer to go to the KHL."

He spent four years in the KHL and then he moved on to Sweden. Today, Jonathan is still on the ice and the possibility of a return to the NHL is still out there. "I mean, yeah, the desire is there. It's just a matter of whether the opportunity to chase after that is worth what you'd be giving up, the stability in Europe."

Perhaps one day, Jonathan can defy the odds — you should never bet against the Sigalet boys. If Jonathan needs inspiration, he can always look to what his big brother pulled off when he took to the ice with the Bruins. "It was unbelievable. He was my idol and hero, always, growing up. So to see him get his chance was pretty awesome.

"I think that was sort of a nice cherry on top, a reward for all the dedication and perseverance. And it was pretty awesome that he at least got to step on the ice."

As for his one night: "One game doesn't even really fell like you made it . . . it's so quick, and over and done with. I never really thought that would have been my only game."

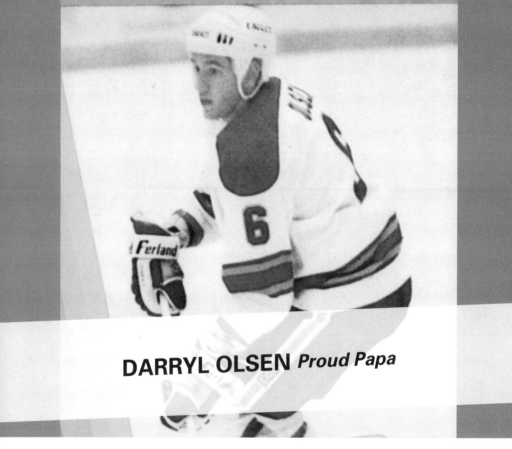

DARRYL OLSEN *Proud Papa*

If making it to the NHL is like having a winning lottery ticket, like a lot of one-gamers say, Darryl Olsen picked the wrong time to purchase his. It's not that his numbers never came up — they did. It's just that Olsen "won" in the wrong place and at the wrong time . . .

Before we get into just why Olsen couldn't cash in, let's establish a little bit about the 6-foot, 180-pound smooth-skating defenceman from Northern Michigan University. His game was offence. During his four-year NCAA career, he racked up 123 points in 154 games. If he was going to make it to the NHL it would have to be as a high-scoring, puck-moving blueliner. At 180 pounds, he knew he wasn't going to make his living pushing guys around; during his first two years of pro in the IHL, he put up 121 points in 148 games.

In his third pro season it all paid off. One of the Flames' top offensive blueliners, Gary Suter, was out of the lineup with an injury. Calgary needed someone with offensive upside on the back end and Olsen was their guy. "I got the call from the coach in Salt Lake. He said, 'We've got some news for you. The Flames just called. You're headed up, buddy.'

He goes, 'You gotta be on a plane in the morning. Make sure you call the trainer. Get your shit and get up there. Best of luck and I hope I never see you again,'" Olsen recalls almost 25 years later.

"It was kind of exciting because that was the year I went into training camp and I had the most points in preseason. I led the team as a defenceman [in scoring]. So it was kind of exciting because I was hoping to get the call and get the call for good. But that didn't happen."

Olsen, who grew up cheering for the Flames, was heading back to play for his hometown team against Steve Yzerman and the Detroit Red Wings on December 14, 1991. He called his folks, then made his way to Alberta. "That whole day was sort of a blur. You walk in, in your suit and tie, and get your under armour on. You walk to your stall and you see your jersey. That's kind of a big deal. Your jersey is in your stall, your name's on it. You're excited and pretty nervous and then . . . I just remember putting my jersey on and going out for warm-up. As you walk down the hallway you can see the fans. You know that your family is going to be there and you skate out on the ice — it's pretty surreal."

Olsen knew he was in the lineup to help provide a little offence. After all, he was replacing Gary Suter. He was in awe of his surroundings, but he had to settle down . . . quickly. "It's all business. You're skating around and you're like, 'Holy shit. I actually have a Flames jersey on.' You look across the ice and you see those guys. But then you've got to regroup and pull your head out of your ass or you're going to look stupid out there."

In those days, the Wings had quite a few players who could make a rookie look stupid. They had Yzerman and they had Lidstrom. But for Olsen it was Sergei Fedorov who might have been the best. "He was just so highly skilled. His skating and his lateral movement was just phenomenal. He was really tough to defend one-on-one, but at the same time that's who you wanted to be against because you wanted to stop him. Like I said, I played in preseason that year. I got to play against Lemieux, Jagr, Brett Hull — a lot of big names. And you were excited to play against those guys. I knew Fedorov and Yzerman were going to be out there. I actually had Fedorov down in front of the net and we exchanged punches to the head."

So maybe Olsen was a little more physical than we're giving him credit for.

Olsen didn't register a point that night. He finished minus two in the 4–3 Detroit overtime win. He had three shots on goal, but it's the one shot he didn't take that still stands out. "I don't know if we were on the power play, but at one point the puck had popped out from behind the net and I was walking in to tee up a one-timer. It was just me and the goalie and I thought, 'You know what? I'm going to snipe this.' And just as I went to take my slapshot, Gary Roberts comes through and steals the puck away from me. I'm like, 'Oh fuck.' I was kind of excited to put that in the back of the net. Like I said, in preseason I led the team in scoring. I kind of wanted to carry on that offensive pace and let those guys know that while Suter's hurt, I could do the job."

A few nights later, Suter was still out of the lineup. The Flames ended up winning a 7–4 game over the Winnipeg Jets. It was the kind of game a small, offensive-minded defenceman would have been right at home in, but Olsen never got the chance to play. "We had nine defenceman getting ready for pre-game warm-up. All nine of us are kind of going, 'What the hell's going on? We can't all go out there.' So we're sitting there in our skates. You're getting ready for the game, mentally prepared. You spent the day getting prepared and then all of a sudden our assistant coach Paul Baxter comes through and says, 'You're not going. You're not going. You're not going.' And I was one of the players not going."

Olsen spent another two weeks with the Flames. He practised with the team, travelled with them, but he never played again. He was sent back to Salt Lake with just one game on his résumé.

Everything about his lotto ticket had been right, except for the fact that the Flames already had offensive defencemen on their roster. "Doug Risebrough told me during my exit interview, 'It's just numbers. We brought you up for a reason. You played very well. We know that you can play at this level.' And then I got sent down.

"It was kind of tough. I had done my job in Salt Lake. I had done my job. I knew I could play. I showed them I could play up there. I put up points. But I also understood. You know, you've got Gary Suter and Al MacInnis. Back then you had two offensive guys and that was it.

The other four of the six guys who were on the team were 6-foot-5, 230 pounds and were basically there to be defensive defenceman and beat the shit out of people."

Olsen went back to Salt Lake and he did what he was supposed to do. He finished the 1991–92 season with 40 points in 59 IHL games. His contract with Flames expired after that summer and he signed on with the Boston Bruins with the intention of cracking their lineup in the fall of 1992. There was just one problem. While the Flames had Suter and MacInnis, the Bruins had a couple of key offensive cogs on their blue line as well. "Again I'm the last guy cut. I'll never forget this as long as I live. I'm in my exit interview with Bruins coach Brian Sutter and he says, 'Lad, I love everything about your game.' And he holds his index finger and his thumb up and you can barely fit a feather through there, and he's like, 'You were this close to making it to the NHL and staying in the NHL.' And you're sitting there going, 'This close? What does a guy have to do for that?' You know what I mean? But then again, I was realistic and you take a look at it. Who did they have? They had Ray Bourque and Glen Wesley. How in the hell am I going to crack that lineup?"

Once again, Olsen was back in the minors. This time it was the AHL, with Providence. The year started off well enough, but then he found himself in the doghouse. "I don't know what happened, but I fell out of the good graces of the head coach, Mike O'Connell. He comes in one day and he's like, 'We're going to loan you out to Atlanta.' I'm like, 'Why?' And he goes, 'Well, management has different plans for you.' I'm like, 'Well, I'm not going to Atlanta.'"

Olsen got on the phone and arranged his own trade to the IHL's San Diego Gulls. When he said no to the Bruins plan to send him to Atlanta, he knew he was not only saying no to hockey in Georgia, he was basically saying goodbye to another shot in the NHL. And he realized that a life in the minors was probably what hockey had in store for him. "That's when I realized, 'It's probably time to start looking at other options — because I'm pretty sure I'm not going back to the NHL.'"

Olsen played in California and then spent another year in Salt Lake — and then he headed for Europe. "I went overseas and loved every minute of it." His final stint was in the WPHL and he retired after the

1999–2000 season. Like a lot of players, Olsen's career timing was off. Just look at how the game is played these days. An undersized point-producing defenceman can thrive. "I probably would have had a long career if I was a defenceman today.

"Even though I played one game, I know in my heart that if I was given an opportunity I could have played 10 years. But you look at the evolution of the game and it just wasn't my time. I know if I was put in a different situation I could have been part of an Al MacInnis and Gary Suter or Ray Bourque and Glen Wesley tandem. You're looking at four Hall of Famers, right? Even still, the one game was a dream come true. I grew up wanting to play for the Calgary Flames and getting drafted by them, and playing that one game was special. I'm more than satisfied with my career."

His playing days over, Olsen has stayed in the game. He set up shop in the Salt Lake area, teaching hockey and power skating. His star pupil shares the same last name. Darryl Olsen's son Dylan is another speedy, smooth-skating defenceman. Unlike his dad, however, the younger Olsen has the size as well. He makes his living in the NHL with the Florida Panthers. "It's phenomenal. He's playing against the best of the best. He's a shut-down defenceman. To watch him at 6-foot-3, 230 pounds, skating the way he skates . . . it's beautiful just to see the life that he's leading and the smile on his face. I would've loved to have lived that life but I'm glad that he got the opportunity and he's taking advantage of it."

For years, Darryl taught and Dylan listened. And he picked up everything his dad was preaching. His dad, who played in a hard-hitting time, could see the game evolving from the rough grudge match it once was into the much faster game we see today. "I knew that this was going to happen, and if you can't skate you can't play. So we worked on that. He's got a hell of a slapshot. He's on the power play at times. When he's utilized on the power play he can move the puck. It's just nice to watch because he does have all the aspects of the game down. And that's a testament to all the hard work he put in as a kid."

Dylan Olsen is now well past his dad on the family's all-time games played list — in fact, he passed Darryl on January 6, 2012, when he played his second NHL game. The old man was smiling, maybe even laughing a little bit as he took it all in. "The TV announcers were pretty well aware. They were like, 'Well, Dylan Olsen's played one more game in the NHL than his father. I wonder how he feels?'"

The old man felt just great.

"I hope he plays a thousand games."

DARIN SCEVIOUR *Proud Papa II*

For almost two years, out of every father-son combo to ever play the game, the Sceviours, dad Darin and son Colton, had a pretty unique distinction. "I was aware of it. I'm not sure how much he dwelled on it," says Darin.

Darin was aware of the Sceviours' infamous spot in the one-game-wonder club. Darin played a single NHL game for the Chicago Blackhawks on February 1, 1987. His son Colton made his NHL debut for the Dallas Stars on February 5, 2011. And then the Sceviours waited for Colton's second outing. And they waited. And waited. And waited. Darin says, "Colton concentrated on getting out of the AHL and doing the best he could, but I was very aware of it. While it was amusing, it was also not amusing at the same time. He experienced the same thing as me, and I felt bad for him."

Finally, after another 100-plus games with the Texas Stars, Colton got the call-up to Dallas. He played in career game number two on January 26, 2013, and he even got an assist to move into the lead on the family's all-time NHL scoring list. Most importantly, Colton passed his old man on the games played list. "He'd played one game for a couple years, until they had some change at the upper management level, and then he got his opportunity with Lindy Ruff and Jim Nill. For the longest time, though, that's all he got. And then after his second game, he said he officially no longer had to listen to me anymore . . . because now he's played more. It was a good line."

Today, Colton Sceviour is a full-time NHLer. A few decades ago that was Darin's goal: make it to the Show on a full-time basis. During his second year in the Chicago Blackhawks organization, the NHL seemed far away for the 22-year-old from Alberta. He was playing in the IHL for the Saginaw Generals in Michigan. Sceviour had split the previous season between the Generals and the AHL's Nova Scotia Oilers. The Blackhawks and Oilers shared the AHL affiliate in Nova Scotia, and if you were one of the Blackhawks' top prospects, you played in Nova Scotia. Sceviour was playing in Michigan — not a good sign. "I'd played in Halifax the year before and then the following year I didn't make the same team. So I didn't think I was one of their top prospects at that time."

However, Saginaw does have one distinct advantage over Halifax. It is a hell of a lot closer to Chicago. On February 1, 1987, the Blackhawks were hosting the Edmonton Oilers and they were unexpectedly down a man. They needed someone, and in a hurry.

The math here is pretty simple. It's 11 a.m. and the Blackhawks are in panic mode and need to get a call-up quick. It's one 1 p.m. in Halifax, which is a three-hour flight away, if you could get a direct flight, which wasn't easy in 1987. So the Hawks did the only thing they could — they phoned Saginaw. "I think I just came off from our practice and our coach said, 'Would you be interested in playing?' And truthfully I thought it was just someone pulling my leg, but it ended up being real."

Sceviour believed it might have been a prank because, like he said, all of Chicago's top prospects were playing for Nova Scotia. But this was for real. "I just jumped on it and got all my stuff and joined the team."

Sceviour took all of his stuff to Chicago, but not all of his stuff ended up in the Windy City. The drive from Saginaw to Chicago can take anywhere from four and a half to five hours. Sceviour and the Blackhawks didn't have that much time, so Sceviour took to the skies. And that, thanks to the guys who unloaded the plane's cargo, jokes Sceviour, is why he only played in one NHL game. "They lost my sticks. I do remember that because I was pretty fussy with the way I played back then. And my sticks didn't show up and I ended up having to use someone else's. So that's what I blame. If I had my own sticks I probably would have stayed for more."

Anyone who's ever picked up a blade knows you have to have your own sticks. It's a feel thing. Sceviour thinks he may have used some of Wayne Presley's lumber that night, but he is not entirely sure. Anyway, the night of February 1, 1987, was just like any other night, until he hit the ice. "It was just hockey, but I didn't realize the magnitude of it until the warm-ups. The game happened to be against the Oilers, so the first time I skated by Wayne Gretzky I realized what was actually happening. I remember skating by him and I remember I had to just make sure I didn't fall over my first time around. It kind of caught me off guard. That was back when the Oilers were that dominant club. So it was pretty exciting."

Chicago was facing off against the best team in hockey. Darin Sceviour woke up in Saginaw, Michigan, and now he was set to play against the Great One in the loudest building in the NHL. Let me rephrase that. *Some of his teammates were about to play against Gretzky.* When the game was about to start, the rookie got his orders from the coach. "It was suggested that if Gretzky was on then I wasn't supposed to stay out there." Aye-aye, sir. Once the score got a little lopsided, Sceviour took the odd shift with the Great One on the other side, but not in the early going. You have to follow the coach's orders.

For an Alberta boy, you would think playing against the Oilers would be a big thing. Rod Phillips would have had the call from the stadium, with thousands of Oilers fans listening on radios across Alberta. Sceviour, though, didn't get caught up in the whole hometown-boy-does-good storyline. In fact, the idea of getting the news out to everybody back home didn't really register with him at all. "I think I phoned my father and I told him I was playing. It wasn't the instant thing that it is now. When someone is doing something we all know about it through Twitter and everything. I didn't get an opportunity to get really involved. I was there in the morning and then I played the game and I was gone the next day."

Before he knew it, Darin Sceviour was back in Saginaw. And then, before he knew anything further, he was in Europe. "I went back to Saginaw and one of the owners from the German team happened to be there to watch me and they offered me a contract right there, right after the game."

Sceviour discussed the matter with his agent, but when Chicago came back with an IHL only deal, he said so long and headed overseas for the first of his four years in Germany. As quickly as it came, his NHL dream was over. "I'm not sure how to explain it. Obviously you're excited about playing, but at the same time it's only a single game. You're hoping for another one. Maybe. I thought I played well enough to make it, or at least get another shot. But I was on the second farm team. So they had the Marc LaVarres and those other guys already in the chute."

In the spring of 1991 Darin Sceviour retired. He had become a bit of a scoring star in Germany. "I actually did very well over there for some reason." Concussion issues forced him out of the game; however, he wasn't done with pro hockey.

Fast forward a decade and a half and Darin's son Colton was beginning his WHL career with the Portland Winter Hawks. In 2007, the Dallas Stars took Colton with the 112th pick in the draft. Twenty years after he tried to crack the NHL, Darin Sceviour was now a hockey dad watching his son attempt the same thing. "I coached him for so many years and obviously had been around his hockey. I probably knew more about what he was doing to make it than what I was doing when I was trying to make it. When I went up, my father knew nothing about the game. He never played, never went to a game until I started playing junior in Lethbridge. Really, he had no influence."

Darin watched his son try to squeeze his way into the world's best hockey league. He was a hands-on hockey dad, with a very unique perspective. "At the beginning you try to give him what you think are constructive comments, but really, at the end of the day, it's not relevant to what their system is and what their teams are and it took me a couple of years to figure that out. I always thought I was one thing away from making it happen for him. But really there's a lot more going on behind the scenes and you don't realize when you're going through it how many layers and layers and layers there are. And one of the factors is luck. That's what a lot of people don't realize. There are some very, very skilled players I played with who never even got the opportunity that I did. The luck factor — I call it a lottery. You've got to be with the right team, at the right time, playing for the right coach, with a need in your position. And that's basically what goes into the lotto number combination for some people."

Colton Sceviour finally won the lottery and broke through. He played his first full season with the Dallas Stars in 2014–15. Darin, who played a single game in 1987, watched his son put up 26 points in 71 games. Is the thrill of watching his son better than the thrill of playing in his own NHL game? "Yeah, much more. It was good — he took a long road and he did have some trying moments.

"It almost seemed like I was more involved with him than I was in my own career. I didn't have much control over my career — not that I had control over his either — but I was able to watch more of his. Basically life revolved around watching him. It was really cool when he got the opportunity."

Darin Sceviour, who now scouts for the Lethbridge Hurricanes, still spends a lot of time watching his son play. One thing he doesn't do, however, is rummage through pictures of his hockey past. Like a lot of one-gamers, the moment just passed him by.

"I don't think I have a picture of it. I never got a training camp photo. There's one floating around the internet that one of my sons found that's quite comical, so they show that to me every once in a while. But I've never been one of those guys who are big on nostalgia. So I don't have a trophy room — I'm not that type of guy. But you always think that it's going to keep going . . . eventually you'll be famous or something and be one of the big guys. And then when it's done you can't un-ring that bell. Once it's over, it's done."

CHAPTER SIX
MAKE YOUR MARK

LARRY KWONG *The Trail Blazer*

It is hard to put into words just what Larry Kwong had to go through to get to his one game — what he was up against is thankfully no longer accepted in society.

Kwong was born in 1923 and grew up in Vernon, B.C. And like thousands of other Canadian kids, he fell in love with Canada's game. But in the eyes of the hockey world, the young man was different. He was Chinese Canadian, and no one in the NHL looked anything like him in the 1930s. But Kwong had a dream: to make a living as a professional hockey player. He got a taste of what he was up against when he left home in 1941, at the age of 18, to play for the legendary Trail Smoke Eaters. "When I went to Trail I said I was going to work in the smelter like all the rest of the hockey players and it turned out that they had a ban on Chinese. So they gave me a job in the hotel as a bellhop. And that was hard to take too."

Like a lot of young Canadian men, including some great hockey players, Kwong was called into the Canadian Army during the Second World War. And then his hockey career took a Hollywood-like twist.

While he was in the army, Kwong played alongside some former and future New York Rangers, including some top-notch talent. "I played with Mac and Neil Colville, and 'Sugar' Jim Henry and Chuck Rayner were the goalies. And we got along pretty good." And that is how the New York Rangers came to discover the 5-foot-6 Kwong.

Kwong made an impression and his new pals brought word of the smooth-skating kid with a quick shot back to New York. When Kwong left the service, the New York Rangers came calling. In 1946, the kid from Vernon found himself in New York City. He made an immediate impression with the Rangers' farm team, the New York Rovers. "I always thought my shot was pretty good. I was smart. My first coach for the Rovers was Freddie Metcalfe. He told me, 'You're really good. I've never seen anybody shoot the puck so fast. Not the speed of the puck but the accuracy and the fast release.' He said, 'You should be up there.'"

Up *there* — as in, with the Rangers in the six-team NHL. But someone who looked like Kwong had never been "up there" before. Larry Kwong was trying to break in to the NHL a decade before the league finally welcomed Willie O'Ree into its midst. Kwong was going up against the near impossible. "I would say the players accepted me," says Kwong. But the fans and management . . . perhaps not so much.

Kwong finished fifth in scoring in his first year on the Rovers. The next year, he went on a tear and wound up with 86 points in 65 games. The Rangers had no choice. They had to give the man whose nickname was "The China Clipper" a shot. On March 13, 1948, they did — but, then again, they really didn't. The Rangers were in Montreal to face the Canadiens and Larry Kwong was about to play in the NHL. On that night, he didn't think about the fact that he was making history as the first Chinese Canadian to play in the NHL. He simply thought about the fact that his childhood dream was about to come true. "It was a big deal because I was up to the professional league, which was my goal. Ever since I was a kid I was trying to get up there. That was big for me, because all the papers had write-ups and all that." But Kwong quickly adds, almost seven decades after that night, "It wasn't what I thought it would be."

The Rangers and Canadiens took to the ice, but Larry Kwong did not. He sat and watched and sat and watched as his teammates and the

Canadiens tore it up at the historic Montreal Forum. Kwong did not get a shift in the first period. He didn't get a shift in the second either. Rangers head coach Frank Boucher had him glued to the bench.

Finally, late in the third, Larry Kwong got on the ice for his first and only shift in the National Hockey League. "I was disappointed that I didn't play more. He got me up there but he never used me. I was dressed but I didn't do too much because I was on the bench all the time. And just at the last minute he threw me in. One shift.

"When he sent me in there, I was quite cold, sitting on the bench all the time. So I was sort of disappointed in that."

Larry Kwong was averaging over a point per game with the Rovers and all he got was one shift for the New York Rangers, who, by the way, did not have a player in their lineup that year who scored at a rate of more than a point per game. And it was a tight game. The Rangers could have used a goal or two more. (The Habs won 3–2.)

That was it for Larry Kwong. After the season he said goodbye to New York and hello to life in Quebec. During the 1930s and 1940s, the Quebec Senior League was one of the best hockey leagues in the world. If the New York Rangers didn't want Larry Kwong, the Valleyfield Braves certainly did: "The manager of the Valleyfield Braves told me, 'Anytime you want to play here you just give me a call,' and that is why I left the Rangers. I went to the new league and I was quite happy there."

Kwong played on a team coached by the great Toe Blake. During his first year with the Braves, he finished third in scoring with 84 points in 63 games. Soon enough, the league would feature a young Jean Béliveau skating for the Quebec Aces. "I played against him three years there. He was the main man for the Quebec Aces. And we played them in the playoffs and beat them and went on to win the Canadian Championship."

In 1950–51, Kwong finished second in the seven-team league-scoring race with 85 points. He was named the league's top player. After being rejected by the New York Rangers, Larry Kwong had found his hockey home. Being named the MVP of a league stacked with great players like Herb Carnegie and Dick Gamble still means a lot to Kwong: "Fondest memory? I would say winning the title of the best player in the league, the Quebec League. That was quite a thrill." It was big news in Quebec, but maybe not so much at home in B.C.

And maybe that's why, in large part, Larry Kwong's story has slipped through the cracks of hockey history, though a Vernon schoolteacher named Chad Soon has done remarkable work in bringing Kwong's story to light, and we should all be thankful for his important efforts. (Chad was instrumental in helping me track down this living hockey legend.)

These days Larry Kwong is well into retirement. Health struggles have led to both of his legs being amputated in 2004 and 2005. He had just one shift in the NHL, but he went on to become a superstar in Quebec, and he also played overseas. Now, all these years later, back where his hockey dreams began, in British Columbia, does he think he got a fair shot from the New York Rangers? "Not really."

Despite everything he went through, Larry Kwong still loves the game of hockey. Before we said goodbye, Larry mentioned one more thing about the game he fell in love with as a child: "I'd like to add that hockey did well for me and I'm glad. I really enjoyed playing, and maybe because I enjoyed it so much I stayed that long and played."

Yes, he played for a long time. For a long time after that one shift with the New York Rangers in 1948.

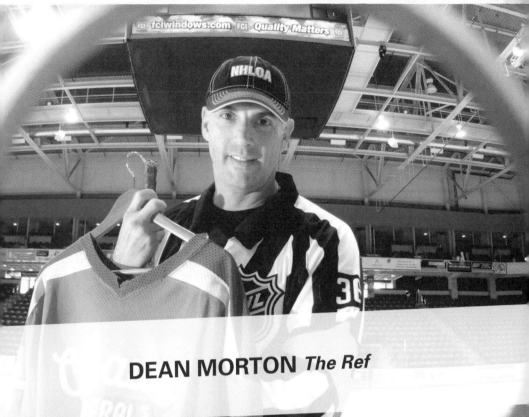

DEAN MORTON *The Ref*

Ron Pietroniro/Metroland Durham Region Media Group

When I catch up with Dean Morton, he's still feeling the effects of a hockey injury from eight months earlier. On a January night in Toronto, Morton took a vicious hit from David Clarkson of the Leafs. Clarkson didn't see Morton. But Morton saw Clarkson. You can hear Morton yell "Clarkie" just moments before impact. But it was too late. Clarkson hammered into Morton and Morton hammered into Clarkson. The ref went down with a broken rib. Rewind the tape about 25 years, though, and it was the guy in stripes handing out the hits at hockey's highest level.

"Things went my way for training camp and the preseason games. It wasn't like I was scoring goals. I'm talking brawly, open-ice hits, mucking in the corners, battling in front of the net. Things were going my way, and it created a buzz within the *Detroit Free Press* and they were covering me as a rookie from nowhere, creating all this stuff in preseason." Morton is taking me back to his days at Red Wings Camp in September 1989. He was a 21-year-old rookie who had put up 186 PIMs the season before as a first-year pro with Adirondack of the AHL. In the fall of '89, the hits happened in intra-squad games. One of Morton's first victims was NHL-vet Paul MacLean. "I grew up with Steve Chiasson and he just says, 'That's a great hit.'"

Morton's madness continued through the exhibition schedule. "In a game against Minnesota, Curt Fraser threated to rip my head off because I was just hitting guys. A Scott Stevens style of hitting . . . open ice, shoulder squared to the body. I wasn't elevating myself. It wasn't how you see these kids hitting today. I was hitting like a linebacker — I had the leverage that I was able to catch their upper body, and then their feet would just flop."

Another big hit came in a preseason game against the Leafs. "I laid out Eddie Olczyk on a suicide pass by Gary Leeman. The next thing I know I've got five Leafs on top of me and another three Red Wings on top of me. And I've got Brian Curran trying to scratch the living shit out of every part of my body he can get to. I'm surprised I still have my eyes. Things kind of snowballed."

They snowballed all the way to Western Canada. Dean Morton was with the Red Wings on their regular season opening road trip to start the 1989–90 season. It was a three-game western swing that started up with a stop in Calgary. On October 5, 1989, Morton, who was all of a sudden Mr. "I'll Hit Anything," found himself on the ice at the Calgary Saddledome against the defending Stanley Cup champs. Morton, who was skating in the AHL the previous season, was now a big-leaguer. If the sight of Morton on the ice was a shock to Red Wings management, after all he was buried on the Wings depth chart when camp began, it was an even bigger shock to Morton. He just tried to let it all soak in.

"They're raising the banner and you're overwhelmed because you go through such a high in training camp and then all of a sudden it's like, 'Well, yeah? That high for me as a young kid is basically a sliver in someone's ass that's played in the league for a while.'"

Morton found himself staring at guys who had starred in the league, future Hall of Famers like Lanny McDonald, Doug Gilmour and Al MacInnis. There was more than a bit of culture shock for a guy who was riding the minor league buses of the AHL in upstate New York just a few months earlier.

"I've got to be honest. The first 10 or 20 minutes of the game I was more in awe than anything. It was just a fog. Everybody always talks about the fog you're in when you play your first game because you don't really realize what's happening until years later."

Still, Dean Morton still has retained something from that night. It's the puck from his one and only NHL goal. It's on what he calls his *I love me wall* at Chez Morton. The goal is also recorded on an old VHS tape, as well. But Morton doesn't need the help of the grainy video to describe the moment.

"We're in the attacking zone and the boys are cycling the puck. Yzerman was out there with Marc Habscheid and they were cycling it down in the right-hand corner. I'm the right defenceman, on the boards, and they keep cycling and cycling. Habby passes it back to me, a nice flat pass; I lay a bit of an off balanced one-timer at the net low. It managed to go through three sets of legs. It doesn't touch anybody and Mike Vernon's screened. And, lo and behold, next thing you know I got my goal and I'm looking around like, 'What the hell just happened?'"

Morton's goal on that night was one of 17 scored in that game, and it looks great on the official game sheet. One of the assists went to Hall of Famer Steve Yzerman, and it was scored on goalie Mike Vernon, who could find himself in the Hall of Fame one day. "Vernon was a sieve, and Yzerman, I kind of taught him a couple things," jokes Morton about a wild night in the Wild West. The Flames won 10–7.

Morton was a healthy scratch for Detroit's next game, in Vancouver. However, he was hopeful that he'd get to lace them up in L.A. for the final game of the road trip. Morton, though, wasn't the only blueliner hoping to get in the lineup against the Kings. Börje Salming spent the last season of his NHL career with the Detroit Red Wings, and at the start of the 1989–90 season he was battling an injury. He didn't play in the Wings' first two games and his status for the third game was up in the air. Morton was thinking he might get the nod. "Börje was still kind of on the fence then."

Morton took the morning skate and followed hockey's unwritten rules for any potential healthy scratch — he was one of the last guys off the ice. "Salming and myself are kind of floating around as the extras with Brent Fedyk and Joe Murphy, and I can't remember the fifth. But then for some reason we decide we're going to Venice Beach to hang out and be cool kids. Well, I hadn't really been to California so Börje's like, 'Why don't we have a beer?' So I said, 'Okay, let's go.'" Morton, who was 99 percent positive he was not going to play that night, tipped back a pop or two.

"So it gets about three o'clock and we head back to the hotel to get cleaned up and we're going to the rink. And Salming being Salming, he kind of looks at me, and he goes, 'By the way, kid, yeah — I'm kind of still hurt. So if anybody's hurt during warm-up you're going in.' So needless to say the two beers I had at the beach might've been a bad idea if I had to go play in the Forum. But I probably would've played better," Morton cackles.

Nobody got hurt in the warm-up, and Morton and the beer in his belly didn't get on the ice against Gretzky and the Kings. When the Wings arrived back in Detroit from the three-game roadie, they gave Morton the news. He was going down to the AHL's Adirondack Red Wings. Looking back on his brief time in the NHL, Morton figures maybe it wasn't the best place for the 21-year-old version of himself to be. "After the Calgary game when we got shellacked, there was a big meeting in Vancouver. I'm sitting in the corner with all this shit that's going on within the room and there was this divide. There was so much going on at that time that to have a young fella like myself in that situation — I'm going, 'This is pro hockey?' There was some stuff being aired out in the locker room. In hindsight, it's probably something I didn't really need to hear. When I did get back to Detroit, Jimmy Devellano and Jacques Demers just said, 'We're going to send you down. We've got to get ourselves lined up before we have you subjected to this shit.' Because we were zero and three and shit was just starting to spiral down even further."

The Wings had started the season with three loses in a row. They'd given up 20 goals in three games. The general consensus seemed to be that there was no reason to expose a rookie to this. Morton was on his way to the minors. Morton returned to Adirondack, where he'd won a Calder Cup the previous spring, and he wasn't exactly devastated with the demotion. He wanted to play a lot of minutes, rack up some solid numbers and let his hockey future take care of itself. Unfortunately, his new boss in upstate New York didn't seem to take a shining to the defenceman. Like a lot of us nine-to-fivers, Morton thought he was doing his job rather well, but Barry Melrose, the Adirondack coach, had a different opinion.

"Maybe complacency had set in, but we were a successful team. Billy Dineen was our coach the year before, and then we go from Bill Dineen to Barry Melrose? You know the ego Barry had. It wasn't much different when he was trying to be a coach.

"I remember Steve Chiasson called me one time and he's like, 'What the frig is going on? You go down there and your head's too big. They say you're not even playing.' And I said, 'Well, Chase, I'm playing probably 25 minutes a game,' and I'm playing all 72 games at the time. And he says, 'Well, they're saying things on the radio from the coaching staff.' And I said, 'Okay, things are changing.'"

Melrose was the boss in Adirondack and he was not impressed. Morton figured no matter what he did in the minors it was not going to be enough to impress Melrose and, in turn, the big club. "Melrose had his thing and then I guess the year later Bryan Murray came in — he was coach-GM and things started changing and then the depth chart just got thrown out the door."

Instead of being the sixth or seventh guy on the Wings depth chart, Morton found himself at the very bottom. And as he puts it: "That's when the suitcase happened." Morton split the 1990–91 season between the AHL, the IHL and the ECHL. The following year was another workout for his suitcase. Morton played in the Colonial League and the AHL. Morton played his final year of pro hockey in 1992–93. He split the season between the Cincinnati Cyclones and the Brantford Smoke — a long way from Detroit and the NHL.

While he was still playing in Brantford, Morton helped out at his family's business. His father-in-law ran a European deli and that kept Morton busy and prepped him for life after hockey. Near the tail-end of his playing career, Morton's future line of work inadvertently presented itself. A number of Colonial League referees were guys Morton knew from the OHL. Every once in a while he would go down to the refs' room "and shoot the shit with the guys." One day someone suggested Morton try his hand at refereeing. "They said, 'Why don't you try this camp.' It was the North American School of Officiating. They were looking for former players."

Morton went to the camp — but he was not a natural. "I was totally out of my element. I had no idea. Wave my arms . . . Why?" Eventually he started getting the gist of it and caught the eye of some OHL and OHA officials. Just two years later he was working the AHL Finals.

Within a few years, Dean Morton found himself back in the NHL. It was Morton 2.0: the former player had transformed into one of the guys in the striped shirts.

Morton missed out on one of his goals: working a game featuring an old buddy. Steve Chiasson died in a car accident on May 3, 1999. They had talked about what it would be like to share the ice, but it never happened. "We kind of just touched on it. I think that was my biggest goal and the biggest disappointment I had when I started getting passed over as a linesman."

He had made it back to the Show — and the kid who'd played just one game for the Wings was calling the shots. Once upon a time he'd played with Steve Yzerman, now he was, at least in the eyes of some, the enemy. "Stevie hated anyone with stripes anyways. He was a lot like my mother. My mother still doesn't understand why I would want to be a referee. Then there are guys like Brendan Shanahan. Shanahan was like, 'I know you from . . . you used to be with the Generals.' Shanny wouldn't know me from the NHL context or the minors because he went right to the NHL, but he remembered me from the OHL. It was funny, but I had to distance myself from that because of the impartiality of it. Because the perception becomes that you're going to have a favourite and all that bullshit, which never happens in our businesses anyway. But people have that perception."

Luckily for Morton there was an older guy in stripes he could relate to — someone who had already walked the path that Morton was following. Back in his playing days, few men messed with Paul Stewart. In the winter of 1975–76, he spent 276 minutes in the penalty box for the

Broome County Dusters of the NAHL. Simply suiting up for a team called the Broome County Dusters makes you pretty tough in my book — the name reeks of tough '70s hockey awesomeness. When you consider the fact that the NAHL was the league that inspired the movie *Slapshot* — well, you can imagine how tough Stewart was. Later, Stewart played in the WHA and he also suited up in 21 games for the Quebec Nordiques in 1979–80. Later, he became a highly respected NHL official. Morton, who was undergoing the same transformation, from bad guy to lawman, had an instant mentor.

"He cared so much. He wanted nothing but the best for a guy like me. He just said, 'You have the ability, you just have to go out and referee.' Back when I started you had to assert yourself sometimes. Because you could let things go — that was just how the game was called. Stewie definitely took me under his wing."

Dean Morton's life makes a great comeback story — the guy who played in NHL for just one night is now on the ice night after night in the National Hockey League. For the man in the stripes, the return eased a lot of tension.

"It took me a good 10 years to come to terms with the fact that people would say, 'Oh, did you play?' I used to say, 'I only played one game. I only scored a goal.' And then the questions would begin. And you'd go through it and it was an embarrassment for me, because I expected more. But then I started officiating in the American Hockey League as a linesman and then I started refereeing and I started seeing how the game had changed. I'm like, 'You know what? There's 700 friggin' guys in the minors, and at best there might be 150 of them that even get a half-decent sniff in the NHL.' So I kind of went, 'I did something pretty special.'"

And when Morton sees one of those young kids that defies the odds and scores his first NHL goal, the referee thinks back to the night when he too found the twine in the world's best hockey league. "You know right away because the celebration is a little more exuberant. And sometimes during the game, when things settle down, I might just go over to a veteran and say, 'That's good for that kid, eh? You know, I did that 25 years ago.'"

BRAD FAST *Making NHL History*

Brad Fast's name will live on forever in NHL history. In just one game, he made his mark. I reached him by phone, but I'm not the first guy to ever call the former Michigan State Spartan.

"A few years ago somebody else called wanting to do an interview. I was kind of wondering if it was a buddy playing a prank on me or something, because they asked if I had the puck or if the Hall of Fame had it. But I had no idea what they were talking about. Then they said, 'You scored the last goal of the last tied game.'"

That's why Brad Fast's name is in the record books. On April 4, 2004, he played his one and only NHL contest with the Carolina Hurricanes. With 2:26 to go in the third, Fast scored to make it 6–6. The game finished that way. It was the final tie in NHL history. "I'll always have that little fun fact."

Fast had a long career, but his only NHL appearance came in only his second year of pro hockey. On a Saturday night early in April 2004, just after Fast and his AHL Lowell Lock Monsters wrapped up a game, he got called into his coach's office. "He asked me how I was feeling. I had a little nagging injury. I told him that everything was good. He said, 'Well great, because you're headed down to Florida to play in the afternoon.'"

There was no time to waste. It was Saturday night and he was in Lowell, Massachusetts. He had to be ready to go for the Hurricanes' final game of the regular season, in Miami, less than 24 hours later. "I got down there and it was just a blur. I mean, I left very early in the morning. Flew in and was running on adrenaline all day — tried to get a nap in once I got to the hotel but that didn't work out very well. And then I hopped on the bus with the team, went to the game. And what a great day that was."

As the game sheet suggests, it was a wild affair. The Hurricanes and Panthers traded shots, and goals, all game long. It was the final day of the regular season for both teams. Neither side was on the way to the playoffs, so this was it. But Fast says nobody was slacking off, and that's still one of the things about that game — the professionalism — that remains with him a dozen or so years later. "From the bus ride on, everybody had such a calm professionalism about them. I mean, it was the last game of the year. I don't know if there was much on the line for either team, but the guys came to play. There wasn't a lack of hits out there as far as I was concerned. There wasn't a lack of intensity. There were a lot of goals being scored. Guys were going hard. I thought that was pretty cool, to get to do something that I always wanted to do. I can't remember the smell of the bench, but I can remember the feeling in the air. It's something that I'll never forget — the excitement that is involved with playing in the NHL."

And how about the excitement of his one and only NHL goal? Only three men have played in a single game and managed to score a goal; Dean Morton, Roland Huard and Brad Fast. This is how it happened for Brad Fast. Fast was on the ice in the final minutes of regulation. The rookie found himself on a rush with a great veteran and a soon-to-be superstar. They were flying up in the ice looking to tie things up for the 'Canes. One of the game's best goalies, Roberto Luongo, was in the Florida crease, looking to keep the Panthers in front.

"We had a rush. I was on the ice with Eric Staal and Rod Brind'Amour. I believe it was four on four — either way, I jumped into the play.

Nothing materialized off of the initial rush, and then Erik Cole and Rod Brind'Amour cycled below the goal line. As I came back across the high slot, Rod Brind'Amour found me in between the top of the circles. I got the pass, took a shot and I got to put my arms up in the air."

Fast sounds pretty casual about the whole thing, but he scored his one and only NHL goal in his one and only NHL game on a potential Hall of Famer. The assists went to a couple of potential Hall of Famers in Brind'Amour and Staal. A bonus? Fast is a former Michigan State Spartan and so is Rod the Bod. "I went to Michigan State and he went there too. He's obviously a legend, but I thought it was extra special that a couple Spartans got to connect. Little did I know that the goal was going to be my only one, but still it was unbelievable to have him feed me that puck."

All of this seemed surreal for a 24-year-old. He wasn't only playing in the NHL, he was scoring. "When you spend your whole life dreaming about doing something like that, it takes a little bit to sink in. I'm a pretty calm guy to begin with, and I was ready for it and I think it sunk in maybe a couple weeks later. When you look back you're like, 'I did what I always wanted to do.' Still, I wasn't satisfied with that. I worked hard to get back there. Unfortunately it never happened again."

Like most men in this book, Fast believed he'd get many more opportunities. He went into the summer of 2004 on an absolute high, and why wouldn't he? A spot on the Hurricanes blue line was waiting for him in the fall of 2004. "I was on top of the world that summer. I was slated to play with the big club, at least to start . . . and then things didn't work out."

It's not that Brad Fast had a bad camp and lost his spot. He didn't have a camp at all. Actually, no one had a camp in the fall of 2004. Fast's luck ran out when a lockout led to the cancellation of the entire 2004–05 NHL season. In life, timing is everything, and Brad Fast's timing was awful — he was ready, but the NHL wasn't playing. Fast spent the year in Lowell, and with the NHL dark, the AHL became the top league on the planet. His Lowell Lock Monsters were loaded with talent — among those on the blue line were Mark Giordano and Mike Commodore. It was a chance for Fast to shine — but he didn't. "To be honest, I didn't have a great year."

Less than a year after scoring a goal in the NHL, Brad Fast suddenly found himself on his way out of the AHL. He was sent down to the Florida Everblades in the East Coast Hockey League. He was a long way from the NHL. His confidence was shattered. It was hard going through the process. "It was tough. I didn't think that I was a good hockey player anymore, but fortunately I had some help along the way. A guy named Paul Henry would call every so often to pick me up. I've got a great family. I've got good friends. My agent was always great about it. I was playing up at the top, and then I was a long way from the top. There were some tough times. I don't know if I was bitter. I know I definitely lost a lot of confidence."

After the 2004–05 season, Fast's contract with the 'Canes came to an end. He moved on and signed a deal with the L.A. Kings and played in 62 games with the Kings' AHL affiliate, the Manchester Monarchs, in 2005–06. That spring, he watched the team he was supposed to be suiting up for, the Carolina Hurricanes, win the Stanley Cup. He watched former teammates lift up the most prized trophy in the game. "I was really excited for them. It would've been really nice to be on that team . . . I was really happy that a lot of guys I got to play with got to do the one thing that everybody wants to do at the end of the year."

When the 2005–06 season wrapped up, Fast was two years removed from his one NHL game. He decided it was time to move on from North America and embarked on his own world tour. Fast signed on with a team in Switzerland. He spent the next few winters travelling the globe, playing in Switzerland, Austria, Germany and South Korea.

"I got my confidence back maybe a little too late to return to the NHL, but I did get it back eventually.

"I was fortunate enough to see some parts of the world that I don't know I'd ever see otherwise. I got to live in Switzerland. I got to live in Austria and Germany and then in South Korea. Not too many North Americans get to spend a large amount of time there. I thought it was really cool."

After a few years of globetrotting, Fast retired. Fast grew up in British Columbia, but he found himself back in Michigan when his playing days came to an end. He trains hockey players in East Lansing, a spot not far from where another one of his favourite hockey memories occurred. "I remember playing in the first big outdoor game in North America — the Cold War: Michigan versus Michigan State. I was lucky to be part of that. I've had some pretty cool opportunities, but I'd say second to the game in the NHL another single-game highlight would definitely be the Cold War."

Fast is still just a young guy, but he already has a lifetime of hockey memories. And we'll be talking about him for a long time thanks to his one NHL marker. (Keep his name in the back of your mind the next time you have to stump a hockey-trivia genius.)

"It'll be a great trivia question. And some people — they won't even understand why we were playing to a tie."

So, was it all worth it? All that time sweating it out, travelling the globe, for just that one NHL game?

"Oh my goodness, was it ever. I wouldn't trade it for anything. Like I said, you get to that level because you're a competitive person. There's no fluke getting there. I wasn't satisfied with just playing one, but at the same time, looking back, I guess I got my chance. I got my shot."

RON LOUSTEL *One Night and 10 Goals*

One of the challenges of writing a book about one-game wonders is tracking them down. When I scrolled through the list of men who suited up just once, I knew I had to talk to Ron Loustel. He has the distinction of giving up the most goals by any goalie who appeared in just one game — 10. If you're a glass half-full type person, however, you will point to the fact that he also made 41 saves.

For the life of me, though, I couldn't find Loustel. He didn't materialize as easily as some of the other guys in this book. My usual research methods drew a blank. Luckily, one of my old colleagues out west had a few connections and came up with his number. I called — and Ron knew what was coming. The first thing I heard over the line from Winnipeg was laughter.

"The game has changed a lot," says Loustel. "It's pretty tight and you don't see that many shots." Think about 51 shots — to put it into context, the Chicago Blackhawks led the NHL in shots on goal per game in 2014–15 with just under 34. On March 27, 1981, Loustel was a very busy 19-year-old.

At the end of the 1980–81 season, Ron Loustel had just finished up with the Saskatoon Blades and was back in his hometown practising with the Jets who had selected him 107th overall in the 1980 Draft. It wasn't long before he found himself in an NHL crease, for real.

"There was a sickness for a couple of the other guys the morning of the game. And I was pretty much told I was going to start that night."

Loustel didn't have much time to prepare. Friends and family packed into the Winnipeg Arena that night to watch Loustel and the Jets take on the Vancouver Canucks. Loustel had played with the Jets in exhibition games, but, as he says, "when it's for real during the season it's a little bit different. The crowd when you step on the ice, it's surreal."

And let's be blunt here. Ron Loustel, who grew up a big Ken Dryden fan, wasn't exactly tending goal for the 1977 Montreal Canadiens. The 1980–81 Winnipeg Jets were not a good hockey team. Want to know how I know? It's pretty simple — their record. The Jets finished the season with nine wins in 80 games and were dead last in the NHL with 32 points. Loustel was starting regular-season game number 74, and there was nothing on the line for the team. He realized early on that he was in trouble. "Pretty much right off the bat Vancouver was buzzing us. So I knew it was going to be a long night."

The Jets jumped out to an early lead, but Vancouver replied with three in the first and added three more in the second. (Think Denis Lemieux in *Slapshot* before the Chiefs turned it around — pucks were going in from everywhere.) Don't ask Loustel for too many specifics from that night though. "I remember there were a lot of shots and a lot of praying," he laughs.

He can't begin to imagine how many odd-man advantages — two-on-ones, breakaways and three-on-twos — he faced that night, but a man Ron watched as a kid stands out. "Tiger Williams — he was just some-body I grew up watching — and he got a hat trick that night, if I recall correctly." For the record, Tiger only scored two that night, but when you stop 10 and save 41, the odd detail might slip by 35 years later.

Loustel says that despite the pucks flying by him, he wasn't looking for a bailout from the bench. "You never look at getting pulled. I think it says you're giving up. And I never really did that." His head coach left him in for the entire game. Loustel was a 19-year-old facing an all-out assault in his first, and it turns out his only, NHL tilt. The coach's advice on that night was . . . well, he didn't really give any to his teenage goalie. "He just left me to be." Final score — Vancouver 10, Winnipeg 2.

Once Loustel's NHL debut was behind him, he met up with a few friends and family for a bite to eat but, understandably, that was about it. "We went home. I was pretty exhausted."

Loustel hung out with the Jets for the rest of the regular season and then joined their top farm team, the Tulsa Oilers, for the playoffs. The next year, he was back in junior for his third season with the Saskatoon Blades. Just a couple of seasons later, Loustel was out of the game. He never got back in another NHL net again. It's crazy when you think about the opportunities that pop up in life. What were you up to when you were 19? "It is kind of surreal that happened before my 20th birthday," Loustel says.

Today, his memories of the night are hazy. "It was so long ago; I can't even remember. From time to time I look at pictures of the game, that's pretty much it."

These days Ron Loustel is in the fur business, something he's been doing since he retired from hockey in 1984. He runs Sydney Gitterman Furs in Winnipeg, and he took a few things from the ice to the business world. "The same mentality applies to business. Structure — everything is structured. And drive. You never give up even when things look bad."

You keep going even if you give up 10 goals. You keep going even after you make 41 saves. After all this time, Ron Loustel holds on to one thing from his single NHL game: a sense of humour. "You gotta. The positive was I made 41 saves. I let in 10, but the next day you come back out and it's 0–0 again."

At least Loustel made his mark, and he's the answer to a great trivia question: who is the goaltender that both gave up the most goals *and* made the most saves in his lone NHL game?

"Yeah I made 41 saves, but I could've stopped a few more," he says, laughing again.

CHAPTER SEVEN
JUNIOR STARS

BRENT KRAHN *The First Rounder*

AP Photo / Tony Gutierrez

It was one of those days that made you smile. Everything seemed to be right in the world of sports.

Full disclosure: I spent a fair bit of time covering Brent Krahn's junior career with the Calgary Hitmen while I was a sports reporter at A-Channel Calgary. Brent was a talented goaltender and a great young kid. His Hitmen were one of the top teams in the WHL. They were loaded with other stars too, including Pavel Brendl, Brad Moran and Kris Beech. The 2000 NHL Draft was held at the Calgary Saddledome, home of both the Hitmen and the NHL Flames. When the Flames stepped up to the stage with the number nine pick, the Dome was buzzing. Would they take Krahn? I was there, and I sure hoped they would. You couldn't help but root for the young kid from Manitoba. Krahn, however, didn't think there was a chance. "I was sitting there thinking, 'There's no way the Flames are going to draft me.' I had meetings with them and I wore my glasses. And the scouting staff and everybody was telling me, 'Why would a goaltender wear glasses to an interview?' And I never thought anything of it. I was like, 'Well, because I have bad eyes. Why do you think I would wear glasses to an interview, right?' I didn't really think of it. I didn't think the interview went all that well. So I thought, 'There's no way Calgary's going to draft me, so I'm going to get to experience another city.'"

Apparently, the Flames found the glasses stylish and Krahn rather charming. The Flames stepped up to the mic: "They said, 'From the Calgary Hitmen,' and I just shot up. 'It's got to be me.' And as I stood up I was like, 'Oh shit, what if it's not me?' So I just kind of start walking, you know, just act like you do this all the time." It only took a second for the Flames to say Krahn's name, but in his mind it seemed like forever. Trying to look cool waiting for his name to be announced, he just kept telling himself, "'They're picking you. They're picking you.' Sure enough they did — but the thought process as I was walking up to the podium was, 'Well, maybe there's another Brent Krahn who plays for the Calgary Hitmen . . .'"

Nope, he was the one and only, and he was now a first-rounder. At that moment, the sky seemed like the limit for the 18-year-old. The Flames had a plan for their number-one pick. "When you get drafted, especially as high as I was, you're always told *this is your plan*. This is what you're going to do." The Flames laid out their plan for how Krahn would develop over the next few seasons and Krahn took it as the written word. Whatever the Flames wanted, he was all in.

"When you're a young kid and you're listening to guys who scout in the National Hockey League, who are in control of your future to some degree, and they say this is what we would like to see you do, you take that as gospel. Like that's exactly what's going to happen, whether I'm awesome or whether I'm terrible, this is my plan."

A plan might have been in place, but the game got in the way. Krahn's body didn't do him any favours, and the injuries started early. He started having problems in his left knee during his second year with the Hitmen. He needed surgery. During his third year in the WHL he needed another. He played another year in the Dub and went under the knife again.

But Krahn battled through. The former first-rounder started his pro career in 2003–04. He split the season between the Las Vegas Wranglers of the East Coast League and the AHL's Lowell Lock Monsters and San

Antonio Rampage. His numbers were solid through 35 games, but a player can only control so much. While Krahn was slugging it out in the minors, the big club made what appeared to be a minor move, but it sent the Flames on an incredible run all the way to the 2004 Stanley Cup Final and buried Brent Krahn on the Flames depth chart. In November 2003, the Flames sent a second-round pick to San Jose for a tender named Miikka Kiprusoff who just couldn't cut it with the Sharks.

Laughing, Krahn says, "I credit Miikka Kiprusoff with the demise of my hockey career."

Kiprusoff became a mainstay in the Flames crease for the next decade. Krahn would get the odd call-up to join the Flames, but all he could do was watch Kiprusoff from the bench. "He was nothing but sensational when I was up for a brief period of time. The way I played goal was all because of Miikka — his mentality, his demeanour, his athleticism, his ability. He was so poised. He was everything I wanted to be in goal. For my money he was the best goaltender in the league for the time he was in Calgary. He was the most consistent goaltender in the National Hockey League.

"He didn't get hurt, stuff didn't bother him. He was just so mentally tough. It's a good story. If somebody else would've taken that spot and maybe not have had the same type of presence, been the same type of goaltender that Miikka was, maybe I'd be talking about it a bit differently."

Maybe someone else would have come in and bottomed out in Calgary. Maybe if that happened Brent Krahn would have gotten his shot with the Flames. But that didn't happen. Miikka Kiprusoff played in Calgary for almost 10 years. "I obviously joke around that he ruined my career, but he was probably the best goaltender I ever had the privilege of watching."

Krahn spent the next few seasons in the AHL, nursing further injuries and watching his peers get their chance in the NHL. "I played with Cam Ward in the American League. I played against Corey Crawford, Pekka Rinne, Ondřej Pavelec, Kari Lehtonen, Antti Niemi. Guys I played against, who in my opinion I played equal to or better than, earned a spot in the National Hockey League."

Krahn played just 14 games for the AHL's Quad City Flames in 2007–08. That summer, the Flames decided to let their former first-rounder go. He was a free agent and eventually inked a deal with the Dallas Stars. The NHL was once the plan for Krahn, but it seemed an awfully long way away. He continued to defy what his banged-up body was telling him and kept on playing in the East Coast League with Las Vegas and in the AHL with the Chicago Wolves. Eventually, his persistence paid off and Krahn got the call. He had spent time on an NHL bench as the backup to Kiprusoff in Calgary, and now he was destined to backup another one of the NHL's top tenders, the Dallas Stars' Marty Turco. On Valentine's Day 2009, the Stars were in Chicago. The Blackhawks were on top 3–1 late in the second, and Krahn, who was the backup, was in the Stars dressing room. "I watched the game on a fit ball with Brenden Morrow. And Momo kind of leans over to me with about 30 seconds left in the second and says, 'Kronner, I think you're going to get your chance.' And I was thinking, 'There's no possible way I'm going in.' Because we had played the New York Rangers the first day I got called up and we beat them 10–2. And I had thought for sure, when there was like five minutes left they would throw me in, just to kind of give me a little taste. So I said, 'Well, there's no way with the game still in hand that they're going to give me a chance to go in the third period.'"

Krahn was wrong. With his Stars being outshot 27–12 after 40 minutes, Dallas head coach Dave Tippet was looking to do something to rally his troops. Apparently, he thought letting Krahn make his NHL debut was the answer. "There was about three minutes left on the intermission clock and Dave comes in and goes, 'Kronner get your gear on and get ready to go.' And I was just fired up. I mean, the boys they were getting it, but I couldn't wipe the smile off my face. I wish I would've had maybe the maturity or presence of mind to calm myself down a bit and realize it was more of an opportunity to get some NHL action, but I viewed it as like, 'Are you serious. I'm about to step foot on the ice in the National Hockey League.'"

Eight years after going in the first round of the 2000 Draft, he was finally going to play in the NHL. That really didn't seem to matter to his opponents. The Blackhawks continued to pour it on. Jonathan Toews scored on Krahn just 42 seconds into the third, not that Krahn cared all that much. "The outcome of the game didn't even matter to me at that point. It was just the fact that I could play in the National Hockey League and say I played in the NHL. So I remember getting out there and just floating. I remember Havlat coming in and taking a shot on me, Byfuglien taking a slapshot. Kane and Toews were out there. I remember going back and playing the puck. Darryl Sydor's going back and he's posting up, expecting Marty Turco to pass him the puck. And I stop it. Behind the net I'm like a deer caught in the headlights. I don't think there's anybody around me but I just fired high and hard around the glass. You know what? I let in three goals on nine shots. But I remember smiling the whole time. I grew up loving that big air horn in Chicago. That was just the epitome of hockey for me and it went off on me three times and I couldn't have been happier."

Chicago won the game 6–2. Krahn let in three goals on nine third-period shots. But he had done it. He finally played in the National Hockey League. "A lot of the guys came up to me and congratulated me. They were really, really good about it. I was disappointed in the outcome of the game, but I was just too ecstatic to be upset at myself and I was smiling from ear to ear. I felt like I had won the Stanley Cup, even though that couldn't be further from the truth. I was just so in the moment it was as if I had a shield of armour around me. You couldn't knock me down I was so inflated."

Krahn was on a high, but he was not delusional. He had no illusions that, after a rough 20 minutes, the Stars were going to put him right back in net the next night. "After that game I thought, 'There goes my chance of making the National Hockey League.'" Once the euphoria of his NHL debut wore off, Krahn eventually got a grasp on the reality of the situation. "I settled down a little bit, and I thought that there would be at least one more opportunity to start, but that wasn't the case."

After two more seasons in the minors, Krahn couldn't continue. Or more accurately, his body couldn't take it anymore. By the time he was 28, he had undergone five knee surgeries and a sports hernia surgery. "My body just gave out. I think by that time I became a little mentally drained with all the injuries. You know, one little thing after another just piled up. As much as I hated leaving hockey, it wasn't even fun anymore because it was play and get injured, play and get injured. You couldn't find a rhythm."

Krahn retired. And he did what very few retired NHLers do: he headed for Alberta's oil sands. "I went roughnecking when I was done hockey. I went and worked the oil rigs for a while. I was working 10- to 14-hour days. I was living out of a hotel, which is nothing new, but I was getting up at six and driving to the rig and working there till six or eight o'clock at night. Do that for 21 days on, seven days off — that was a reality check."

For a brief time, Krahn and his agent thought about a comeback — he was thinking Europe — but the injuries were just too much. "We felt around, my agent and I. We basically got the same response from everybody: 'We would love to have you, but your track record kind of speaks for itself. We're not gonna pay you to sit on the sidelines.' It was good. I was happy I was forced out and I didn't end up playing till I was 35 or 36, just getting by because I couldn't let go. I was very fortunate to have somebody make that decision for me."

With some helpful advice from Colin Patterson and Ron Stern, a couple of former Calgary Flames, Krahn landed a job in downtown Calgary. He works as a salesman for an oil company. And in the winter of 2014, on the heels of the Sochi Olympics, Krahn found himself back in his old haunt, the Calgary Saddledome. Some of the Flames were back in town at the tail end of the Olympic break. They were skating and they needed a goaltender. Krahn answered the bell for four skates. "It was crazy because I remember when I played I tried so hard. And I went on the ice and I was grossly out of shape and just kind of went through the basics and had fun. The guys weren't giving me an inch either, which was hilarious. I mean I played with Giordano, I played with Hudler. I played with a bunch of the guys. So they were fucking around and having a good time and seeing if I could actually make saves at the NHL level. Let's be real, I wasn't going down a whole lot but I thoroughly, thoroughly enjoyed it. It was great. I had so much fun. I nearly died twice, but I had a great time."

Krahn's buddies still have a good time razzing him about his 20 minutes in the NHL. They point out that Henrik Lundqvist was selected 205th overall in the 2000 Draft, 196 picks behind their friend. But they also point out that Krahn played 20 more minutes than they ever did. "You have to look at it in a very positive manner, that you achieved something that every young man who plays dreams of — playing in the National Hockey League. So in one way, it's quite the achievement — it's quite the accomplishment — but on the flipside . . . I view it, sometimes, as . . . I could've done more. I still held on to that competitiveness when I was done. Saying, 'You know I got 20 minutes,' was great. But my competitive nature said, 'I should've worked harder. I should've done something to get more time, to get more of an opportunity. There's no bitterness, but when I look back 20 minutes wasn't enough. It comes from a positive place when people say, 'You played 20 more minutes than I did.' But you didn't go through the things I went through or that other guys go through at that level."

If there's one thing Krahn wonders about, it's that day the Flames took him with the ninth overall pick. He never viewed himself as first-round material and, let's face it, a lot of pressure comes with being a first-round selection. Krahn never felt he was the kind of guy who deserved any big-time hype coming out of junior. "I was the type of person that never really thought I deserved any of it. I always thought, 'There's no way. I'm not that guy, no way.' I would rather not be talked about in that way. It made me very uncomfortable. I often wondered, hindsight being 20-20, what would have happened if I would've been drafted at 60-something. I kind of started from the top and worked my way down throughout my career, and with my mentality I rather would've . . ."

Krahn trails off. Maybe that would have changed something.

"If you would've asked me when I was 10 years old, 'You can do all this for just 20 minutes in the National Hockey League, would you do it?' Absolutely. But once you get there, your goals change."

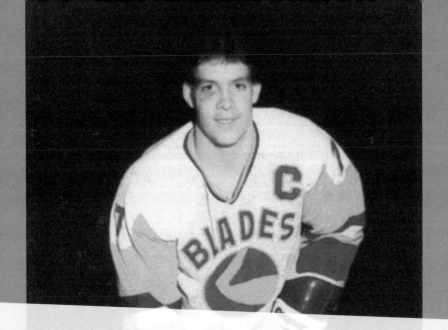

DAVE CHARTIER *Wheat Kings and Bigger Things*

One thing Dave Chartier can tell you more than 30 years removed from his single NHL game is, "In the grand scheme of things it's not a big deal. It's just a sport." Hockey is still something Chartier loves, but one New Year's Eve at the old Winnipeg Arena didn't exactly change the world. But it was still a big night for a 19-year-old who grew up in St. Lazare, Manitoba. Friends, family and acquaintances were among the 14,167 attendees who watched the Washington Capitals down Chartier's Winnipeg Jets 5–3 on the last night of 1980 and were probably telling the stranger in the seat beside them that they knew Dave Chartier. "It was overwhelming for me. You had 14,000 people in the big rink screaming and yelling. If I would have had a little time to prepare, I think I could have stayed," says Chartier.

There was absolutely no time for Chartier to prep for his NHL debut. One night he was tearing things up for the Brandon Wheat Kings — he put up an unreal 124 points and 295 PIMs in the WHL in 1980–81 — and the next night he was in the Show. "It was New Year's Eve and we had just played the night before. And then here I am skating the next day. We had a hell of a run with the Wheat Kings trying to make the playoffs, so we're playing every day. I'm playing every second shift or whatever. And then they called me up and I had nothing in the tank."

Think back to when you were a kid, to one of those nights that you thought would last forever, or one of those times that you thought would just be the start of an epic journey. Chances are you had a great time — but do you really remember all the details? After all, this was a night that you expected to be the first of many. The same can be said about Dave Chartier's first NHL game. It was a great event — but nothing specific stands out. After all, it was supposed to be the start of his NHL career, not the beginning and end. "It's just like the movies. You walk in and you see your stall with your name on it and then you look around and you don't see anything else. And then I see a chalkboard and on the chalkboard it says these are the lines for Washington and these are the guys, and that's all I remember."

With a little further prodding, though, one thing does come to Chartier's mind. It happened when there was a scrum in front of the Jets bench. "I do remember a guy taking a water bottle and spraying Archie Henderson. And then he turned around and I was thinking, 'You know, maybe I should jump the bench and fight the guy.' But the guy that did it was our goon, Jimmy Mann, and I thought, 'Holy gee.'" Despite his massive PIMs totals in the WHL, the 170-pound Chartier knew there was no need for him to stand up to Jimmy Mann. That could have been Chartier's one chance to find the game sheet. He was held pointless and without a penalty in the Jets' 5–3 loss, and the next thing Chartier knew, he was on his way out of town. The NHL club wanted Chartier to stick around, but the WHL's Wheat Kings were in need of their leading scorer's services. They wanted him back in junior. The Wheat Kings got their wish.

"The Jets wanted me to play against Philly the next night, but the Wheat Kings were playing in Regina that night. So I drove back to Brandon and bussed to Regina and played because we were trying to make the playoffs. A little bit political . . . or I would have played." Political, as in, the Jets were pretty much out of the playoff picture by January 1, 1981, while the Wheat Kings were in the hunt and needed

Chartier's hands. Besides, the Jets would get plenty of other looks at him down the road — at least that's the way it seemed at the time.

"With Winnipeg, I was just going up there for a test. John Ferguson loved me because of the way I played. He wanted me to be the Stan Smyl–type. The Bob Nystrom–type guy who just loved to score."

Chartier went back to Brandon and back to scoring. He led the Wheat Kings and finished eighth in the WHL scoring race. But for me, it's his 295 PIMs (sixth in the WHL) that stand out. Penalty minutes that high weren't all that unusual in the rough and tumble WHL in 1981. But almost 300 for a guy who also notched 124 points? It was simply a matter of survival for the 5-foot-10, 170-pounder. And as Chartier explains it, that lesson in survival came courtesy of Jim McTaggart of the Saskatoon Blades. "I was going away from the play and I didn't have the puck and nobody was looking. He slashed me and broke my wrist. Right then I said, 'If I don't start being dirty I'm going to get killed.'"

Chartier began his full-time pro career in the fall of 1981. He spent the season in the CHL with the Tulsa Oilers. "You're a 10th-round draft choice — you're not supposed to be there in the first place. Tenth rounders gotta work their way up, and they're going to have to fight their way up, and if they don't, it doesn't matter.

"I was the leading scorer in the first 15 or 20 games in Tulsa, and then I sat on the bench. I don't know, I might have said something. I was pretty lippy back then, so I don't know what I said but I think I pissed somebody off." Chartier finished his first pro season with 18 goals, 17 assists and 35 points in 74 games. And aside from scoring, Chartier kept playing his edgy or, as he calls it, dirty game that first year as well. He had 126 PIMs.

"We were in Tulsa, Oklahoma, and this big goofball, I can't remember his name, he was running me so I put my stick on the boards and his gut went through my stick and he snapped it. He turns around and toma-hawks me over the head, and Bones [Rick Bowness] just fights him right on the spot. Not a question asked."

That spring, Chartier got another taste of the NHL. He was called up to the Jets for their playoff run against St. Louis, but all he did was watch.

If someone would have gone down with an injury, Chartier would have gone in. But that never happened.

After two more seasons in the AHL, Chartier's pro career was cut short. Back in his junior days he'd injured his knee on a hit from Dirk Graham. By the time he was in his mid-20s, the pain was just too much. A demotion to the Fort Wayne Komets didn't help matters either. "They sent me down to Fort Wayne for a bit and my legs went. You know when a machine goes, *chit chit chit chit chit*. My knees started hurting and I just said, 'Enough.'

"It seemed like I had to do all the fighting all over again. Because everybody I beat up in the Western Hockey League was in Fort Wayne — all the guys who weren't good enough to play were a little tougher — so I had to start fighting again. And so I said, 'Ah shit, who needs this?' For 300 bucks a week — you know it didn't even pay my rent. I didn't like getting beat up that bad . . . I went home."

Chartier went back to Manitoba. At 23, he was a retired hockey player and he started a landscaping company. He also went to work in the mines. Now he's a lead planner in a maintenance department. Sometimes, the guys at work will bring up the fact that he once was a high-scoring hockey player, but Chartier doesn't go around advertising it. He does wish he had a few old tapes to show his kids that the old man knew how to put the puck in the net. "I have a son and a daughter, and my son knows I was pretty intense when I played, but he has never seen the finesse part. He knows I was really good around the net but he doesn't realize how good."

Chartier still laces them up from time to time. And he says he still has the hands. "Even today, I'm 54 years old and I can score anytime I want to. And they look at me and say, 'How can you do that?' And I say, 'I don't know. Why wouldn't you fake the shot and freeze the goaltender and snap it high?'"

Dave's brother Scott also came close to playing in the NHL — painfully close, literally and figuratively. The younger Scott was much bigger than his older brother and almost found himself on Anaheim's roster once upon a time. *Almost.* "I always tease my brother — at least I played one game. I used to tease him quite a bit, eh? I don't tease him anymore because he's 6-foot-4 and he should have played for many years, but he broke his ankle the day before he was supposed to play."

The tough breaks of the game aren't lost on Dave Chartier. When I ask if all the blood, sweat and tears that he put into hockey were worth his one night in the NHL, his answer may surprise you: "Everybody says at least you made it. At least you were there for one game. I've had a lot go wrong with me in the last couple of years. I got septic arthritis. I've got herniated discs from hockey. I got my knees operated on 20 times. I've got shoulders that have torn tendons in them because of the way I played. My body now is starting to give up a bit."

This is a guy who's been telling me about the game with stories riddled with laughter. I have to ask: would you give up your single game for your health?

"I'd trade my health for the one game . . . But I wouldn't change anything. I'm sort of contradicting myself, but everything I've done has been for a reason. And everything I've done followed me for the rest of my life. I was a leader everywhere I went. Now with the work I do, I lead people. I talk to people. I try to motivate people. I'm honest with people and that's a big thing." Those are all traits Chartier picked up from hockey. He also picked up a few bucks during that one game with the Jets, which he spent rather wisely all those years ago.

"That one game set up my life. It bought me my wedding ring for 275 bucks. That's what I bought." He and his wife, Cheryl, have been married for 35 years.

DARREN BOYKO *Hanging in the Hall*

When you walk into the Hockey Hall of Fame, you can feel hockey's magic. And when you step into the Trophy Room, sketches of the greatest to ever play the game look upon you as you search for their names on the Art Ross, Vezina and Hart trophies. And then there's the Stanley Cup. There's a pretty good chance you're not going to run into Guy Lafleur or Wayne Gretzky as you scan for their names, but a man who played in one game for the Winnipeg Jets is usually at the Hall from Monday to Friday.

Darren Boyko is the Hockey Hall of Fame's manager of special projects and international business. On October 19, 1988, he was a centre for the Winnipeg Jets in a 5–2 home loss against the Boston Bruins. It was his single NHL game. And if you think that's good enough to make him an NHLer, he says that's simply not the case.

"If people ask me if I played in the NHL I always say no, because essentially that's true. I did not. But then they will go, 'Well, you played in Winnipeg.' I go, 'Not really. I played in Europe.'"

Boyko may not think of himself as an NHLer, but thanks to a lengthy pro career in Europe, he thinks of himself as a pro hockey player. His one shot in the NHL came early in the 1988–89 season. Boyko, a 5-foot-9 169-pound centre, was way down on the Jets depth chart. He was buried behind Dale Hawerchuk, Thomas Steen and Laurie Boschman. "That leaves the fourth-line spot and you better be doing something. Otherwise goodbye and good luck."

Boyko took the road less travelled to Winnipeg. Following his Western Hockey League career, he spent two years at the University of Toronto before playing overseas in Finland. But in the fall of 1988, he decided to give North America another crack. That's how he found himself suiting up for the Jets in the old Winnipeg Arena.

Boyko was on the NHL roster, but he wasn't playing. Finally on October 19, he got a spot in the starting lineup. "I had probably sat for close to a month. I was just on the roster, not playing."

"The coach doesn't know me at all. I'm some freak show from Europe. He doesn't know I'm Canadian . . . I don't know, I played and got in the game. We played like crap. I got two or three shifts. I don't honestly know how much ice time I got.

"I'm not thinking that this is my first and last game . . . I would've done something that you'd be able to see on the highlights," he says, laughing.

After the game, the Jets told Boyko that he was on his way out. Since he was on a one-way deal, he had the option of returning to Finland instead of going down to the American League. He chose Helsinki over Moncton. Boyko headed back overseas and scored 30 points in 34 games for HIFK Helsinki. And because he was still under contract with the Jets, once his season in Helsinki wrapped up he joined the Moncton Hawks. When the AHL playoffs came to a close, so did Darren Boyko's North American professional career.

He spent the next seven seasons in Helsinki and split one more between Germany and Sweden. His return to Europe could not have gone better. Three of Boyko's four kids were born in Finland and he got an MBA from the Helsinki International School of Economics. And on the ice, just as he had been in junior, he became a scoring star. Following his career, he was inducted into the Finnish Hockey Hall of Fame. He was the first Canadian ever inducted into that Hall.

"That was pretty cool. I know Carl Brewer played there. He played for my club way back in the day. I think he only played one season, but he coached there, so he was in the Hall as a builder. So I was technically the first foreign *player*. That was quite nice, an honour. I tell everybody the reason I'm in is because there were three people on the selection committee: my wife, my mom and my grandmother . . . and I got in by two to one." The easily likable Boyko is also very modest. During his 474 games with HIFK Helsinki he scored 406 points.

But his Finnish Hall of Fame career almost never happened. Remember how Boyko was buried on the depth chart in Winnipeg behind some very talented centres back in 1988–89? Well just one year later, in 1989–90, another centre jumped ahead of Boyko on Helsinki's depth chart. And this guy was going to be tough to beat. In the fall of 1989, the Russians were coming. The fall of communism opened the gateway to the west for Russia's best hockey players, and one of them, one of the greatest centres of all time, Igor Larionov, was set to join HIFK Helsinki.

"Our club signed him and they weren't going to keep both of us . . . So they were going to let me go. Fortunately for me, I guess you could say, they let him out of his contract so he could sign with Vancouver."

Boyko continued his European stint in Helsinki. It was a career he never saw coming. Like every other Canadian kid, he aspired to the NHL. And the Jets weren't his only choice. Following his WHL days and during his time at the University of Toronto, he had chances to join the Vancouver Canucks and the Philadelphia Flyers as well. It's the missed opportunity of joining the Flyers that still gets to Boyko. Instead of joining his old U of T coach Mike Keenan in Philly, Boyko went for Winnipeg.

"The year I signed with Winnipeg, Philly also offered me a deal but it was a two-way and I ended up in Winnipeg in a one-way. So I took it. That probably wasn't the greatest move, but you think you have a chance when you sign a one-way.

"I think that was the biggest mistake I ever made . . . not going to Philly. Because Keenan knew me and was okay with the way I played."

Boyko's one shot in the NHL came when he was 23, and it was the only shot he ever got. Was it a fair shot? Maybe — maybe not. But that's the business. He only got a few shifts and ended up a minus one. "Later that summer, one of the assistant coaches, who I knew from junior, told me that they blamed the goal on me," Boyko says, laughing. "And that was my last shift. That's how it goes if you don't impress."

Hockey gave Darren Boyko a chance to see Europe. It gave him a chance to get a degree from the University of Toronto and an MBA from Helsinki. But hockey can also leave a mark.

"I could've squeaked out a couple of years. I know I could have. But that's just the way it goes. I mean everybody has their chance.

"You don't want just one chance in the NHL, do you? No. You want a career."

TRENT KAESE *The Big Book of British Scoring*

We've already met two of the three men who played in a single NHL game and managed to score a goal. On March 25, 1989, at the Quebec Colisée, Trent Kaese of the Buffalo Sabres could have made it four. And who knows, if he had found the back of the net that night maybe he would have gotten into game number two. Kaese, fresh from Rochester of the AHL, led the Sabres with five shots in their 4–1 loss to the Nordiques.

"I think Ron Tugnutt was in goal, if I can remember correctly. He kind of robbed me. I was in front. That was the one really good scoring chance I had. The puck came flying out of the corner and I got it but I had to kind of pick it up on my backhand and turn it to my forehand. I had a guy checking me, so Tugnutt came flying across the crease. He made a two-pad stack kind of save. And even the guys on the bench said, 'He robbed you,'" Kaese laughs all these years later.

Of course, because this game was at the tail end of a decade that featured wide-open hockey, one chance led to another. "It was funny, because after that scoring chance, Peter Šťastný went back down the other way and they had a scoring chance. The puck got turned over and they went down and then they had a chance. My dad kind of finds that funny."

Kaese got the call to join the Sabres during his second year as a pro. He was putting up respectable numbers with the Rochester Americans with 20 points in 45 games, but wasn't expecting to go to the NHL. In fact, he didn't even think the call was *the* call. "I got a phone call when I was in Rochester. And I thought, you know what the guys do in the minors, they do some pranks . . . and I said, 'Stop bullshitting me.' I thought it was Joe Reekie actually. I said, 'That's enough, Joe. Good one.' And then I ended up on a flight up to Quebec City."

Kaese spent the night in a Quebec City hotel and then went through the usual game-day routine with his new teammates. When he checked into the Sabres dressing room at the Colisée, it didn't take long for him to realize this was the big time. Trent Kaese was about to play in his first NHL game. One of his teammates, Mark Napier, was about to play in his 1,000th. "I was sitting in the dressing room, and they were kind of celebrating Napier's 1,000th game. I'm playing number one. And it really kind of sunk in right then and there. You know you're getting dressed with all of those guys — Andreychuk, Turgeon — who have all played for many years."

When Kaese got out on the ice for warm-up, he saw a familiar face that helped him to ease into things. At least that's what he thinks. "Once I was on the ice, Joe Sakic came up to me and started skating around with me." Kaese and Sakic had crossed paths back in their WHL days.

"He was happy to see me. And I couldn't understand a word he was saying because I was so nervous. But it was kind of special because he came right up to me and said, 'Good to see you. You look great.' So it just goes to show you how much of a professional he really was, and that he didn't ignore his roots. That's the kind of guy he is."

Sakic, of course, went on to score 625 regular-season goals. Kaese as we mentioned, came oh so close to . . . one. And it really was a baptism by fire for Kaese that night at the Colisée. The Nordiques had three future Hall of Famers in their lineup. "You're just playing and you don't realize it. The Stastny brothers were playing on the other team and

Michel Goulet was there. You know, you don't think of them as being big guys until you play against them. And you know they are big, big guys and very talented too."

And then it was over and Kaese was on his way back to the minors. "I thought I'd played a pretty good game for my first time in the NHL. I mean, a lot of guys get two or three shifts. You know, I probably played — to get five shots on goal — 14, 16 shifts. I thought I did okay, but the guys who were out injured were much better than me. I think Ray Sheppard was out and they had one other right winger out."

Kaese spent a few more years playing in the minors before it was time for a change. He went overseas to England. And that's where Trent Kaese put up some eye-popping numbers. To be more exact, they're Gretzky-like. During the 1993–94 season with the Milton Keynes Kings of the British Hockey League, Trent Kaese scored 119 goals and added 106 assists for 225 points in 53 games. He's the first to admit that he wasn't exactly playing against NHL competition, but, man, those numbers look fun. "The competition wasn't really stiff. I played with an amazing player who came out of Boston College, Danny Shea. We did some lighting up. There were a lot of goals scored every shift. The league got better and better as things went on. It was just the early stages there."

Here's my favourite part about Kaese's 225 points. They were good enough to finish only ninth in the BHL scoring race. (Man, that sounds like my kind of league.) Playing in England also gave the one-time NHLer something other than an opportunity to rack up points. It gave him a chance to get ready for life after hockey. He met his wife in England. They've now been married for more than two decades and have a couple of boys. "England was where my life kind of started rolling . . . the other end of things as you step out of hockey."

Kaese is in the golf business now. He is the owner and general manager of the Cottonwood Golf Course in Nanaimo, British Columbia. He's known around town these days as much for his life on the links as he is for his life on the ice. "I'd probably say 50-50. People will come and ask me questions and say, 'Hey, you made it all the way, not very many people get to do that.'"

And that last statement is very true. Not very many people make it for even one night. It's a message Kaese passes on to minor-hockey players: enjoy the game, and if the pro-life happens, it happens. But the odds of making it are stacked against every kid (or parent) who dreams of life in the NHL. "I do talk to minor-hockey associations about some of those situations — that you work so hard and then you only get a chance to play one game. And that's how hard it is. Even for Nanaimo, where I live right now, no one else has made it since I was there. That's a long time. It just goes to show you it's not an easy road.

"I wish that I was maybe more dedicated through the summer and worked at it some more and did some more off-ice training. But that just wasn't really what happened back in the late '80s. You just kind of went and did whatever. You did your training and got in shape but not to the extent you see now on the Nike commercials, which everyone is doing today."

Kaese has a few reminders around his home of that night at the Colisée. There's an old tape of the game, but he says, "I don't even know where that is." There are a few pictures and a painting of his night with the Sabres that his wife had painted for him. There's no jersey though. Kaese likes to joke that the Sabres retired his number. He wore number 39 that night. It's the same number Dominik Hašek wore for the Sabres, and it now hangs over the Buffalo ice. "That's a conversation I had with a reporter once. We had a chuckle, saying my number was getting retired . . ."

Trent Kaese still plays hockey. In fact, he skates on a beer-league team with his old Sabres teammate Doug Bodger. They golf together as well. (Bodger lives only about five minutes away.) Talking to Trent Kaese, you get the sense that he doesn't dwell on the fact that he played only in one game. "I'm certainly not complaining. I'm obviously blessed that I got the one game and, no matter what, they can't take it away from me."

MIKE KEATING *If I Can Make It There . . .*

Sometimes when you're in *the moment*, you don't know it's *the moment*. Mike Keating had his moment on January 29, 1978. He was 21 years old. Like a lot of 21-year-olds, Mike Keating thought his moment was going to last forever. He was playing in his first, and only, National Hockey League game. As far as he knows, his moment was never captured. He didn't bring a camera. He doesn't have a picture from his one and only NHL game. After the game, he took off his New York Rangers sweater, and he never put it on again. "My advice for young kids today: if you get called up, get pictures taken."

Mike Keating was a high-scoring winger during his Junior days with the Hamilton Fincups. On May 16, 1976, Mike Keating and the Fincups won the Memorial Cup with a 5–2 win over the New Westminster Bruins. The following season, Keating and the Fincups moved to St. Catharines. Keating finished second on the team with 112 points. He was sandwiched between the team's leading scorer, Dale McCourt, and Ric Seiling. McCourt and Seiling combined to play in 1,290 NHL regular season games. Keating played in one. "I had it pretty easy in my career when I was young in Toronto. I didn't have to work real hard at stuff. The guy upstairs gave me some nice talent, but when you get to the Show you got to realize every other guy was gifted too and they might've worked a little bit harder."

Keating got his up-close-and-personal look at life in the Show during his first year as a pro. He was playing for the New Haven Nighthawks in the AHL when he got the news: "Parker MacDonald was the coach in New Haven, and he just called me and said, 'Hey, listen. You and Kenny Hodge got to get on a flight. You're going to New York to play L.A. tomorrow night.' Kenny Hodge is Kenny Hodge. It was probably a pain in the ass for him to do it; for me it was like, are you kidding me?"

MacDonald was not kidding. Keating and Hodge, who were living together in New Haven at the time, made their way to New York. The Nighthawks were on the road, so the roommates caught the first flight to New York City. As soon as Keating pulled up to the World's Most Famous Arena, he knew he had hit the big time. "I'll never forget it. I was getting out of the cab. I've been to Madison Square Garden before with the Rangers but I never got to play there. I signed my contract and stuff the summer prior but to be able to actually walk in and say, 'I'm playing tonight!' You look back now and you think there's going to be more games, but, hey, that's what you do. You live and learn."

Keating and his Rangers took on the L.A. Kings. He looked at the Kings crease that night and he saw Rogie Vachon. He looked across the ice and he saw Marcel Dionne. The Kings led 3–1 after one. By the end of the night, the Kings skated out of MSG with a 4–1 win. Keating was a minus one and his NHL career was finished. "I did think I was going to be up a little longer because that's kind of what they indicated. And then a day or so later, I think after practice, they said, 'You know you're going back down.' They brought up a guy from New Haven, a guy by the name of Jerry Byers. He was a left winger, great guy. They brought him up when they sent me down."

Just a year and a half after playing his first NHL game, Mike Keating retired. He spent the 1978–79 and 1979–80 seasons in the AHL and the IHL. And he produced. Keating had 116 points in 133 games. But in the spring of 1980, when he was just 23 years old, Mike Keating walked away from professional hockey, although he kept the skates on until he was well into his forties. "Why did I call it a career? I would tell you the same thing I told someone from the *Toronto Star* years ago. In fact, Don Cherry, who I don't know, I guess they interviewed him and he said, 'Well, I think he made a good move.' I realized I'm pursuing something that's passing me. I maybe didn't put the effort in or whatever but I gotta eventually get a job and I'm getting married. I want to have a family. So that's why I did it."

Keating is very honest about his career; he was loaded with talent, he just didn't make it past one game in the NHL. And he freely admits, like a lot of young guys playing pro hockey in the late 1970s, he had a good time. Take for instance, his first trip to New York City after the Rangers drafted him in 1977. "When I was drafted Brent Imlach, Punch's son, was my agent. Anyway, he says, 'Okay I've been in contact with John Ferguson. I've got you a plane ticket. You're flying down to New York.' I think it was a Thursday or Friday, and it was the July 4 long weekend, and then I was going to be flying back two days later. So they had a hotel room for us and everything. I flew into New York. A limo guy met me with a sign and drove me to Madison Square Garden. I went in, signed a contract and had pictures taken. Fergie, Ronnie Duguay and Lucien DeBlois were there. And then Dave Farrish, who I knew, and Steve Vickers, who is a Scarborough guy like me, were also there, and I never even stayed a night in the hotel."

The party was on. "We went out to Long Island. I went out and stayed on Long Island with Donnie Murdoch and Maloney. I was a kid, right. I didn't really have any money on me. I didn't expect to be staying there. Farrish gave me $400. He said, 'Just pay me at training camp.' I was like, 'Oh, okay.' I told my fiancée at the time I'd be back Sunday. I came back a week later. I'm not kidding you. I went, 'This is pretty cool. I think I can hang out here [in New York City] for a while."

As you can imagine, with an off-season party that seemed to never stop, off-ice conditioning in 1976 was a tad different than what we see nowadays. "Training camp was a couple of skates a day and then off to the pub. That's what it was. If I look at my stats through junior and pro, I probably got most of my points and most of my goals from just before

Christmas and on because I didn't really work out a lot in the summer. I played some golf, did this, did that, and by the time Christmas came, I finally was in good shape. It's crazy.

"I'll be very honest with you. I mean, I might not be able to show you where a lot of rinks are in the cities I played in, but I can show you where a couple of the pubs are, and that's the way it was back then. We didn't do the training that these guys do today. They are machines today. We practised and then we went for breakfast and then we went for beers."

Keating had his moments on the ice aside from his one night in the Show. He can't say enough about Phil Esposito: "He was a tremendous, tremendous, tremendous guy with rookies. He just welcomed you. Whether you were at practice, a game or at the pub, you were part of the team. I don't want to mention names, but there were a couple guys I've met in my career that were kind of PRs to rookies. You know what I mean? But I just found him to be a hell of a nice guy."

And in one preseason game, Keating even got to play on a line with Esposito, and it paid off. "I scored a goal in an exhibition game against Boston in Providence. And I played with Espo and Lucien DeBlois. Even though it was exhibition, it was still a goal to me."

And along the way, Keating even played in Toledo with a career minor-leaguer by the name of Mike Eruzione. In 1978–79 Mike Eruzione finished fourth on the Toledo Goaldiggers with 72 points. Keating was seventh with 53 points. "Rouzie wasn't just a guy I played with, he was a very good friend of mine. I had a Corvette at the time and someone cut me off, and I had no ride home. So Rouzie said, 'Well, listen, I'd love to go to Toronto. Why don't we just hook up in my van?' So, he came and stayed at my parents' for a couple days. In his old van, I'll never forget, we blew a front tire around London and just about went off the road."

The next year, in 1980 Eruzione joined the U.S. Olympic team. Soon enough, Eruzione was wearing the C for Team USA. "When I saw he was named captain, I thought, 'Of all guys to be named captain.' Like Ruze, he's a great guy, but I just didn't see him being named captain with the coach they had."

It turns out Eruzione was the perfect captain for Herb Brooks in Lake Placid. You know the rest of the story — Eruzione, who gave Mike Keating a ride up to Toronto in his beat-up old van in the spring of 1979, scored the game winner in the Miracle on Ice less than a year later. Keating, of course, watched his old buddy snipe from the high slot against the Soviets. "I swear to God, I was so happy for him because he is a hell of a nice guy."

When you talk to Mike Keating, you get a sense that it's the people and the friendships, not the goals and assists, that stick with him all these years after his hockey career came to a close. "Like my sister-in-law. When we were young, we'd go to Santa's Village and take the kids. Everywhere we went I would know somebody. She would say to me, 'Is there anywhere we can go where you don't know somebody?' I went, 'Hey, that's the beauty of hockey!'"

The friendships remain. Keating and his old Memorial Cup team-mates still get together for reunions. "It's incredible. It really is. You don't lose that bond."

If you ask Mike Keating if he was a hockey player, he will admit that he was. But an NHLer? Not so much. From time to time, a co-worker or someone he knows might bring up the topic. "They might come to me and say, 'Oh, man. I heard you played.' I say, 'Yeah, I did. But don't get too excited. It was a plane trip up and a plane trip back to the minors.'"

"I have no regrets. I played one game. I probably should've played a lot more, but that was all on me. It wasn't on New York management. It wasn't on anybody else. But I can also look in the mirror and say, 'Man, you had a pretty good career.' Because when I was playing, one in 100,000 got to lace them up for a game. So I can put myself in that category. But I honestly have no regrets."

Except for maybe one. He doesn't have one picture from the night he played for the New York Rangers against the L.A. Kings at Madison Square Garden. That night can live on only in his memory. "I don't any-more, but I coached in Toronto for about 14 years. Once, we went down to Michigan State University, when the kids were in their draft year, their Bantam year. On the Sunday morning before we left, they had a big breakfast for us with a couple of young teams that were there and they asked me if I could say a few words. And I told them, 'Listen, don't make the same mistake I did. Try to keep mementos or pictures of those special things.' As a kid, you don't think about it."

But as a man you do. Even if that moment only lasted for one night.

CHAPTER EIGHT
SKATING WITH THE STARS

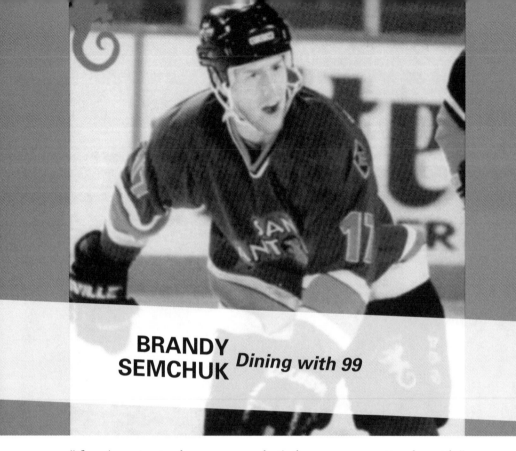

BRANDY SEMCHUK *Dining with 99*

"If you're going to play one game, that's the guy you want to play with." Brandy Semchuk is a TV account executive in Fresno, California. The "one guy" he's talking about is the man many call the greatest player of all time: Wayne Gretzky.

During the 1992–93 season, a 21-year-old Semchuk suited up for his sole NHL game. But don't think of Brandy Semchuk as just a one-gamer. He was part of L.A.'s first-ever run to a Stanley Cup Final, a dinner companion to the Great One and an eyewitness to one of the most infamous events in Stanley Cup history.

Brandy Semchuk was a decent prospect. The Kings took him in the second round, 28th overall, in the 1990 NHL Draft. He was known as a speedster, a responsible right winger who put up 24 points in 60 games with Canada's national team the previous winter. He also ran into his fair share of injuries during his first two pro seasons. In 1991–92 he managed to get into only 20 games between the International and East Coast Leagues.

The following season, Semchuk was having a solid year with the

Phoenix Roadrunners and hoping for a call-up to the Kings. "I was kind of injury plagued, but I had really started to put a good season together. The Kings had, I think, the oldest team in the league at the time. When you have Gretzky, there's no such thing as a youth movement. So it was just kind of a wait-and-see, put your time in."

And that's what Semchuk did. Then, in early March, he got the call. "It was against the Flames. And my hometown is Calgary, so I was very excited and nervous. You know, you call the folks and friends and say, 'I'm getting called up.'"

Semchuk headed for L.A. He checked into his team hotel the day before the game, made a few calls, went to bed, woke up and joined his teammates for the pre-game skate. The 21-year-old walked into the Kings room. All the stars were there: Robitaille, Kurri and, of course, Gretzky. Were his knees trembling? After all, he was in the presence of The Great One. The answer is a resounding no.

"I'd probably played in 10 to 15 exhibition games and been to three training camps with Gretzky. So . . . it was kind of like, 'Hey, kid, good to see you up here.' I had gotten to know the guys over the previous training camps and exhibition games. The thing with Gretzky was that he was such a nice guy — to everybody. I think the locker room was a place where he could really be himself. He wasn't as guarded. He loved to hear stories. Just kind of shoot the breeze. So do all those guys. You know how hockey players are. They're good guys. Nobody is resentful that you're coming up. They're just happy for you and want to see you do well."

Semchuk took the stress-free morning skate, and the next thing he knew, it was game time: the Kings versus the Flames in a tilt that actually counted in the standings. If the nerves weren't a thing at the morning skate, they came with the opening faceoff. "I remember my legs were like Jell-O. I think I was probably fourth line. Probably three shifts a period kind of thing. I think I was with Jimmy Carson. I can't remember who was on the left side. I got a penalty. A charging or a roughing penalty. So I got my name on the board." (Any player knows that if you're going to show up, make sure everybody knows you were there. And the summary from that night shows that Semchuk took a penalty at 5:08 of the third.)

Other than that penalty, though, Semchuk says his one night in the Show was not all that spectacular. "It was pretty uneventful. I was just really happy to be there. Looking back, I kind of recall the feeling as surreal . . . a big crowd, warm building, noisy, just not really in your comfort zone, trying not to make a mistake, kind of overthinking everything. It was great. At the time you think it's just the start."

But it wasn't the start. After the Kings' 6–2 win, he was sent down to the minors and given the usual advice, "They said, 'Go down, keep working hard and you'll be back up.' So I did that."

In reality, this was where Brandy Semchuk's NHL adventure truly began. He had his one game at the "Fabulous Forum," but there is much more to the story. Brandy Semchuk went back to Phoenix and worked hard. And he did get called up again — for the adventure of a lifetime — even though he never played in another NHL game.

When the playoffs started in the fall of 1993, Brandy joined the Kings for what would become, until recently, the most glorious playoff run in franchise history. "I ended up getting called back as one of the Black Aces."

The Kings playoff drive started with a first-round match-up against Semchuk's hometown Flames. The Kings were on the road to start the series. And that is when Semchuk secured his dinner companion for the next two months.

"We get into Calgary and we're getting checked in and just hanging out in the lobby, and Gretzky comes down and literally grabs anyone within his line of sight and says, 'Let's go for dinner.'" The Kings ended up winning the game that followed that meal. So Semchuk kept dining with the Great One.

"Gretzky, being as superstitious as he was, had to have the same people out with him whenever we were on the road. So we were going to Hy's Steakhouse in Toronto, and whenever he was going out for dinner he would make sure that the lineup was the same. He was dropping thousands per meal — it was insane, but it was so cool." When Semchuk tells this story all these years later he's still electric with delight. The thought of his young 21-year-old self dining with greatest to ever play the game still makes him smile. It was storytelling time and story-making time with greatest scorer in NHL history.

"There were a bunch of guys just telling stories and listening to Gretzky. When he spoke he had an audience. We just kind of sat there in awe, wondering, 'Is this really happening?'"

Of course, we know the rest of the story — or at least we think we do. The Kings kept winning and eventually found themselves in the Stanley Cup Final at the Montreal Forum. The Kings took Game 1 by a score of 4–1 at the Montreal Forum on June 1, 1993. Then two nights later, on a night that still lives on in NHL history, the Habs won Game 2 in overtime, 3–2. With 1:45 to go in the third and the Habs down 2–1, Montreal head coach Jacques Demers asked for a measurement on Marty McSorley's stick. He had an illegal curve. The Habs went on the power play.

With 1:13 to go in regulation and with Montreal goaltender Patrick Roy on the bench, Éric Desjardins one-timed a Vincent Damphousse pass through traffic and beat Kelly Hrudey to tie the game at two. Then in overtime, Desjardins did it again. He scored his third goal of the night, squeaking the puck through a desperate Hrudey to give the Canadiens the win. The series was tied at one, but it was all Montreal from that point on.

The Habs swept the next three games to win the series and the Stanley Cup 4–1. Many say the tide turned on the illegal-curve call, on a gamble by Demers and the Habs. After all, if the Canadiens' plan backfired and McSorley's stick was legal, L.A. would have gone on the power play. But Brandy Semchuk says the Habs didn't gamble at all. He and the rest of the Kings' Black Aces, he explains, had a front row seat to "Operation Illegal Curve."

Semchuk and his fellow Black Aces went through their usual routine on the morning of Game 2, and they saw something, that all these years later seems more than a little interesting. "There were five or six of us. We stayed after practice. We were actually in the locker room getting undressed and one of the stick boys for the Canadiens came in. And you don't think anything of it at the time, but he was checking all the sticks. Grabbing them and looking at the curves, checking the flex out and you think, 'It's just a stick boy.' You know, a fan of the game that's looking at Robitaille's stick and McSorley's stick." McSorley's stick — that's what

Semchuk says the stick boy found most interesting. Or, more accurately, the curve of McSorley's blade. "The little bastard was taking mental notes of the curves, so the Canadiens knew exactly who they were going after." Semchuk is still ticked all these years later. The Habs, he says, found exactly what they were looking for on the morning of June 3, 1993. "And it cost us a ring."

Once the final wrapped up, Brandy Semchuk figured he was only at the beginning of his NHL adventure. But timing is everything in hockey. He was going into the option year of his contract and his agent was saying, "'You need to play your option out.' I had a gut feeling that it wasn't a good idea. I'd been injured and the Kings had really been patient with me. So I kind of had a bad feeling. I think it was Nick Beverly . . . I talked to him and he kind of expressed his disappointment. But you've got your agent telling you that you're going to tear it up. You're going to have teams lining up for you."

But no NHL teams lined up. Just a few months after dining with Wayne Gretzky and skating at the Montreal Forum, Brandy Semchuk suffered an eye injury. "I had the injury shortly into the season and that was it. I couldn't get a tryout with anybody when I detached my retina. And then you know you're screwed. You don't have a contract underneath you, and that was it. I was never really the same after that anyways. Lost a lot of vision. Missed a lot of time. And then you're a liability."

Semchuk only played in two games for the Kings' top farm team in 1993–94. He spent the rest of the year in the East Coast Hockey League. The following season he started a four-year journey though the minor leagues with stops in San Antonio, Nashville, Columbus, Fresno and Shreveport. After 39 games with Fresno Falcons of the WCHL in 1998–99, his career was over.

"I think I had the talent to play for a while. I had the size. I think I could have found my place as a third-line guy, especially with my speed. I was probably regarded as one of the fastest guys to play the game at that time. Looking back, I think I could have turned out a little career. Could I have worked harder in the summer? Yes. Should I have not got into some bad habits and things like that? Definitely. So I wouldn't say I'm content with my career . . . I was 21. I was just kind of really finding my game, and then with some bad advice and an unfortunate injury, that was it."

So Semchuk doesn't use the word "content" when describing his hockey career, but he did get to live the dream, at least for a brief while. He got to dine with the king of the Kings, he got to skate in an NHL game and he even got to ride on Bruce McNall's famous "Air McNall" jet. "That was cool. We had catered dinners. They had the massage table going there. It was wild."

Semchuk coached minor hockey in California for a number of years and says, "You wouldn't believe how far that one game's gotten me. You're running a hockey camp and you put 'former L.A. King' on there, especially in California, it carries some weight.

"It's something to be proud of. There's such a small number of people who get to play at that level. I would have liked to have had a long career, of course, but I'm still proud of what I was able to do."

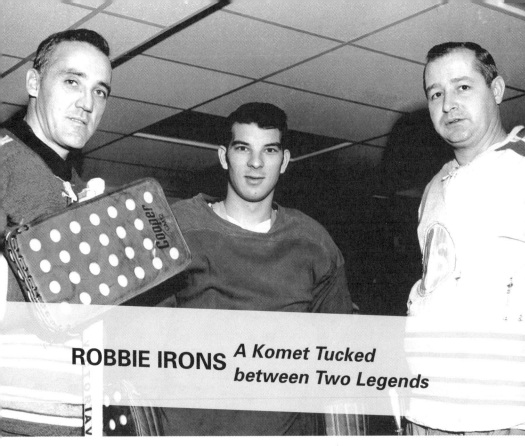

ROBBIE IRONS *A Komet Tucked between Two Legends*

Three minutes, that's it. Three minutes. That's the amount of time a 22-year-old Robbie Irons played for the St. Louis Blues on November 13, 1968. You might think you wouldn't have much of a story to tell after only three minutes in an NHL crease. But those three minutes in the Blues' net have given Robbie Irons a story he can tell forever. Those three minutes also helped change the way NHL coaches use their 'tenders.

These days Robbie Irons is a happily retired former goalie. After his playing career came to an end, he worked at Pepsi for more than 30 years. But he is still involved in hockey. Tune into a Fort Wayne Komets broadcast and you'll hear Irons providing colour commentary. After all, Robbie Irons is a legend in Fort Wayne, Indiana. He spent 12 years in goal for the Komets, and his number 30 was retired by the team. But Irons didn't just play for the Komets — once upon a time, he shared an NHL crease with two of the greatest goaltenders to ever play the game.

In the fall of 1968, a young Scotty Bowman was the bench boss for the expansion St. Louis Blues. The team was in their second year in the league. They were solid in goal, with two future Hall of Famers, Glenn

Hall and Jacques Plante, between the pipes. But what would the Blues look like in goal in just a few years' time? After all, Hall was 37 and Plante was 39. Their advanced age helped Irons end up with the Blues.

"The way Bowman had it laid out was that I was going to be in St. Louis for the first two months of the season and then I would go to Kansas City for the last four months. And they would bring another rookie up," says Irons. Now Bowman's plan wasn't exactly an apprenticeship for the young goalies as much as it was a way for Bowman and the Blues to build the team's minor-league system. Irons knew his role: sit on the bench while either Hall or Plante played. If Hall played, Plante would be in the stands. If Plante played, Hall would be in the stands. Either way, Irons would be stuck to the bench, unless fate intervened.

"I think reality was looking me right in the face there — I wasn't trying to compete and beat those guys out. I was just happy to have the opportunity to be there."

But still, when you're 22 and sitting on an NHL bench, in uniform, just inches away from the ice, the thought has to cross your mind . . . what if I actually get to play? "You always had to be prepared and ready to go," Irons says, "which I always felt I was."

One night in 1968, Irons was prepared as fate intervened. The Blues were at Madison Square Garden wrapping up the final game of a six-game road trip. Glenn Hall got the start in goal and as per usual Robbie Irons got his seat on the bench. But he wasn't sitting for long.

The Rangers' Vic Hadfield opened the scoring just 76 seconds into the game. The goal did not sit well with Hall, who on that night was wearing a mask for the first time in his NHL career. "A high slapshot or something," says Irons. "It went over Hall's shoulder. And he got all upset and came charging out at referee Vern Buffey, and he ended up bumping him. And that was enough. They threw him out. And then it was, 'Robbie, in you go.'"

Just like that, Robbie Irons's NHL career was about to begin. But not so fast — remember, the always cerebral Scotty Bowman was the Blues coach. Bowman was only 35 at the time, but even at that young age, he was still way ahead of the game. Robbie Irons was about to get a glimpse into the brilliant, calculating mind of Scotty Bowman.

"Bowman said, 'I want you to go out there and take a warm-up and then I want you to come over and see me.' I say, 'Okay.' So in I went and I came over to the bench and he says, 'I want you to sit here for a second, tell him you got hit in the ankle or something.'" Irons did what any young aspiring NHL goaltender would do. He listened to his coach. For some reason Bowman wanted this goaltending switch to take as long as possible. It went on and on.

"All the time he's delaying the referee is getting upset. Emile Francis, the coach and general manager of New York, was getting all upset. So it went on for about four or five minutes and finally the referees turned around and said, 'That's enough. Let's get this going. Get him in the net.'"

With that Robbie Irons headed toward the St. Louis Blues goal. He was on one of the biggest stages in sports, at Madison Square Garden in front of 15,738 fans. He was an NHL goaltender — but not for long.

"We were down 1–0 but I was feeling better every second . . . and then all of a sudden I looked over and they're waving to me from the bench and Jacques Plante is there. Dressed."

Robbie Irons's night was over. He'd played three minutes before Jacques Plante took over. At the time, it was the least amount of time ever played by an NHL goaltender. For Bowman and the Blues, Irons's three-minute cameo was all part of the plan. The stalling, the pretend your ankle's hurt and hang around the bench, was all done so Jacques Plante could head to the Blues dressing room, put on his gear and get into the game as soon as possible.

"The guys all said, 'Good going, you did what you had to do.' I remember Lynn Patrick, the general manager at the time, came down to the bench and he just sort of tapped me on the shoulder and he said, 'You did what we wanted you to do. Thank you.' So it was a nice compliment from a pretty nice guy. So that was it and then we went on and we won the hockey game 3–1 and all hell broke loose. Emile Francis raised hell that we were delaying the game. Made it look bush league. And I think New York raised such a stink that the NHL turned around within the next week or two and said, 'That's enough. The two goalies that you have dressed for a regular-season game must start and finish or you gotta use a forward player in the net.' It actually changed the rule in the NHL."

So, when you think about it, Robbie Irons's three minutes were more than just three minutes. They helped change the game. Scotty Bowman had a plan, and Irons just happened to be the man to execute it, even if he really didn't have any idea of what was happening at the time. "And that was the thing with Bowman, he always seemed to be ahead of the curve on little things like that. That's what he had. So Glenn Hall and Jacques Plante, they knew all about what was going to happen, I would imagine. I seemed to be the only one who was in the dark about it. It was an experience I will never forget."

Irons is anything but bitter about the experience. If anything, he wishes he had a chance to play a little more in the minor leagues during the 1968–69 season. He played in only 24 games that year, though he did end up playing in some preseason games with the Blues during the years after his three-minute emergency cameo. "Every year I played I felt a little better. I played one game in St. Louis, a full house against Minnesota. I think Plante played the first two periods, I played the third. I think we won 4–0, so, you know, I was feeling a little better. My games in Kansas City [with the Blues' farm team] . . . I felt pretty good about those. It was just a matter of was I going to get another try? Was I going to get another shot?"

Irons never did.

It wasn't long before the Blues released him and he eventually found his way to Fort Wayne. He never left. His second tour of duty with the Komets started in 1971. It lasted until 1981.

"It was a great place to play. My alternative was to go back to Toronto and get a job and possibly play senior hockey out in Barrie or some place like that. I knew a couple of guys up there. But the Komets kept calling me back after the summer. And my wife and I kept going back and finally we decided to stay and have a family here."

Robbie Irons is a fixture in Fort Wayne. All these years later, however, the memory of his one night in an NHL crease is still with him. His son found a picture of Irons at a Blues practice with Plante and Hall and it proudly hangs in the living room of his home. Sure, Irons played only three minutes in the NHL, but the memories of those three minutes can last a lifetime. This is a man who played with legends.

DEAN CLARK *A Drop of Oil*

"My first year of organized hockey in Saint Albert was played on out-door ice. So when you go from that to playing with a great hockey team in the Coliseum in Edmonton in front of all your friends and family, that's pretty surreal," says Dean Clark, a one-time Edmonton Oiler and long-time WHL coach.

In January 1984, Clark laced them up with one of the greatest teams in the history of the game. He was playing for the Kamloops Junior Oilers when he started the new year in the best way he could have imagined. The Oilers had a rash of injuries and they put in a call to Kamloops coach Bill LaForge. The NHL franchise wanted Clark to head to Edmonton right away and join the big team. But there was trouble. "We were fogged in in Kamloops and I couldn't get a flight out."

And when Clark says he was fogged in, he was really fogged in. We're not talking about a 30-minute delay. It was 48 hours before he got a flight out of Kamloops. "There was a panic that I wouldn't make it. I was a little bit concerned that I would never get there. But everything worked out."

Well, almost everything. Clark made it to Edmonton but his sticks didn't. And instead of a few days of practice with the Oilers, he arrived on a Friday, laced them up for one practice and then played against the Hartford Whalers on Hockey Night in Canada on Saturday. "Obviously I wanted to go in there and help them for as long as they needed me. They had a great team back then. There were lots of great players though, so I ended up playing only one game. I just wanted to make sure I didn't screw up."

Great team is an understatement. You know the names: Gretzky, Messier, Kurri, Fuhr, Anderson, Lowe and Coffey. The 19-year-old Clark, however, wasn't what you would call awestruck. An Alberta boy, he'd played for Mark Messier's dad, Doug, as a youngster. And he knew most of the guys from training camp.

So when did it finally hit Clark that he wasn't skating on an outdoor rink in St. Albert? "A little bit in warm-up. You know, you go out there, and of course nobody's wearing a helmet. That moment was pretty cool. I knew all my friends and family were there and they were watching. I mean it was pretty cool during the anthem as well. And then I just got on the ice for the first shift; I was a little bit nervous, and then after that I was fine."

Clark centred a line with Pat Conacher and another junior call-up — Steve Graves. Naturally, he didn't set a record for most minutes played in a single game. "I think the total amount of shifts was four." Clark took it all in, while he was on the ice and while he was on the bench. He got to witness some history as well. The Oilers won the game 5–3, and it was sealed with an empty netter by Wayne Gretzky with 43 seconds to go. It was Gretzky's 50th goal of the season. Too bad it took so long for the Oilers to put this one away. "The plan was to get us [Clark and Graves] some time with Gretzky, but unfortunately the game was too close and that's just the way that Slats [Glen Sather] rolled the lines."

Clark, the future coach, didn't keep his eyes just on his teammates. He was checking out the guy who was rolling the lines. Sure, Glen Sather had a ton to work with on the 1984 Edmonton Oilers, but that doesn't mean it was easy. Sather, however, was smart enough to know that when you have the horses, you let them go.

"He let the guys go out and perform. That was the biggest thing. They had a really good dynamic on the coaching staff because they had Slats — he was the motivator, he'd get guys fired up — and then they had John Muckler, who was a real technical guy, and Ted Green to help out as well. So the staff was really, really unique and good for that group. They were smart enough to let the creativity happen and if they needed to be reined in a little bit, then Slats was there to do that. 'Let's move the puck. Let's get it up the ice,' was what they wanted to do. Attack.

"Wayne Gretzky, the best guy to probably ever to play the game, would think three and four steps ahead and had the ability to put the puck in areas where people were going. He was by far way ahead of everybody when it came to those types of things. They were such a close-knit group. They played hard together. They had fun together. It was a really, really good group."

Clark's stay in Edmonton was short. He was sent back to Kamloops thinking that the NHL life was well within his reach. "I think at that time I thought, 'I got my taste now . . . I've just got to work on getting back.' Unfortunately, that never happened. But I thought for sure this is what I'd like to do. Obviously I knew the curve to potentially crack the Oilers was steep."

But within hours of arriving back in Kamloops, Dean Clark's hockey future took a drastic turn. In his first game back with the Junior Oilers, he separated his shoulder. "That was the beginning of the end."

Clark returned to Kamloops the next year as an over-ager. The Junior Oilers became the Blazers. Clark re-injured his shoulder early in the second half of the season. Then he injured his other shoulder. He was finished for the year and his junior career was over. The Blazers had a young rookie head coach by the name of Ken Hitchcock, however, who made him an assistant. Just like that, Dean Clark was on to the next stage of his career — at least for the time being. "I stayed there for the rest of the year. Hitch wanted me to come back the next year and continue helping." Mom and Dad had other plans though. They wanted their young son to get an education. Clark headed off to the Northern Alberta Institute of Technology, where he crossed paths with another great coach, Perry Pearn.

After stints with the NAIT Ooks and the Alberta Golden Bears, where he hurt his shoulder again, Dean Clark's playing days were over. He went to work as a journeyman power lineman. He was about as far away from skating with the Edmonton Oilers as you could imagine. Soon enough though, hockey came calling again. Midway through the hockey season Clark's old Junior A team — the St. Albert Saints — were looking for an assistant coach. He stepped in. The next year he was the head coach and his Saints won the Alberta Junior League title. Soon, one of the most notorious incidents in the history of the game would kick off a 17-year WHL journey for Clark.

In 1996, the Graham James scandal shocked the hockey world. James, who was the coach of the Calgary Hitmen, resigned in September of that year, just days before police confirmed he was being investigated for sexually abusing two former players while he was the head coach of the Swift Current Broncos. Suddenly, the Hitmen were a franchise in turmoil. They needed a new coach, but much more importantly, they needed a real leader for their young players. They turned to Dean Clark. "The best thing for me at that time was I had no idea what I was getting myself into. I just kind of did it the way I felt it should be done. I sure felt bad for the kids. You know how the media can be at times.

"There seemed to be a black cloud around us that whole year. It's funny, I think we won only 15 games that first year. I was there when the team was sold to the Flames, and Lauren Johnson, who was the president of the Hitmen at the time and who had hired me, made sure that my contract was included in the sale — that I continued coaching — which was obviously very honourable of him."

It was a wise move. Clark and his players turned the team around and essentially saved the franchise. The team that had a "black cloud" hanging over it won 40 games in Clark's second year with the team. And in the spring of 1999, Clark's Hitmen won the WHL championship. "We emerged from such a terrible thing to be such a great team, a great franchise. There are a lot of guys who went on to be teachers and different things that I'm just as proud of because life is what it is. You know, whether you're going to be a hockey player or you're going to do something else, what you learn from playing on a team and all the life experiences that you have certainly helps you prepare for some of the things that might happen further along in your life."

Clark eventually went on to other WHL jobs in Brandon, Kamloops and Prince George. He's been out of the coaching business for a couple of years now, however, and back in the power business. He says he would welcome a return to the bench under the right circumstances. "I was fortunate enough to do a World Juniors with Claude Julien and Todd McLellan. Those guys have gone on to some pretty successful careers in the NHL. I mean, it would be nice to do that, but at the end of the day those opportunities didn't materialize for whatever reason. And some of that was my own doing and now I've got myself back in the power-line business. And I'm enjoying that for a change. It's been two and a half years since I was let go by Prince George and that's part of the game — as a coach you get hired to be fired. You figure that out in a hurry."

As for the circumstances that surrounded Clark's playing days, he doesn't think about it much. Who knows what would have happened if Dean Clark was drafted by a team like the New Jersey Devils, who might have needed some help, instead of the super-stacked Oilers. But *What if?* is an easy game to play. Before Clark joined the Kamloops Junior Oilers he was on a full scholarship at Michigan's Ferris State University in the NCAA. What if he had stayed at Ferris State instead of joining Kamloops? "In hindsight, if I would've stayed maybe I never would've never received the injury that I did."

The bottom line is Dean Clark played, at least for one night, for one of the greatest hockey teams of all time. "I don't think too much about it. I played a little beer-league a couple years ago, and when you sit back and the guys ask for stories I guess you realize how fortunate you were. I had an opportunity to play on a team that was one of the best. I think in the *Hockey News* it was voted the second greatest team of all time. A guy came to my house when that issue came out. He said, 'Hey, look. Your name's on this team. It's the second-greatest team ever.'" Clark was quick to add, "'With one game played.' A lot of people ask me if I got a ring, all that kind of stuff. But obviously I didn't."

Clark jokes that he's still waiting for an invitation to the Oilers' 30th anniversary party for the 1984 Cup champs. But when you think about it, the one game was kind of fitting for Clark. I ask him if he would define himself as a player or as a coach, and it's clear he's all coach. In fact, looking back on his playing days, he could see how he was made for a life behind the bench. "I had some leadership as a player. I'm probably more of a coach than a player, because even when I played I was kind of the Reggie Dunlop."

Which of course prompts me to ask the only possible follow-up question when you hear mention of the greatest fictional player-coach the game has ever known: Did you have the Reggie Dunlop all-leather suit? Sadly, the answer is no, but Clark still rocked some ice slacks. "Back then it was the Cooper-all. We wore the long pants in juniors. And I think I did have the black leather tie."

JEROME MRAZEK *A Holy Intervention*

Hockey Hall of Fame

"Mo-ses. Mo-ses." In the 1970s, there was no nastier place for a team to visit than the Philadelphia Spectrum. The Broad Street Bullies were big and mean. And so were their fans. But on the night of February 7, 1976, the NHL's meanest fans found religion. "It was an interesting situation and a little bit comical. And maybe even unfortunate at this point. There were about six or seven minutes left in the game and the fans started chanting Moses, which was my nickname back then," says the now clean-shaven Jerome Mrazek, who rocked quite the beard back in his Philly days.

Mrazek got the nickname in the fall of 1975. "Actually Dave Schultz's brother gave me that name — Country Ray Schultz was his handle. We were getting on an elevator and he said, 'Moses are you getting in?' This was during training camp. I didn't know anybody so the name Moses stuck for the rest of the time I was affiliated with Philadelphia."

Fast forward a few months and the Flyers were well in control of the St. Louis Blues — 6–1 late in the third. Mrazek had been with the Flyers for a couple of months but he was the backup goalie. And when I say backup, I really mean backup. He had yet to see a second of action. But Moses was about to find his calling. On this night, the Philly fans wanted Moses. The chanting continued and got louder and louder. "They were chanting, 'Mo-ses, Mo-ses,' and I didn't know what to do. You know, what do you do? You sit there as a call-up and a player, you don't look around and say, 'Mr. Shero, can I go in?' You just wait for the call. It either comes or it doesn't."

Finally, Flyers head coach Fred Shero answered the prayers of the Philly faithful, even though it took him a little while. "Because Bobby Taylor had been the constant backup in Philadelphia for two or three years, he was trying to remember what my name was and he was saying, 'Bobby? Ah . . .' You know, kind of fumbling through. And I guess some people would have said that was typical of Fred. Some people say he was oblivious to some things, but others say he was a pretty astute fellow. And finally he called my name."

Moses wasn't going to climb a mountain, but after 15 or 20 games with Flyers he was finally going to climb off the bench. There was just one problem — or more like two problems — for the goalie. He was missing his glove and blocker. Since he figured this night was going to be like any of the other 20 or so he spent on the bench, he had already shipped his glove and blocker back to the dressing room. Playing goal in the NHL can be tough at the best of times, but without a glove and blocker it's impossible — even for a guy named Moses. "The equipment guy ran up the lane and got my gloves. What are the odds that Fred calls my name in this particular game and I just sent my gloves up the way?"

When the equipment finally returned, Mrazek climbed off the bench and into NHL game number one. If Moses was looking for a miracle, he wasn't going to get one. The main problem with a goalie getting thrust into a game with six minutes to go is obvious and it goes like this: *Thou Shalt Not Have a Decent Chance to Warm Up.* "I finally get out there and I went down to my knees on basically the first shot . . . which I didn't often do, because I wasn't a butterfly goaltender. And there was a huge rebound and a simple goal."

Just like that, Mrazek gave up his first NHL marker: Gary Unger had beaten him on a power play with 4:06 to go. Mrazek didn't face another shot. The Flyers scored two more and Mrazek's night was over. It was an 8–2 Philadelphia victory.

Mrazek stayed on with the Flyers but he never got in another game. But at least Shero knew his name now: "I hadn't been sure if Fred knew who I was. I was just the backup, some guy."

Mrazek might have just been "some guy" but he was the backup on a great team. Bernie Parent had gone down with an injury and Wayne Stephenson handled most of the duties — all but those six minutes. Still, Mrazek was living the life of an NHLer on one of the best teams of the '70s. He got to see legends like Reggie Leach, Bill Barber and Bobby Clarke — up close. "It was very interesting to be sitting there at the start of a game and everybody is ready. And everybody was waiting for Clarkie to give the nod. As a young guy or call-up, you're looking around and even though you've been there for 20 games or so you're still respectfully waiting. Clarkie puts on his gloves, gives you the nod and then you go. It was great. They were good to me. Clarkie was very good to me. Just a really good experience — a lot of fun."

The fun for a 24-year-old bearded western-Canadian kid who literally wore his boots to work every day, or at least tried to, took place off the ice as well. "They nailed my work boots to the top of my dressing-room stall one time. In those days I was kind of a free spirit and wore work boots all the time. I don't know if they had enough of that or if they wanted to just do something to the rookie." For the record, Mrazek figures Reggie Leach was the ringleader.

"Of course you're pretty awestruck anyway, being around all the guys. Sitting in the room, it was all business. And to me that was the most significant part of it; everybody knew Clarkie was the boss. So you didn't do anything before he said so."

Although Mrazek appreciated his time with the Flyers, he does wish things had gone a little differently. "I was just filler at the end of a game, which was nice. It would have been more significant had I been the starter for a game. I remember some other game situations, in preseason, more. Other than, probably, the goal. It wasn't as if I had time to soak it in and say, 'Hey, I've made it.'

"At that level you probably always assume that you'll get another opportunity." But Mrazek spent most of the following season in the AHL with Springfield, where he had a bloated 5.38 goals against average in what he calls "a horrible season for everybody who was in Springfield." Then it was a year split between Maine and Hershey. "Near the end of that season I got shipped to Hershey and didn't get an opportunity to play in the Calder Cup. Then things started to unravel. And then you find yourself out of a job and out of professional hockey and you kind of wonder what happened."

Mrazek's professional career came to an end in the spring of 1978; just a couple of years earlier he had been in the NHL. "In hindsight, perhaps if I had had an agent . . . At that time some guys had agents, but when you're a little bit younger and newer you didn't have an agent speaking for you. So had I had an agent, I may have gotten the opportunity either to play more or go somewhere else because someone else would have been speaking for me. And that's regrettable. But you make decisions and that's the way it is. You move along. It was probably most difficult getting out of hockey because you have this dream and you have these expectations and you've always been the top of the ladder. And because others expect you to make it, you expect to make it. And then you have to re-evaluate your life. Now what am I going to do? Who am I? That readjustment is probably the biggest adjustment of a person's life. It's career changing, it's life changing."

How long did it take for Mrazek to find his way after hockey?

"I'd say several years, quite honestly." He worked in the restaurant business, was in the sign-painting business and real estate, but finally found what he was looking for in retail management.

Mrazek grew up in western Canada and that's where he lives today. Years after he played in the NHL, he's still not sure he ever really made it. "If I had been there just a little bit longer maybe I could feel like I made it. But you tell people about your short story and what they say is, 'Well, you were there.' So in as much as I feel I didn't really meet my goals, other people look at it and say, 'You know, this guy has been there and he has some hockey knowledge.' And I guess, as I'm involved here with hockey locally, people still ask me questions. That's gratifying."

But still, six minutes were not enough for the man they used to call Moses. "I never reached the goals or met those expectations I had as a young person. I've moved on, but maybe there's still a void there somewhere."

CHAPTER NINE
LIFERS

DON WADDELL *A Life in the Game*

"I have the jersey I wore," Don Waddell tells me. That night was a life-time ago for the hockey lifer, but once we start talking, the memories come flooding back. It probably helps that he has the game sheet from his one game as well.

"When I was up in the NHL offices, Colin Campbell went and looked and found the actual game sheet. That was back when the league used to have everyone send in the game sheet, so he made a copy to keep in their file and he gave me the actual game sheet that is all handwritten. So I carried that around for three or four years, getting any player I saw who was on it to sign it." The names from that night when Don Waddell's Kings played the New York Rangers sound like a who's who of hockey from the early 1980s: Dionne, Simmer, Greschner and Duguay. And on January 28, 1981, future NHL head coach, GM and president Don Waddell was there as well.

Waddell started that year playing defence with the Houston Apollos of the Central League. But in a not-so-uncommon scene from the '70s and early '80s, the Apollos folded just after Christmas. "We went to get on a plane and we had no tickets . . . and then the team folded and they started sending players everywhere."

Waddell was shipped to his home state of Michigan to play for the Saginaw Gears of the International Hockey League. Waddell was only in Saginaw for a couple of weeks when he got the call. "It was kind of interesting because I got the call after practice, back before cell phones. I think it took them three hours to track me down. So I got the call and had to be on a flight within the next hour. I had to hurry to the arena to get my stuff, so I really didn't have a lot of time to think about it. I was rushing around to get to a flight. I remember the game was on a Wednesday. I caught the last flight to L.A. on Tuesday night. My initial thoughts were probably more panic than anything, not so much about playing but the logistics of getting everything together. I can remember landing in L.A. It was probably nine o'clock at night, which would have been midnight back in the east. I started calling some of my family, saying, 'Hey, guess where I am?'"

Waddell had hit the big time in his first year of pro. He took the morning skate with the Kings and he learned that yes, he was going to play. Two defenceman were hurt and Waddell went straight into the Kings lineup. That night at the Fabulous Forum, he looked across the ice and saw Tom Laidlaw, his old college teammate from Northern Michigan. "Tom and I were defence partners for four years. With him being on the other team, that made it a little special.

"It was warm-up and we were skating around. He said, 'What the hell are you doing here?'"

When Waddell took to the ice for the Kings, his partner on the blue line was a man with one of the best handles in league history: Jerry "King Kong" Korab. Korab was a huge 6-foot-3, 220-pound defenceman who put up some decent offensive numbers and hit hard. It didn't take Waddell long to feel the wrath of King Kong. "On one of the first shifts, if not the first, Ron Greschner, who was playing for the Rangers at that time, was playing left wing and I was the right defenceman. He came down on me on a one-on-one and big King Kong came over and tried to throw that patented hip check on him and missed and took me out. And Greschner goes in on a breakaway and top shelfs it on Mario Lessard."

Waddell was a minus one. How does he remember it so vividly? Well, the pain of the hit from King Kong likely helped things sink in — plus Waddell has a great photo of the aftereffects of King Kong's wrath.

"Art Kaminsky was my agent at the time and somehow he got a hold of this picture and he sent it to me. And I'm lying on my stomach; it looks like I'm just relaxed, putting my hands on my chin, watching Greschner score his goal. It's an unbelievable picture."

That was the only blemish of the night for Waddell, who finished minus one in a 6–2 Kings loss. But he didn't hop right back on a flight to Saginaw; he stuck around and practised with the Kings. He just couldn't get into another game. There were other positives though — he was in Hollywood, and the money was good. "I stayed up for a while and took a couple more pre-game warm-ups but never dressed again. I stayed up for probably 15 or 17 days. I remember getting that first paycheque. I was making $75,000 at the NHL level. A kid that grew up in Detroit with a big family, and a very low income, and you get a paycheque like that? You're like, 'I have enough money to live the rest of my life.'

"The guy that kind of looked out for me and took me down to the beach and to lunch a couple of times was Mike Murphy. I remember he had a little two-seater sports car. So sometimes I'd head down there with him, but I didn't always get to be the passenger on the way back," he says, laughing.

As a trained journalist, I can see that no follow-up question is required.

Eventually, Waddell's California dreaming came to an end and he was shipped back to the Gears. But things were pretty dreamy in Saginaw as well. Waddell's team swept the Kalamazoo Wings 4–0 in the IHL Final to win the Turner Cup. Fresh off a title win in his first year as a pro, Waddell went to camp the next year full of confidence. The Kings started their preseason in Victoria, British Columbia. "I played some exhibition games. That was my second year pro and I thought I had a chance to stay. Then they made a coaching change. Bob Berry was the coach when I was there and then Parker MacDonald took over. I think I played three exhibition games that year and actually went to L.A. When they cut the squad down, I think there were roughly 28 of us who travelled back down to L.A. to continue camp. Before the season started I ended up getting sent back down."

Waddell was back in Saginaw, but he didn't pout. He went to work putting up points from the blue line — lots of them. (Waddell had 95 in 77 games with the Gears.) He was named the IHL's Defenceman of the Year for the 1981–82 season. But he never got the call. He split the next season between the Gears and the New Haven Nighthawks of the AHL. And again he didn't get the call. That's when thoughts of a post-playing career, of a life in coaching or in management, started to creep in. He kept playing, though. "I went to Europe and played for a couple of years. When I was in college, I can remember telling myself that I wasn't going to bounce around the minors, you know. I was going to give it a shot and if things didn't work out . . . But actually, when I started playing I loved it so much I said, 'You know, I'm going to do this for a few years.' Then after playing four or five years I came back from Europe and I knew that I wanted to stay in the game."

Waddell did eventually step away from the game, or at least he tried. He only played in 10 games in 1986–87. And then he started a portable toilet business. He knows it comes with its share of jokes, but he was doing well.

"It was a company called Porta John. It was a national company. So I bought territorial rights for southeast Michigan and northwest Ohio. I had a friend that had done this and I knew how he did with it. So I had the opportunity and I ended up keeping it for five years. When I bought it I think I had 25 portable toilets, and when I sold it I had over 1,500. I ended up getting some big contracts with the city of Detroit for all the things they do during the summer."

Eventually, though, the game Waddell loved so much came looking for him. He got a call from Rick Dudley, who was running the Flint Spirits in the IHL. Dudley needed a defenceman. "I decided, what the heck. I missed it." Waddell was playing again, and he was also moonlighting with his portable toilet business. The two went together seamlessly.

"I can remember joining the team one time in Fort Wayne, and I had parked my Porta John truck in the Fort Wayne Civic Centre parking lot.

And I went in and played a game and then got back in my truck to go back to work the next day."

Waddell returned to Flint the next year as a player–assistant coach. The following year, Dudley left the team and Waddell took over as the head coach and GM. Just like that, Waddell, who had envisioned himself as a coach or an exec just a few years into his pro career, was running an IHL team. He was just past his 30th birthday. "I was in way over my head. We had a tough year."

Waddell took over a team that wasn't affiliated with an NHL club. He combed North America for players and he went through a ton of them. "I think I went through 60-some players that year. It's like your fantasy team. How can I make it better right now? So I always thought, 'Well, maybe this guy would be better.' And back then you didn't have guaranteed contracts, you had 24-hour contracts. You could cut guys anytime you wanted."

His time in Flint helped Waddell learn that he preferred management over coaching. His next stop was in San Diego, where he helped build the expansion Gulls. He's been on the management side — as a GM and president — ever since. With the exception of 85 games behind the Atlanta Thrashers bench, he's worked in management in Orlando, Detroit, Pittsburgh, Atlanta and now Carolina. Waddell has also served USA Hockey in a management role and was one of the final cuts from the Miracle on Ice team. Those experiences set him up for the management style he's now practised for over two decades. "When I became a GM, I made sure every player that comes through is important to the organization. Some are going to play for us and some aren't. I've been fortunate to get to where I'm at and if somebody needs 10 minutes or two hours with you, you gotta give them the time. I truly believe that.

"As a player I never knew where I stood. No one ever said to me, 'Go down and work on this and you'll get another chance.' Those things never got talked about. When you got called up it was a simple phone call and when you got sent down it was, 'Here's your plane ticket, kid.' And that was basically it.

"The communication back in the '80s, and even when I first got into coaching, is much different than it is today, and what it needs to be today. You had no relationships with your coaches or your managers."

Don Waddell was one of those players he speaks of. He still gets a kick out of looking over that old game sheet, and he wouldn't trade that night for anything. "When you consider the number of players that play and try to make it to the NHL, the percentages are against you — most players don't make it. So to be able to say that I played one game in the National Hockey League, I'm very proud of that. To be a kid from Detroit and to get that opportunity, it was unbelievable. Being in the business, people ask, 'Did you play in the NHL?' I actually just did a speaking engagement and the question came up and I said, 'I did.' I said, 'When you go to the record book you're going to be amazed at those stats.' How many guys have had the opportunity to play in the NHL, coach in the NHL, be a GM in the NHL and be a president in the NHL? And it all starts with that one game."

He still has his old number 29 jersey from that game, and he can thank his wife for that. About 10 years ago she tracked it down. Waddell's wife found an old Kings trainer who pointed her to a guy who had bags of Kings jerseys. "He didn't even charge her. I remember she said, 'I tried to pay him for it and he wouldn't take any money. He was happy he could find it.'

"She gave it to me and said, 'I wish you could still fit in this.'"

BLAIR MACKASEY *The Unintentional Hockey Lifer*

Blair MacKasey wasn't a typical teenager growing up in Montreal in the early 1970s. Unlike kids who had time to goof around and hang out until the wee hours, MacKasey's schedule was full. And we're not talking on a daily basis, we're talking on a yearly basis. "I probably missed out on the social side of being a teenager, but I had the opportunity to grow up in the Montreal Forum playing for the Jr. Canadiens. And as soon as the season was over I'd head out to Jerry Park and practise with the Expos for a couple of weeks before I was assigned to wherever I was going. And as soon as the baseball season was over I'd come home and it would be time for hockey training camp."

These days MacKasey would be known as a two-sport phenom. Back in 1972 he was just Blair, a young man who played Major Junior Hockey and Minor League Baseball. And it's not like he was the only one doing it. Michel Dion, another hot hockey prospect, was one of his teammates with the Cocoa Beach Expos of the Florida Gulf Coast League. "I was a first baseman, Ellis Valentine was the right fielder and the two catchers were Michel Dion and a guy by the name of Gary Carter."

When MacKasey showed up in Cocoa Beach in 1972, that Carter kid was a big-time shortstop coming out of California. The Expos had other plans for the future Hall of Famer. "I was a first baseman and Carter was a shortstop and Michel was a catcher. When Carter got down there, he was excited they were going to make him into a first baseman. When I arrived about a week later they decided he was going to be a catcher. So I like to think that maybe I had something to do with him being a Hall of Famer," MacKasey says, laughing. After a season in the Gulf Coast League, MacKasey headed back to Montreal for another season of junior hockey. The next summer he played Class A ball for the Expos in Jamestown, New York. And though he was still only a kid, he had to make a decision: was he going to make his future playing baseball or hockey?

"The Expos kind of forced me to make a choice. I was really only playing half a season all the time and the chances of making it, especially for a positional player like myself, are slim. Being in Class A ball, it's a long way to go to the Major Leagues, especially if you're not a pitcher. I was a lot closer to playing in the NHL than I was to playing Major League Baseball, so it was an easy decision to make."

Fast forward a couple of years, and Blair MacKasey had one year of minor league hockey under his belt. He was at training camp for the Toronto Maple Leafs and he just kept hanging around. Unlike a lot of men who played a single game in the NHL, MacKasey never got the thrill of "getting the call." Instead, he made a solid Leafs team right out of training camp in the fall of 1976. "Randy Carlyle and I were the two rookies to start the season. Between the two of us, we had well over a thousand games in the league." I like the way that MacKasey looks at things — and it should be noted that those two Leafs rookies went on to win one Norris Trophy between them as well. When MacKasey looked around the bench he saw players like Darryl Sittler, Lanny McDonald, Börje Salming and Tiger Williams. There were a couple of legends behind the bench as well. Red Kelly was the head coach and Johnny Bower was his assistant. Before MacKasey's first NHL game, his Hall of Fame coach had a request. "I was a right shot and at that time there weren't a lot of right defenceman around, so I had always played the right side. In this particular game, Claire Alexander was also a right shot and we were paired together. So Red said to me, 'Can you play left side?' I said, 'Hell, I'll play anywhere.' I kind of got thrown right into the fire and not only was it my first NHL game, it was probably one of the few times I'd ever played left defence." You don't say no to Red Kelly. MacKasey was a rookie and he was smart enough to know that if he wanted to stick around, he better do what his coach wanted.

On October 5, 1976, in front of an unfortunately typical Rockies crowd of 7,359, Blair MacKasey, the right-handed shooting defenceman, lined up on the left side of the point for the Leafs. He was just a couple of years removed from his part-time gig as a baseball player. Perhaps his old baseball instincts kicked in when MacKasey let his lumber fly early. "I took a penalty in the very first shift of the game: cross-checking in front of the net. I think it was the first recorded statistic of that year."

It was definitely the first recorded stat of the year for the Leafs, and it came 2:59 into the first. Unfortunately, the second recorded statistic of the year came just 18 seconds later when the Rockies' Larry Skinner gave the home side a 1–0 lead with his first NHL goal. "We ended up losing 4–2, and then I got sent down to Dallas shortly after that. And the rest of the year was kind of a mess."

The year was a mess because a back injury that MacKasey had in junior flared up and got worse. When he played for the Montreal Junior Canadiens, he'd slid into the boards and damaged his back. As time went on, the pain became less and less bearable. "Arthritis had developed in my back. It got to the point where it was really, really bothering me. It was bothering my sciatic nerves. The Leafs' orthopedic surgeon at the time was David Hastings and he said, 'This needs to be fixed.'"

MacKasey and the Leafs didn't wait for the season to end. He underwent surgery around Christmas. "That was the season. That was my opportunity . . . right there."

The surgery essentially ended MacKasey's career, or at least his shot at a return to the NHL. He was never the same player. "I don't know if the rehab techniques were as good then, or if there were any rehab techniques really to speak of, I just never got back. I never got the mobility back and I just really struggled after that."

He played another 54 games with the Leafs' farm team in Dallas in 1977–78, and he tried his luck at another Leafs camp but it just wasn't working. Blair MacKasey was done with pro hockey at the age of 22. "Rather than spending my time in the minors and kicking around, I just came back to the family business. I'd felt I'd had enough and I quit and came home and went to work."

MacKasey joined his family's commercial printing business and hockey was the furthest thing from his mind. "When I retired I really didn't go near a rink. I think that's pretty common. I really stayed away for about a year."

Eventually he stumbled into coaching minor hockey. A couple of friends wanted the former pro to help out with their sons' Atom team. The next thing the former pro knew, he was coaching 9- and 10-year-olds. He enjoyed it and went back to help out with minor-hockey players the following year as well. "For five or six years, I just enjoyed the coaching. Coached Bantam one year, coached Midget one year, Peewee . . . wherever they needed someone to fill in."

MacKasey ended up coaching the Midget AAA Lac St. Louis Lions. The team won a national title in 1993. That caught the eye of the Quebec Major Junior Hockey League. Suddenly, the guy who was just helping out was a hot commodity. The next season, MacKasey moved to Major Junior as the head coach of the Granby Bisons. He spent the next two seasons in Drummondville, Quebec, with the Voltigeurs. Once upon a time, he was a teammate of a future star named Gary Carter. In 1994, Blair MacKasey was coaching a future star named Daniel Brière. "The first time I saw Danny was at training camp his first year, and he was all of 144 pounds. He went out and he played five or six exhibition games and he was pretty average, to be honest with you. I was kind of saying to myself, 'It's going to take this kid a while to figure it out, but he's going to be a pretty good 19-year-old, and he may even be a good over-age junior.' And then the season started and he went out in the first game and he got six points. From there I think he ended up with 123, and there was no stopping him. The kid was dynamic. I obviously had a soft spot in my heart for Danny because he overcame a lot with the size factor and everything. A lot of people didn't give him a chance. He's one of the great people in the game."

Here's the kicker, during the entire time that MacKasey was climbing up the coaching ranks, he was still working at his family's printing business. His coaching career just happened — he had no intention of becoming a big-time coach when he retired. "I would basically be at work in the morning and then I would head to the rink in the afternoon. It became 24/7. Plus I had four young kids at home. It was tough to put it all together."

After two years in Drummondville, MacKasey had a chance to move to the NHL ranks as a scout. The job would provide him with more time to be around his family. "Winnipeg at the time, the year they were moving to Phoenix, was looking for a so-called 'part time scout,' someone to do the Quebec League and colleges in the eastern U.S. They asked if I'd be interested, and I was. I did that for six years and enjoyed it. Again, I was just content to do that."

After six years with Coyotes, MacKasey moved on to Hockey Canada. All these moves seemed to occur organically. Hockey Canada led MacKasey to his current employer, the Minnesota Wild. The kid who played one game in the NHL, who retired at 22 and stayed away from a rink for a year, who got into coaching just to help out his buddies and who still worked in the family business while coaching the Drummondville Voltigeurs, is now the director of player personnel for the Minnesota Wild. "I certainly wasn't looking to make a career out of it. I did it because I enjoyed it. Which may be the right way to do it."

MacKasey's coaching career started at one of the lowest levels of the game because his buddies thought an old pro, a former NHLer, would be a great fit for their kids. His pro experience, that single NHL game, has helped open up a lot of doors. But the only time he thinks of that one game is when someone like me picks up the phone. "I kind of wished I'd played two games and then people would stop talking to me about being a one-game wonder," he says. "But I really don't dwell on it very much. I look at it as a positive experience. Some people might ask, 'How come you didn't play more?' or 'How come you didn't make the major leagues?' or this and that. Everybody wants to do more. It didn't happen. But it was a great experience and probably had a real positive effect on me going forward.

"There was certainly nothing negative in it. I know a lot of guys play and they get bitter for whatever reason. They felt maybe they didn't get a chance. I've never felt that way. I don't tend to dwell on things."

MacKasey's time as a coach, scout and front-office guy far exceeds his one night in the NHL. Everything, however, has helped him develop an outlook on the game he still shares with young players. "The game is a means to an end. You get as much out of it as you can. And when it's over, it's over. No regrets, and then you walk away. I don't know how many kids I've said that to. It is what it is and you're not going to change it. And if you get one game or if you get a thousand games, then good for you."

MIKE MURRAY *I Should Have Shot*

"I remember it like it was yesterday. I had some speed coming down the right side and I beat Norm Maciver one-on-one to come in on a two-on-one with Brian Propp. And I should have just shot, instead of trying to make a great pass through the D-man."

Some guys can't recall too much from their one game in the NHL — Mike Murray is not one of those guys. On the line from his office in Knoxville, Tennessee, the GM and part owner of the Knoxville Ice Bears is taking me on an extremely detailed account of his one and only night in the Show.

Murray was taken in the fifth round of the 1984 Draft, 104th overall, by the New York Islanders. While he was still in junior, the Isles traded his rights from their "we were just a dynasty" club to the soon-to-be new powerhouse of the then–Wales Conference, the Philadelphia Flyers. Murray had his first NHL camp with the Islanders and then got a look at life in Philly. "It was almost like going from a country club to boot camp. Philly was doing all of the stuff, the testing that they're doing today. So it was an eye-opener. I went straight to Hershey."

During Murray's second year in Hershey, he got the call to join the Flyers. He had gotten called up to the NHL before but was always a healthy scratch. This time, he figured things were different. Murray and his mates were in Newmarket, Ontario, to take on the Baby Leafs. It was kind of a homecoming for an Ontario boy like Murray, but then he was on the move. "My whole family was there. I planned on getting up for breakfast and going to eat with them before the pre-game skate. And that's when I got the call and they flew me right to New York. And I thought, 'Well, if they're going through all this, maybe there's a chance I will dress.'"

One of the problems Murray ran into when he was the property of the Philadelphia Flyers was that the team was stacked. He also says the Flyers' young coach, Mike Keenan, didn't take all that kindly to younger players. "He wasn't a big fan of rookies."

No matter, Murray was on the next flight to the Big Apple to hope-fully suit up against the Rangers at the world's most famous arena. He landed in New York and then had to find his way to the team hotel. "The cab ride from the airport to meet the team was crazy enough." Then Murray checked into the hotel. Life in the NHL sure was different than in the minors. "Just going from the hotel lobby . . . with all the people just kind of gawking at you."

On March 15, 1988, Mike Murray pulled his Flyers sweater over his head and stepped out onto the ice at Madison Square Garden for warm-up. He was 21 and about to play in his first NHL game. He looked the part, with a fine head of hockey hair, and Rangers fans, being the pas-sionate bunch that they are, welcomed him warmly. "I'm flying around in warm-up and trying to get my bearings and trying to convince myself 'This is like any other game, like any other game.' And I noticed, right in front of the penalty box, and this was when the glass was a little lower, this guy looks at me and says, 'Hey, Murray. Who the eff are you?' And I just started cracking up. I think Ron Hextall and Don Nachbaur, they were really close to me, and we just started laughing. It kind of broke the ice. And that was fun."

With the warm-up in the books, it was game time. The hunch Murray had back in Newmarket was bang on: he was going to play. And like I said, Mike Murray remembers the details. Here he is on his first

NHL shift, or at least what he thought was going to be his first NHL shift. "Keenan goes, 'Murray's line's up.' And I'm like, 'Shit. I gotta go.' You know it was only the fourth shift of the game. So Peter Zezel's coming off and I go to jump and about three guys tackle me. He meant Murray Craven. So I was like, 'Oh, shit.' That would have been my first shift — too many men on the ice. My parents were watching back home on TV. My God, that would have been funny."

Soon enough Murray settled in and aside from the bright lights and huge crowd, hockey in the NHL was just hockey. "The thing that was really cool was once you got there, you notice it's the same game you've always played. The passes are crisper, and you stay in your lane. And then once you realize you can hang there, the frustrating thing is when you get sent back down. It's like, 'Man, I was right there.' It's nothing different than what I know . . . so that was a little frustrating. When I got sent down it was like the puck was on a string."

Two nights later, he was back in a Flyers uniform getting ready to warm up at the Spectrum for a game against the Chicago Blackhawks. Enter coach Keenan. "Before warm-up, I'm kind of getting a little nervous. I'm taking a leak at the urinal and Keenan comes and stands right beside me. And we're both looking ahead and he says, 'Hey, there may be a chance that you're not going tonight. So have a good warm-up and we'll see how things go.' And I'm like, 'Why?' And he says, 'Well, we're going to see if Murray Craven's ready to go. If he's ready to go, we'll let you know.'"

Mike Murray took his warm-up. On his way back to the Flyers dressing room he got yanked aside. He was a healthy scratch again. Mike Murray almost played in game number two — he came *that* close to not being in this book. But that's pro hockey. "I was just like, 'Shit, this sucks.'"

So what did Mike Murray do? He went back down to Hershey and helped the Bears win the Calder Cup. And he still thought good times were ahead, that his little taste of NHL life at Madison Square Garden was just the beginning. But Murray was back in Hershey the next year, and, like any other minor-leaguer, he was combing over the transaction wire in the morning newspaper, seeing if anything was opening up in the NHL. "You never wish any ill will on any other player . . . but guys are always looking at transactions — who got hurt, who got called up."

Murray split the 1988–89 season between the American and International Leagues, and then he moved to Germany for a year. "I went down to block a shot my last year in Hershey and broke my foot. So I didn't really finish as strong as I should have. So I ended up in Germany."

Following his year in Germany, Murray began a long hockey odyssey through a number of leagues: the East Coast League, a year in Denmark, the United League. He ultimately found a home in Knoxville, Tennessee, where he met his wife and had a family: "Twenty games turned into 20-plus years."

Over the course of his career, Mike Murray collected his fair share of stories. Some of them go back to his earliest days with the Flyers. It seems Keenan made an impression right from the start. During an exhibition game, Murray and his linemate Rick Tocchet headed for the Philly bench and a line change. "For some reason I always put up my blade when I was sitting on the bench [pretty much everyone else keeps their blade down]. And there was a whistle and everything was kind of quiet. Keenan comes right up behind me and says, 'Murray, turn your effing stick around and get ready to play!' He scared the shit right out of me. And Tocchet's dying laughing. And I'm like, 'Geez, don't do that shit to me. I'm trying to focus here.'"

Mike Murray's pro career lasted from the 1986–87 season until 2002–03. There were a few years of retirement jammed in there, but it adds up to a significant hockey odyssey. So was it worth it? "Oh absolutely, there's not a doubt. I can almost remember shift by shift. Would I have hoped to have a lot more NHL games? Yeah, but, you know, it's very cool to remember."

His staff in Knoxville reminds him of his glory days all the time. "My staff likes to pull up my Wikipedia page with my mullet . . . my hockey hair."

And just imagine if the kid with the hockey hair would have shot on that two-on-one with Brian Propp at Madison Square Garden on March 15, 1988, instead of passing to the veteran. It's a thought that does creep into Murray's mind. "Scoring at that moment might have changed things too."

KIRK TOMLINSON *The Total Package*

You never know where a one-gamer is going to turn up. My search for Kirk Tomlinson ended in my home province of Nova Scotia. Tomlinson lives just outside of Halifax, in Hammonds Plains. He and his wife moved there after his pro coaching days came to an end. After a few years of working in downtown Halifax, he was hired by a local minor-hockey association to be their development coach. A development coach for minor hockey? Things sure have changed since Tomlinson and I were young. "When I played growing up it was you fend for yourself, and you figured it out as you went," says Tomlinson.

If all goes well, maybe one or two of Tomlinson's young protégés will make it to the NHL one day. But the chances of making it to the NHL are about the same as winning the lottery. One night in 1988 it was Kirk Tomlinson who had the winning ticket. Tomlinson was taken 75th overall by Minnesota in the 1986 Draft. A couple of years later, he was playing for the Oshawa Generals, when the phone rang.

"I was sick in bed. I stayed home from school and I wasn't at practice and coach called me and said 'How you feeling tonight?' kind of stuff.

'Oh, you know. I'm not feeling great.' Paul Theriault was the coach; I called him Red Beard. He said, 'Well, that's too bad because Minnesota just called you up. You're playing in Toronto tonight.'"

A call like that is likely the world's best cure for a headache, the flu, a cold — you name it. "I felt better instantly. I got into my brown Dodge Dart and drove up to Maple Leaf Gardens. I pulled into the private parking and went in and played my first and only game."

Can you imagine, you're lying in bed — sick — and then you get a call like that? Tomlinson had all kinds of thoughts racing through his head as he cruised west on Highway 401 from Oshawa to Toronto in his trusty Dodge Dart. "It's what every kid in Canada who plays hockey dreams of . . . that opportunity to get your chance to play in the NHL. And you're going, 'What's it going to be like? Who am I going to sit beside? Am I going to contribute?'"

Soon enough, the 19-year-old Toronto boy was at the Gardens. Of course the first thing he did after he got off the phone with Red Beard was call his parents. "Once I called my parents, they definitely spread the word and I ended up buying a barrel full of tickets. It cost me more money in tickets than I made that game." But really, who cares? This story isn't about money — it's about realizing your dream has become a reality the moment you walk into that dressing room.

"Your stomach kind of drops and you're looking for your name up top. I remember that the guys were already there so I was probably the last one in the dressing room. So I pulled in and I drop my Genny's bag in the middle of the floor. And I remember the trainer coming over and hooking me up and taking my skates and making sure they were good. And they gave me my socks and I wore number 31, which is Larry DePalma's number. And he was out of the lineup that night so I had to wear 31, which turns out to be my lucky number. My twin daughters were born on December 31. I was married on the 31st. And I wore 31 in my only NHL game."

Tomlinson's only NHL game was far from just another date on the calendar in a long and dreadful season for Minnesota, who went on to finish the year with just 19 wins. This was "The Return Match." Back on January 6 at Maple Leaf Gardens, in one of the most infamous moments of the season, Minnesota's Dino Ciccarelli swung his stick several times at the head of Toronto's Luke Richardson. Ciccarelli was thrown out of the game and received a match penalty for intent to injure. He was suspended for 10 games. Later that summer, Ciccarelli was fined $1,000 in court and ordered to spend a day in jail. On the night of February 24, 1988, Dino Ciccarelli and the North Stars were back in Toronto for the first time since the incident. "I was known for a little bit of fisticuffs here and there so I was on the line with Dino.

"Without anybody saying anything, you knew the situation. If there was going to be retribution it would've been that game, and it would've probably happened pretty quickly."

If Tomlinson was nervous, you wouldn't know it, and if fireworks were about to go off, he didn't really seem to care. The first thing Tomlinson did during warm-up was soak up the atmosphere and aura of Maple Leaf Gardens. Of course in 1988, Tomlinson had to look the part. "Oh yeah. No helmet . . . I had the flow going. I had the long curly hair whipping through warm-up." Now this is where the story gets even better. Remember, Tomlinson's first NHL game is in his hometown. It's the kind of moment you'd want to last forever. "One of the best parts about warm-up was that the net broke. So there was a major delay and I ended up wheeling around the ice during that time, waving to all the fans, trying to find all my friends in the stands. It was awesome."

Yep, right before faceoff, thousands of fans waited impatiently for a net to be fixed and for the game to start. The only one who didn't seem to mind was Tomlinson. And there was another bonus. The on-ice delay meant the new guy in the Minnesota lineup got lots of love from the men calling the game on television. "They talked about me. A kid out of junior, an Oshawa boy, coming up. They needed to fill that space when the net broke and they really chatted me up. I got my camera time. The whole works."

Finally, it was time to get down to business. Tomlinson didn't have to wait long for his first shift. The kid who was on his way to racking up 200 PIMs in the OHL that year started for Minnesota on a line with Ciccarelli. Maybe the fans in the stands were expecting retribution for what Ciccarelli did to Richardson. Maybe a few players were too. But on this night, the old Chuck Norris Division didn't quite live up to its name.

"Nothing went down. It was pretty mild, pretty tame game." In fact, there wasn't a single tilt in a 4–2 Leafs win. Tomlinson finished even on the night with no shots on goal and no penalty minutes. After his cameo at Maple Leafs Gardens, it was back to Oshawa for the rest of the season. His ultimate plan was to start a pro career and end up in the NHL for a very long time.

"It's like when I bought my first car when I signed my first contract. You think the money is not going to stop. You think, 'I'm going to play in the NHL. I'm going to play the average of six to eight years.' And it's the same thing when you get that call-up. You're young, you're 18 and you get a chance to play. You think, 'Here we go. This is the start.' But yeah, things happen. And you have to be in the right place at the right time and have the right characteristics to fit in and mesh with the team."

Tomlinson's junior credentials were outstanding. He was a captain with the Hamilton Steelheads. He was an OHL All-Star. But for some reason, Kirk Tomlinson just couldn't adjust to life in the pros. "It was tough going up to the American Hockey League. I wish I could've played Major Junior my whole life. I had success there. I could be tough and I could score goals. In the East Coast they called me 'The Total Package.' I'd go out there and fight twice and score a couple. It's just that next level . . . the quickness, the puck movement and the speed. It was something that I wasn't capable of — I gave all my effort. I just wasn't able to make that adjustment."

Tomlinson didn't go down without a fight, literally. His stats at the minor league level are staggering. Like Tomlinson says, he sure was the Total Package in the East Coast League. In 1990–91, he put up 83 points and 385 PIMs in 57 games for the Nashville Knights. But like he says, adjusting to the AHL was another story. That same season, in eight games with the AHL's Adirondack Red Wings he had just two assists and a whopping 62 PIMs.

"I'm trying to teach kids now, even at the Atom level, that it's those transferable skills. The game changes at every jump and you have to have the qualities, the transferable skills, that get you to the next level and get you to that next step."

These days, Tomlinson spends his time with the next generation of players. He's hoping that what he learned over the course of his pro career, both as a player and a coach, can help today's kids enjoy the game. And, who knows, maybe one day one of them will make it. Now, thanks to the internet, Kirk Tomlinson's players know who he is. Or to put it more precisely, they know who he used to be. "There were hundreds of fights online. And it got to a point that when I applied for the Canada Games Team with Hockey Nova Scotia, the high-performance program, I'd come to the rink and the kids would go, 'I saw your fight on YouTube. I saw your fight.' So I went and asked all the people who posted them and all the sites that had all my fights if they would kindly take them down. I gave them the reasons and you only find one or two on there now. I was trying to turn the page and a new leaf. I didn't want a six- or seven-year-old coming up and looking at me as a fighter and not a mentor."

Kirk Tomlinson is all about hockey. It's a game he teaches, it's a game he loves. His one night at Maple Leaf Gardens will never leave his thoughts, but other games, with the Nashville Knights, the Hamilton Steelheads, the Oshawa Generals and the Peoria Rivermen, just to name a few of his teams, helped turn him into a hockey lifer. "That one game didn't change my life, but playing hockey changed my life — playing in the American Hockey League, playing Major Junior. The game itself is in my blood and that's who I am to this day. I wake up every morning and I work in hockey and I wouldn't credit it to that one game, but I credit it to the game as a whole."

CHAPTER 10
THE KING OF
THE ONE-GAMERS

DON CHERRY *A Night at the Forum and So Much More*

Photo courtesy of Rogers Sportsnet

There is a king of one-gamers, and his name is Don Cherry. The man is also the King of Saturday night. For many of us, he's been the face of the game for the better part of four decades thanks to "Coach's Corner" on *Hockey Night in Canada*. I feel like I grew up with Don — he would visit our house every Christmas when my brother and I would pop the latest edition of *Rock'em Sock'em Hockey* into the VCR.

Years before he was the coach of the Boston Bruins and years before he became a national icon, Cherry was a 21-year-old first-year pro trying to make his way into the National Hockey League. "I was playing in Hershey and in my very first year," says Cherry. "We didn't make the playoffs and Fernie Flaman got hurt for the Boston Bruins. They were in the Stanley Cup semifinals playing Montreal. I got the call from Hershey. Another fellow and I, Norm Corcoran, came up to be standby."

Cherry had put up some solid numbers in his first season in the American League. He had seven goals and 13 assists for 20 points in 63 games. But the Bruins weren't calling him up for his offence. The Hershey rookie also led the team with 125 PIMs. On game day in

Montreal, following the morning skate, Cherry got the news: he wasn't on standby any longer — he was going to play that night against Jean Béliveau, Boom Boom Geoffrion and the Montreal Canadiens. There would be no Rocket Richard in the lineup. He was suspended for the playoffs because of a March 13 incident in Boston. Richard attacked Bruin Hal Laycoe after he was high-sticked and punched a linesman who tried to break up the ruckus. Richard's suspension led to the Richard Riots in Montreal on March 17, 1955. When Don Cherry showed up for his game at the Forum on March 31, he wouldn't have to worry about the Rocket. "I was very, very nervous and I couldn't believe the whiteness of the ice. That's what got me . . . the whiteness of the ice at the Forum and the crowd going nuts."

Boston didn't waste any time getting the rookie into the action and Cherry didn't have much time to admire that beautiful ice. He started the game on the Bruins blue line in front of 13,594 fans. The Habs held a 3–1 series lead. A Montreal win that night and Cherry's season was over. "I was overwhelmed. It was like you were in a dream world. You know how they say it's just another game and it's the same thing as the American Hockey League? It wasn't. You look over and you see the Canadiens sweaters and the Boston sweaters. Imagine walking right into the semifinals. Not the regular season. And to start in the nuthouse of the Forum? They had a great team. It was something to see Bernie Geoffrion coming down on you. It was really overwhelming."

But the tough defenceman had a job to do and tried to play the style of game that got him all the way to the NHL. All of it was captured forever in a photo that showed up in the papers the next day. "I cross-checked Béliveau and I knocked him down. So that was my claim to fame." Cherry finally got a chance to remind Jean of the moment decades later. "About 30 years later, I met Jean at a banquet. I told him the story. I said, 'Jean, do you remember me?' He says, 'Oh yeah, Donnie. I remember. On the bench they said, "Be careful of that number 23, he's good,"'" a laughing Cherry says.

It was all Canadiens on the night of March 31, 1955. The Habs won 5–1 and took the series in five games. They then went on to lose the Cup to Detroit in seven. "And I took a regular shift and I was even. I started the game. That's how much they thought of me, eh? How you can drop in one year . . . it's amazing."

Cherry's fall down the Bruins depth chart can be traced to something that took place in the summer of 1955. The Bruins said their so longs to Cherry after the series against Montreal with the intention of giving him a more than decent shot at camp the following fall. "They were really, really ticked at me because I'd got hurt playing baseball before. They said, 'Look, Don, you got a good future here. Everything is going along good." The Bruins had just one warning for the young defenceman: *don't play baseball*. Cherry went home that summer — he eventually picked up a bat and ball.

"I broke my shoulder playing baseball like a fool." With a spot on the Bruins dangling in front of him, Cherry now had a shoulder dangling at his side. "I dove for a ball and I was a pretty good fielder. I dove for a ball and I didn't roll quite as well as I should have and I landed on my shoulder and I separated it."

Still, there was no stopping Don Cherry. He wasn't going to miss training camp with a spot on the Bruins blue line on the line. And even though he was up for the task, his shoulder was not. He went to camp, but ended up playing that entire season in the minors with a wire holding his shoulder together. When he was on the ice, blood soaked through his sweater. He'd try to shoot the puck, but he couldn't get anything on it. "Bill Quackenbush, I'll never forget, he was getting older and I took a shot and he turned to Milt Schmidt and said, 'He's got a worse shot than me.'

"The wire was coming up through the skin, if you could believe it, while I was playing. I'd hit somebody and it would just go nuts, coming through."

It wasn't so much his shot that ticked off the hockey powers though, it was the simple fact that Don Cherry had disobeyed the Bruins. They told him not to play, but he did. And worse, he got injured. "In those days you had your one shot, and if you blew it and if you got in their bad books . . . I was sentenced to Siberia for the next 22 years."

Cherry had come so close. But when the Bruins 1955 training camp was over, he watched his dreams literally roll down the highway. "It was a tough time in my life, I'll tell you. They left me in Hershey. I remember them driving away, the Boston Bruins were driving away, going back to Boston from the Hershey training camp. I was very sad.

"One of the cruellest things that ever happened was that training camp."

That's when his 22-year sentence began: Cherry's life in the minor leagues. He eventually escaped Siberia in 1974, when he finally returned to Boston to coach the Bruins. "I showed them. I came back and coached their team."

For one night in 1955, Don Cherry lived the dream and proved to the hockey world that he could be an NHLer. Perhaps the greatest parts about that night were the simple things that don't show up in a game summary. Like the fact that Don Cherry's mom got to see him play in his only NHL game. "Believe it or not my mother came up from Kingston on the train and she came to the game with a big shopping bag. She saw me play. After the game I met her in a little restaurant outside. And she had to catch the train back to Kingston that night. And she gave me this big bag of cookies, eh? Cakes and all that. And then I had to go meet the players and they all made fun of me. And we went to the bar after, and they caught a train back to Boston at about 12 o'clock. And they made fun of me, but they ate all my cookies and stuff on the train.

"I was on cloud nine on the train with all the Boston Bruins. It was like a dream come true. And I thought it was going to go on forever. Unfortunately that was my last time in the NHL."

Until, of course, he returned to coach in Boston.

Don Cherry was known as a player's coach. He gave guys who wouldn't get a shot elsewhere a chance to play with his Bruins. And if the Bruins or, later on, his Colorado Rockies were in Toronto on a Saturday night, he'd send a local kid out on the ice to be in the starting lineup. "One time I started a left winger on defence because I knew how much it meant to him. I looked out on the ice, at the Gardens, and there were tears rolling down his face. This kid was so emotional. His name was Peter Sturgeon and he only played a couple of games in the National Hockey League."

Cherry got to experience the way the game was handled by its upper powers in 1955. That's not how he wanted to handle things when he was in charge. "When I became a coach I had a little more feeling for the players than those guys who were absolutely, I have to say it, heartless."

I ask Cherry if his one game in the NHL helped shape him into the man we know today — into a coach who won a Jack Adams and into one of the most famous broadcasters the game has ever seen.

"I don't think so. I think my 22 years in the minors led to it. I spent 16 years as a player and then I went on as general manager and coach in Rochester. So that's what taught me. That's what taught me the toughness," he says with a laugh. "When you play a game and travel all night and get in at six and then play the next game and spend the whole weekend on the bus, that toughens you up for the rest of the world.

"I wasn't one of those guys who could sleep on the bus, and I remember at four o'clock in the morning I'd see the farmers getting up, milking the cows. I used to say I'd be better off being a farmer."

But Don Cherry was a hockey player. And of course, the king of the one-gamers, the final say in a book like this has to go to the coach: "I was bitter for a long time. But then you think back about it and at least they brought me up. They thought enough of me to bring me up. I ruined my own chance.

"Always remember: if a guy builds one bridge, he's a bridge builder. That's the way I saw it. At least I made the one game. People can make fun . . . 'Oh he only played one game in the National Hockey League.' But at least I played one game in the National Hockey League. And that's a lot more than a lot of people."

Acknowledgements

It is hard to believe just how much work goes into putting a little book like this together. There are so many people who have made this book possible, including you, for picking up a copy and supporting my passion for an off-the-wall hockey topic. So thank you.

Incredible thanks go out to the men in this book who allowed me to share their stories. It was a great pleasure getting to talk to these players. At first, a lot of them thought my phone call was a joke, but they soon learned that I was genuinely interested in their stories. They were beyond generous with their time and candour. So a huge thank you goes out to the 40 men who shared their stories and photos with me and made this book possible.

Thank you to my literary agent Brian Wood for once again taking on a passion project of mine. This seems to be a pattern. My writing will never make Brian and me rich, but he shares the same energy for hidden stories of the game that I seem to have. So thank you, Brian, for your continued support.

Thank you to everyone at ECW Press for taking another chance on me. To Jack David and David Caron, thank you for your continued faith in my writing. My editors Michael Holmes and Laura Pastore are miracle workers. They are the reason my writing seems clear and concise and my endless typos have been eliminated from the end product. Thanks to Sarah Dunn for working on the publicity and everyone else who makes ECW tick.

Thanks to Jeff Marek for writing the foreword to this book. Jeff and I were originally going to work on this project together — we had the same idea for a book — but Jeff is one busy dude. Aside from being one of the best hockey hosts on the continent and a podcasting superstar, he has a beautiful mind when it comes to the game and its colourful history. If there's a hockey story that you're longing to hear, chances are Jeff "Palm Isle" Marek knows it.

Very special thanks to a number of people who went beyond the call of duty and did not hesitate when I reached out for help, including: Paul Patskou (one of the sharpest hockey minds you'll ever meet), Steve Hogle of the Saskatoon Blades, Kevin Dickie and Scott Landry at Acadia University, the Saint John Sea Dogs, Barry Trenholm at the Pictou County Sports Hall of Fame, Trevor Stienburg at St. Mary's University, St. Michael's College, Joe Babik at the ECHL, Denis Boisvert at the LNAH, Jean-Michel Tremblay of the Marquis de Jonquiere, Timothy Gassen of the WHA Hall of Fame, Peter Hanlon of the Calgary Flames, Chad Soon, Eric Francis, the Hutchman, the Fort Wayne Komets, Jeff Maher, Grant Roberts, James Hurst, the Carolina Hurricanes, Aaron Sickman of the Minnesota Wild, Justin Van Dette, Mr. Raditch, the Nova Scotia Sport Hall of Fame, Brian Lewis at the Hamilton Sports Hall of Fame, Greg Pilling, John Shannon, Jesse Duke, Neil Smith, Hugh Townsend, James Dalzell, Gus Fahey, Maco Belkovec, Steve Chapman from the ECHL, Gordie Dwyer and countless others.

Thank you, internet. I gathered a large number of stats for this book from hockeydb.com, hockey-reference.com and The Hockey Summary Project — as they like to say "the information used herein was obtained free of charge and is copyrighted by The Hockey Summary Project. For more information about the Hockey Summary Project